No. 2944
$24.95

# Country Furniture

## 114 Traditional Projects

*Percy W. Blandford*

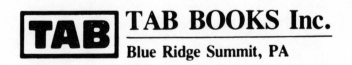

**TAB** **TAB BOOKS Inc.**

Blue Ridge Summit, PA

FIRST EDITION

FIRST PRINTING

Copyright © 1988 by TAB BOOKS Inc.

Printed in the United States of America

Library of Congress Cataloging in Publication Data

Blandford, Percy W.
   Country furniture.

   Includes index.
   1. Country furniture—United States.  I. Title.
TT194.B53  1988    749.213    88-8564
ISBN 0-8306-1444-3
ISBN 0-8306-2944-0 (pbk.)

Questions regarding the content of this book
should be addressed to:

   Reader Inquiry Branch
   TAB BOOKS Inc.
   Blue Ridge Summit, PA 17294-0214

Cover photograph courtesy of NuTone, A Division of Scovill.

# Introduction

There is an undeniable attraction about furniture that has a handmade one-off appearance. Any individually made piece will stand out from the mass-produced furniture that many people have to accept. The individual piece might be a modern design using plywood or particleboard, the same as used extensively in factory furniture production, but there is something difficult to define about solid wood that makes it more attractive. The craftsman, whether amateur or professional, who uses solid wood at least for the major part of a project is making the most worthwhile piece of furniture and carrying on a tradition built up from the days of the first settlers and their ancestors in Britain and other parts of Europe.

Such work is collectively known as *Country Furniture*, but it can have a place in any home, whether town or country—in fact anywhere that beauty is seen in furniture that is made to last and designed to satisfy a purpose exceptionally well. It might not have the flourishes and embellishments often added to modern furniture to disguise the fact that they are made from particleboard without satisfactory joints, but much of the attraction of solid-wood construction is in the grain pattern and exposed joints.

In the days before the Industrial Revolution and the use of machines to aid quantity production, trees were felled and the wood converted to boards laboriously by hand. There is no virtue in handwork for its own sake, and many routine jobs are better done today by machine, but in those days a worker was determined to make the best use of his hard-won wood. As a result, he produced some furniture designs that can be models for our work today. You can use machines to take the hard work out of sawing and planing, and you might find particular value in using a router for rabbetting and molding. If you want the article you are making to have the qualities that only come from handwork however, you must remove the evidence of machine work, such as the ripples on the surfaces that come from machine planing or joints that are obviously machine-cut.

In making country furniture you have much to learn from your ancestors, particularly those from New England, Virginia, and elsewhere on the Atlantic coast as well as the Latin influence that entered from the south. The earliest work was necessarily hasty and simple rather than durable, because of the need to use things immediately, but some of these "primitive" pieces have survived and can serve as models for modern reproductions that are still useful and decorative in their own

way. If you are short on woodworking experience or have few tools, these things have the advantage of being simple to make.

When settlements developed into towns and the comforts of life became more important, the quality of furniture improved. It is the period roughly from the middle of the eighteenth century to late in the nineteenth century that produced much of the good-quality furniture that is worth copying. The terms *Colonial* and *Early American* are used, but there are no clearly defined periods. In Britain it was the time when the influence of the great cabinetmakers was felt, but American design was finding its own way. The Shakers exerted considerable influence, with their accents on simplicity and fitness for purpose.

There was an almost unlimited supply of wood to be had, almost within reach, and some furniture was influenced by the type of wood available. Something like a table, however, had to satisfy certain criteria whatever the wood and how many hundreds of miles apart the makers were, so designs were not vastly different.

More use was made of paint on early furniture. It might cover poor workmanship, but more often it disguised mixed woods. Windsor chair design came from England, where chairs were stained and polished. A large number of American Windsor chairs were made of several woods and finished with paint.

In this book it is assumed in nearly all projects that you wish to make things that finish in the manner and fashion of the early carpenters. This means that anything but solid wood would not be authentic. Where plywood would not be obvious, it is suggested. Joints are those that could be cut by hand, although mechanical aids could be used. Designs are those that follow tradition, since most people will want to equip a room in a "country" manner. Although a television set or a microwave oven might be disguised by a piece of country furniture, there is nothing of a hybrid type described here.

This is not a book on techniques, and some knowledge of woodworking is assumed. There is something for everyone, however, with many very simple projects as well as others to suit more experienced readers. Some projects involve the use of a lathe, but this can be a small and simple procedure. If you cannot turn your own parts, such things as knobs, finials, and spindles can be bought.

In the materials lists, widths and thicknesses are finished sizes, but lengths are full. Sizes on drawings and in lists are all in inches, unless marked otherwise.

The projects in this book are completely described, but variations are possible. Visits to museums or furniture collections will show what can be done.

I believe that making furniture adapted to modern needs from the styles developed by our ancestors can be very satisfying, both in the making and subsequent using. Apart from what is gained in that way, there is the additional satisfaction of knowing you are keeping alive a tradition of good craftsmanship that is not very evident today.

# One

# *Simple Small Assemblies*

Many of the earliest pieces of furniture made by the newly arrived settlers were comparatively crude and nearly always nailed together. Despite the primitive design and construction, there was a certain attractiveness about many of the items that supplemented their obvious usefulness. As the methods of construction are so simple, these assemblies make good pieces of work for anyone unsure about their ability to cut joints and deal with more advanced furniture.

The original items were made of solid wood, often irregularly cut and probably not planed. Joints were made with cut nails and no glue. How close you get to the original concepts depends on your intentions. If you want to make a reasonable replica, you will use similar methods. If you want to make something modern of the same appearance, but with no attempt to keep details like the original, you can use machine-planed wood or even plywood, and manufactured nails supplemented with glue. Between these extremes you can compromise by hand-finishing wood and using modern nails sunk and covered with stopping.

Common nails today are made from wire with round heads. These heads showing on a surface would not be authentic in a reproduction. You could use small-headed nails, called casing, floor-

ing, or finishing, then punch them below the surface and fill the holes with stopping. That would be better than having the common round heads exposed.

There are still specialist manufacturers of cut nails that have a similar appearance to those used in original construction. The body of the nail has a squared taper. The head can be just a projection to one side or an elliptical shape, which can be flat or domed in a variety of patterns. The patterned heads give character to the finished article.

Whatever nails are used, particularly near edges, it is advisable to drill for them. Make the holes almost a clearance size in the upper piece of wood, then make an undersize hole in the lower piece. Much depends on the wood. In some hardwoods the lower hole should be full depth and not much smaller than the nail diameter. In some softwoods you may use a shorter and smaller hole or no hole at all.

You can increase strength by driving nails alternate ways in a dovetail fashion. If there is an open end, as in the top of a box, drive two nails close together for extra strength. The general nail spacing will depend on the construction, but gaps between the nails equal to three or four times the thickness of the wood will look right.

## HANGING SQUARE BOX

Hanging boxes of many types and sizes were once used. One could be used in the kitchen today for various odds and ends. A box could hold a plant in a pot. Outside it could be used for clothespins. Sizes can suit your needs, but the one in Fig. 1-1A is based on 6-inch edges.

Make the back first (Fig. 1-1B) with its grain vertical. Make the grain on the sides and front horizontal (Fig. 1-1C). Assemble these parts. Make the bottom slightly oversize and plane its edges after nailing on (Fig. 1-1D).

There could be a lift-off lid (Fig. 1-1E). Add strips underneath to locate it and a finger hole in the top for gripping it.

### Materials List for Hanging Square Box

| | |
|---|---|
| 1 back | 1/2 × 6 × 11 |
| 2 sides | 1/2 × 6 × 7 |
| 1 front | 1/2 × 6 × 8 |
| 1 bottom | 1/2 × 7 × 8 |

## PIPE BOX

Long clay smoking pipes were stored in a box that did not project much from the wall. Wicks or spills for transferring a light from the fire were kept in a similar box. A similar box today might be used for other storage, but it makes a good holder for a display of dried flowers.

General construction is the same as the previous box in Fig. 1-1, but all parts have their grain vertical (Fig. 1-2). Curve the top and make a V cut in the front. In any box the bottom is stronger if it comes within the other parts (Fig. 1-2B). Join the sides to the back and fit the bottom between them, then nail on the front last.

### Materials List for Pipe Box

| | |
|---|---|
| 1 back | 1/2 × 4 × 15 |
| 1 front | 1/2 × 5 × 11 |
| 2 sides | 1/2 × 3 × 11 |
| 1 bottom | 1/2 × 2 1/2 × 5 |

## BOX WITH SHELF

A variation on a hanging box had a shelf below. The shelf might have been for matches, knives, or various small items. One modern use for a box would be for shoe-cleaning materials, with brushes in the box and polishes on the shelf.

The box could be made with a simple outline similar to the earlier boxes, but this one is shown with curved decoration (Fig. 1-3A). Sizes can suit your needs or available wood. Those shown should suit many purposes (Fig. 1-3B).

Mark out the back first (Fig. 1-3C) with the positions of the other parts and the shape of the top. Make the two crosspieces (Fig. 1-3D), the two sides to overlap them, and the back (Fig. 1-3E). Cut the top of the back to shape and drill the hanging hole. Nail together the parts made so far.

Mark out the front (Fig. 1-3F) to match these assembled parts. For the notch, mark the center of the hole and draw lines to it, then drill a 3/4-inch hole and saw into it. Nail the front on and trim level any excess wood at the edges.

### Materials List for Box with Shelf

| | |
|---|---|
| 1 back | 1/2 × 9 × 18 |
| 2 crosspieces | 1/2 × 3 1/2 × 10 × 11 |
| 2 sides | 1/2 × 4 × 14 |
| 1 front | 1/2 × 10 |

## BOX WITH DRAWER

A tall narrow box was commonly used for wicks as well as pipes, then matches could be kept in a small drawer below. Such a hanging box is decorative in a room with country furniture, even if you now find other uses for it. This box (Fig. 1-4A) is a compact size (Fig. 1-4B). The only slight complication is the making of the drawer.

The main construction is very similar to the box in Fig. 1-3. Mark out the back first and shape its top. Make the front so it is the same width and fits between the sides, which have sloping top edges (Fig. 1-4C). Cut away the front for easy access.

Make up the box completely, with glue as well as nails. Be careful to get the parts of the bottom compartment parallel and square so that the drawer will slide easily.

The drawer is a box that fits into the space with its front level with the other parts. For the

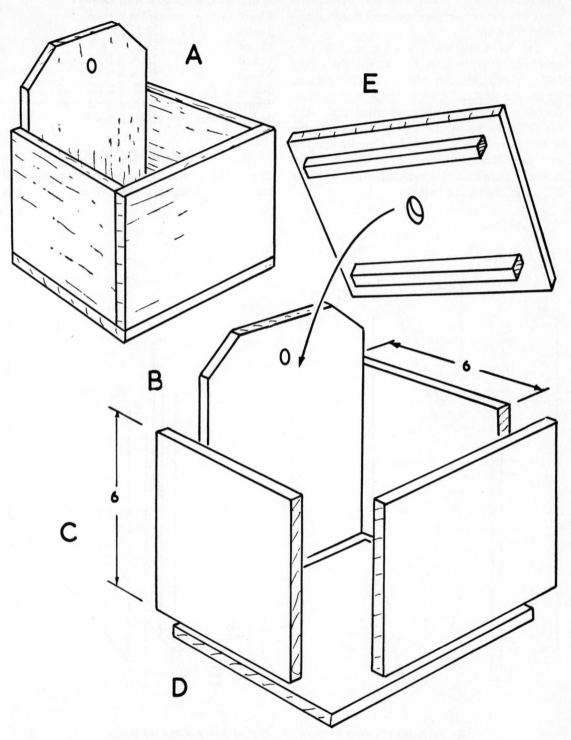

Fig. 1-1. A hanging square box can be left open or given a lifting lid.

sake of appearance, the front should overlap the sides and the bottom, without nail heads showing at the front.

Cut the front to size to make an easy fit in the opening. Notch its ends to take the sides (Fig. 1-4D). Notch the lower edge to take the bottom, for the neatest finish. Except for the notched front, the box is a simple nailed construction (Fig. 1-4E). Set the nails below the surface and plane the wood, if necessary, to make the drawer run smoothly. There could be just a block of wood for a handle, but a turned wood knob to fit into a hole (Fig. 1-4F) would be better.

## Materials List for Box with Drawer

| | |
|---|---|
| 1 back | 1/2 × 4 × 16 |
| 2 sides | 21/2 × 5 × 12 |
| 1 shelf | 21/2 × 4 × 5 |
| 1 shelf | 1/2 × 4 1/2 × 5 |
| 1 front | 1/2 × 4 × 9 |
| drawer front | 2 1/2 × 2 1/2 × 15 |
| drawer parts | 2 3/8 × 2 1/2 × 15 |
| drawer bottom | 2 3/8 × 5 × 5 |

## CRANBERRY SCOOP

You might not want to gather cranberries, but if you do, this scoop is as effective as it always has

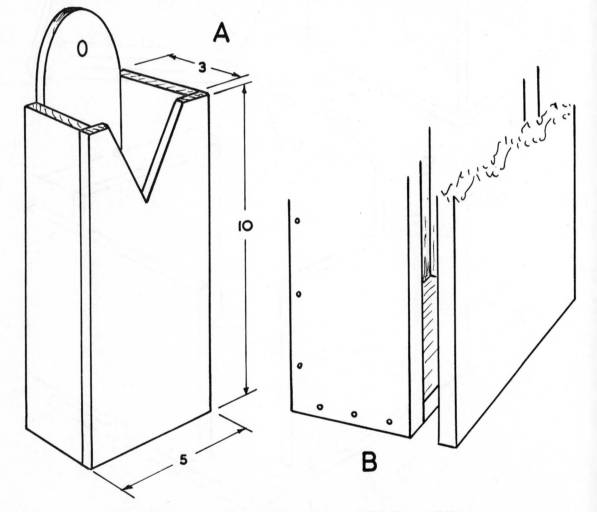

Fig. 1-2. A box originally intended for clay pipes will hold any tall things.

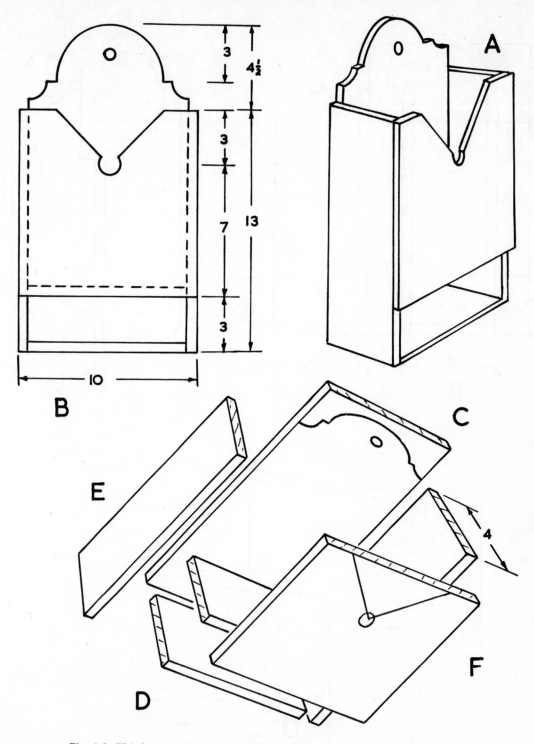

A

O

B

10

3 4½
3
7 13
3

C

O

E

D

F

4

Fig. 1-3. This hanging box with a shelf is suitable for shoe-cleaning materials.

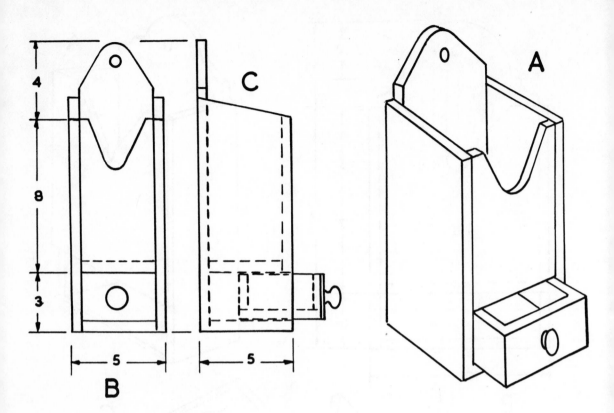

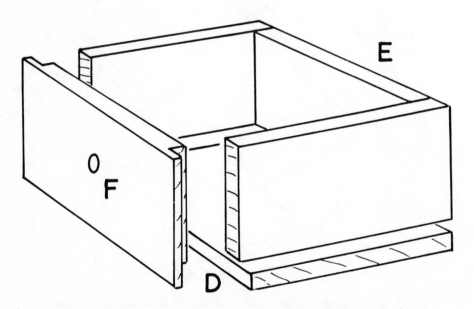

Fig. 1-4. This box can hold wick or pipes and store matches in the drawer.

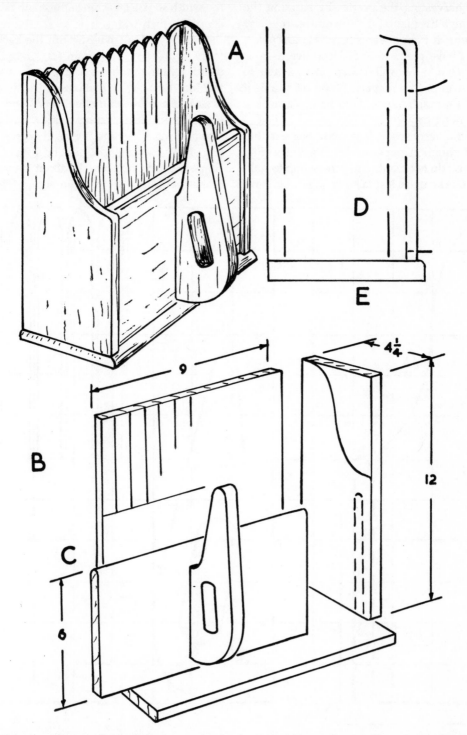

Fig. 1-5. *This scoop was intended for gathering cranberries, but it could be stood on a table to display flowers or hold magazines.*

been for harvesting the berries by running the edge through the plants. As a furniture accessory in the home, it is an obvious conversation piece, but it can have practical and decorative uses as well. Attach it to the wall or stand it on a table to hold a flower or fern display. Stood on a table it becomes a magazine rack. Laid flat on a desk it can be a filing tray.

This cranberry scoop (Fig. 1-5A) is a size that will hold common papers and magazines (Fig. 1-5B). If you do not want to use the scoop to hold papers, you can make it smaller or larger, but have the width so you an arrange the comb with pieces about 3/4 inch wide.

Hardwood is advised, with the back having fairly straight vertical grain for strength in the comb. Join the parts with glue and nails, which will look best if sunk and covered with stopping.

Make the two ends (Fig. 1-6A) and mark on them the positions of other parts. Cut the back to size and mark the spacing of the comb tongues (Fig. 1-6B). Saw the tongues and trim the tops to shape. Reduce the points to about 1/4 inch thick. Make the front with its grain across (Fig. 1-5C).

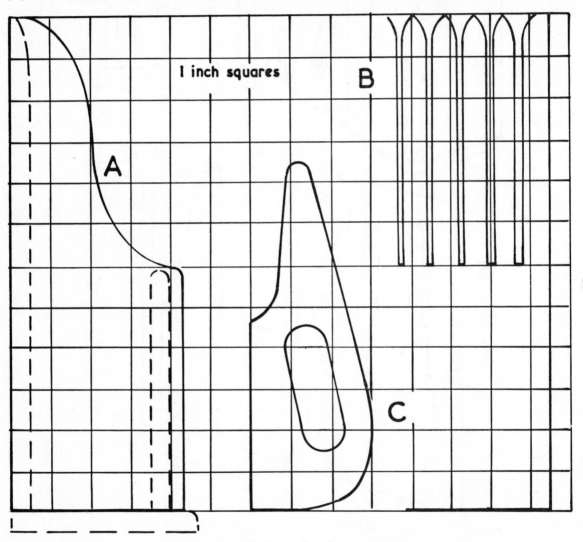

Fig. 1-6. Sizes and shapes of cranberry scoop parts.

Cut the handle (Fig. 1-6C) to shape and make the finger hole by drilling two holes and cutting away the waste. Round the edges. Attach the handle to the front with nails or screws from the inside. Round exposed edges of the front and ends. Join the ends to the back level and to the front set back (Fig. 1-5D). Make the bottom level at the back, but project it 1/4 inch on the other edges (Fig. 1-5E).

## Materials List for Cranberry Scoop

| | |
|---|---|
| 2 ends | 1/2 × 4 1/2 × 13 |
| 1 back | 1/2 × 9 × 13 |
| 1 front | 1/2 × 6 × 10 |
| 1 bottom | 1/2 × 4 1/2 × 12 |
| 1 handle | 3/4 × 3 × 9 |

## SHAKER CANDLE SCONCE

The Shaker's habit of hanging things from pegs extended to their shelves to hold candlesticks. You might not want to put a peg rail around a room, but a replica of a Shaker candle sconce can be hung from a single peg. You might not want to use it for a candle, but it could support an ornament, a plant in a pot, or something similar.

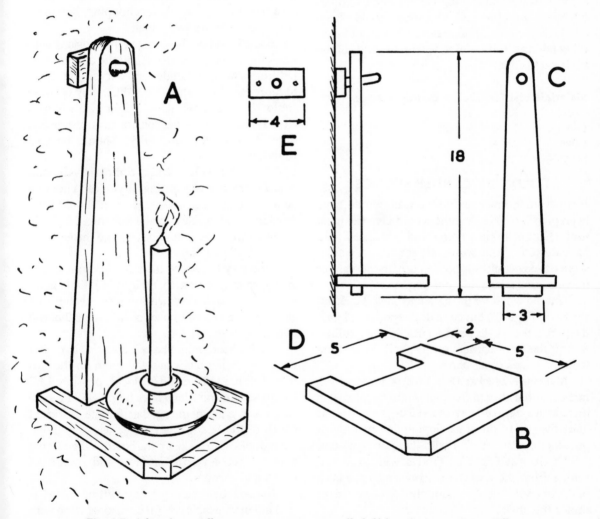

Fig. 1-7. A hanging candle sconce can serve as a small shelf for other purposes as well.

This sconce (Fig. 1-7A) has the simplicity of the Shaker design and a shelf area about 5 inches square (Fig. 1-7B), but any sizes could be used. Keep the back long, so gravity holds the shelf level.

Make the back parallel to above the shelf level, then taper to 2 inches at the top (Fig. 1-7C). Round the top and drill a hanging hole. Because of the weakness of end grain, put the hole lower than the center of the top curve.

Cut the notch in the shelf (Fig. 1-7D) a close fit on the back. Join the two parts with glue and nails or screws. See that they are square.

The peg (Fig. 1-7E) is a block of wood with a 1/2-inch dowel rod at a slight angle and two holes for screws into the wall. The shelf should tilt up a little above horizontal to reduce the risk of anything falling off. If necessary, trim the ends of the shelf extensions.

**Materials List for Shaker Candle Sconce**

| 1 back | 3/4 × 3 × 19 |
| 1 shelf | 2 3/4 × 5 × 8 |
| 1 peg | 3/4 × 2 × 5 |

## COLONIAL CANDLE SCONCE

A small shelf, bracketed to the wall, would have been placed where a candle would give the most useful light in an early home, and its maker would have decorated this sconce attractively. A similar sconce today could support an ornament, vase of flowers, or a plant in a pot (Fig. 1-8A).

Cut the wood for the back and shelf. Mark out the back (Fig 1-8B) but cut a dado groove 1/4 inch deep for the shelf before cutting the outline. Round the front corners of the shelf. Round the forward edges of all parts.

Make the bracket (Fig 1-8C) 4 inches by 5 inches with a curved front. It might be advisable to make it 1 degree more than 90 degrees to eliminate the risk of the shelf sloping downwards. If possible, cut the bracket with its grain diagonal.

Fit the shelf into its groove with glue and screws from the back. Use screws into the back of the bracket, but glue alone should be sufficient under the shelf.

**Materials List for Colonial Candle Sconce**

| 1 back | 3/4 × 8 × 19 |
| 1 shelf | 3/4 × 6 × 9 |
| 1 bracket | 3/4 × 5 × 9 |

## CUTTING BOARDS

Anyone preparing food needs a surface to cut or chop on. Early cooks probably used any available piece of wood, then special boards were made and kept. Any wood, except those that are resinous or aromatic, can be used, but lighter-colored hardwoods look best and give the best service. A board can be any size, though 6 inches square is about the minimum working area. Cutting could be done on a board 1/2 inch thick; for chopping, however, it would be better twice that.

Some early boards were given extensions with holes for hanging (Fig. 1-9A) and the outlines varied from simple rectangles and curves (Fig. 1-9B) to more fanciful shapes (Fig. 1-9C). Any of those could be made now; some might also serve as cheese boards. Whether for practical use or just decoration, corners and edges should be well rounded.

The snag with a wide, comparatively thin board is the risk of warping. If you can choose a board that has been quartersawn, it should keep its shape. Such a board can be recognized by looking at its end—the grain lines will go through the thickness (Fig. 1-9D).

One way to reduce the risk of warping is to glue several strips together (Fig. 1-9E). Early glues were less reliable, but with modern waterproof glues, you can make a board of any shape that will withstand washing.

Such a board might be called *butcher block*, but the true butcher block has end grain on the surface. This has to be made of blocks, possibly 1 1/2 inches square and 1 inch thick (Fig. 1-9F). Prepare strips and glue them together for the sufficient width of the board, then cut across (Fig. 1-9G) enough pieces to make up the board. When all the glue has set, level the surfaces and round the edges and corners.

A good treatment for any cutting board is soaking in vegetable oil. An occasional wipe with

oil will then keep the wood clean and reduce water absorption.

## BLACKSMITH BOX

A shoeing smith or farrier has to work quickly while his metal is red hot. He must know exactly what he will do when he draws the iron from the fire and have all the tools needed ready within reach. To help in this he has devised a tool box to suit his needs. There have been variations, but

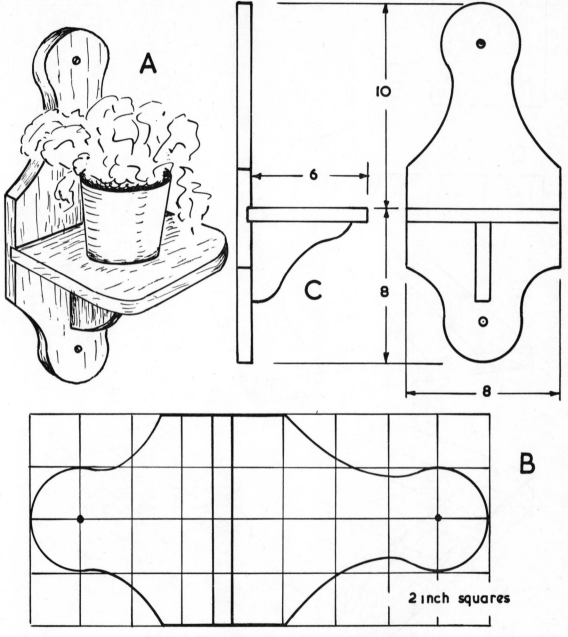

Fig. 1-8. This candle sconce makes a good display shelf.

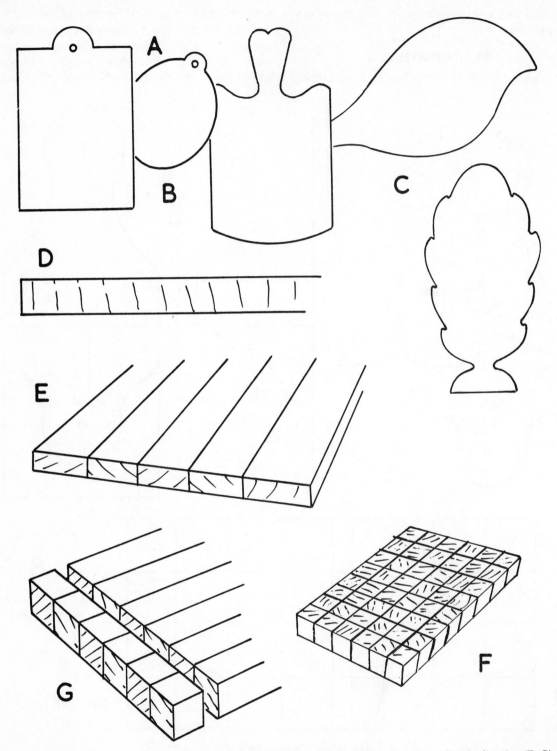

Fig. 1-9. Cutting boards can be made in many shapes (A, B, C,) and should take advantage of grain direction (D-G).

in general the box follows the pattern of this project (Fig. 1-10). It is unlikely you will want to use the box for its original purpose, but it might have a use in your shop. Painted and maybe stencilled, it could serve as a display stand or a magazine rack in your home.

The suggested sizes (Fig.1-11A) suit tools, but the tray will take magazines, the shelf will hold

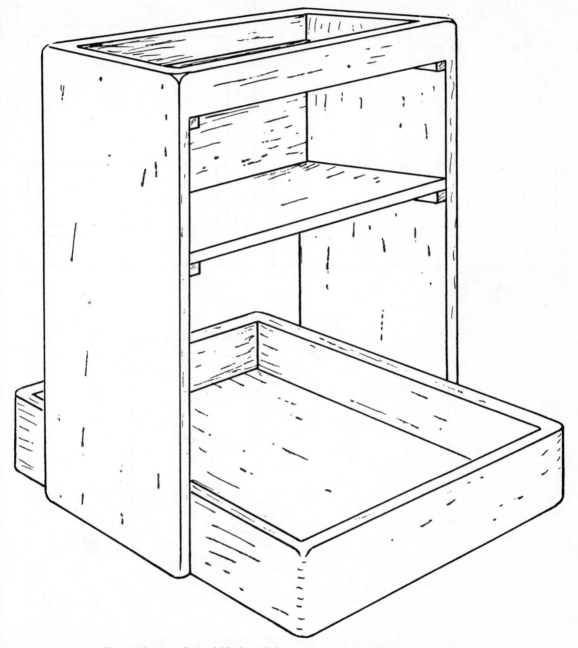

Fig. 1-10. A traditional blacksmith box makes a useful rack in shop or home.

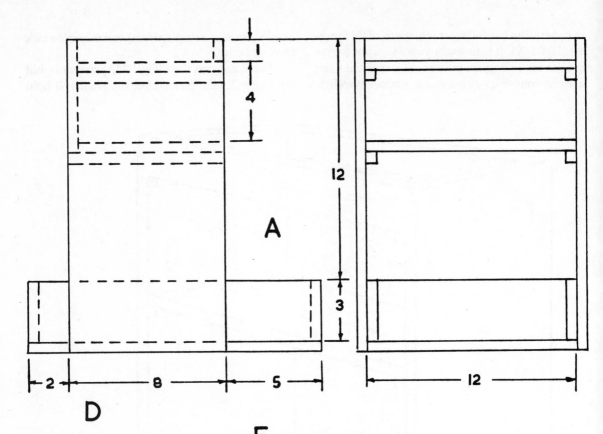

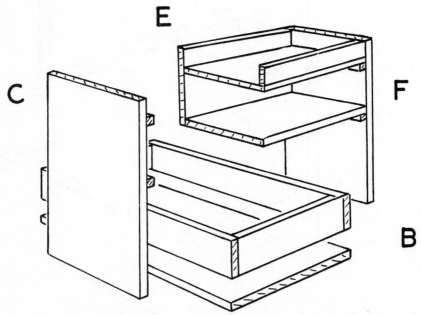

Fig. 1-11. Sizes and construction of the blacksmith box.

books, and the top will serve as a table or a place for sewing or hobby items. All of the parts are wood at least 1/2 inch thick. Construction could be with cut nails, if you want to keep an old appearance, or you could use modern nails, set and covered with stopping.

The bottom is a simple tray (Fig. 1-11B), glued and nailed. The two sides (Fig. 1-11C) are off-center to give easier access to the box at the front (Fig. 1-11D).

The two shelves meet a closed back, and there is a strip across the front to make the top into a tray (Fig. 1-11E). Support the shelves on strips (Fig. 1-11F) and glue as well as nail all parts. Round all edges and corners. In use, a blacksmith would have worn the wood away considerably, so if you want the box to look old, *distress* it heavily. Blocks under the corners could form feet if you want to paint or varnish the box and stand it on a carpet beside a chair.

## Materials List for Blacksmith Box

| | |
|---|---|
| 2 tray sides | 1/2 × 3 × 17 |
| 2 tray ends | 1/2 × 3 × 13 |
| 1 tray bottom | 1/2 × 12 × 17 |
| 2 uprights | 1/2 × 8 × 18 |
| 2 shelves | 1/2 × 7 1/2 × 14 |
| 1 back | 1/2 × 5 × 14 |
| 1 front | 1/2 × 1 × 14 |
| 4 strips | 1/2 × 1/2 × 9 |

# Two

# Shelves

One of the first requirements in an early home would have been to get things off the floor. The first floor was probably dirt, so supports around the walls were needed for cleanliness as well as convenience. This meant that some of the first woodwork undertaken was the making of shelves. In a home equipped with country furniture, there are many shelves and other hanging furnishings that can be made as replicas or close reproductions of similar items made in the early settlement of this country.

Many modern shelving projects have straight lines due to the use of machined wood. Achieving a straight edge or surface was a difficult undertaking, to be avoided if possible. That might explain why there are more curves in many early racks, shelves, cupboards, and similar assemblies mounted on a wall. If what should be straight had errors in it, the fault was obvious. If the available wood was not straight and the edge was cut to a curved pattern, slight errors were not so obvious. If a pair of shaped ends did not match exactly, a casual observer was not as likely to notice the difference as he would if a straight edge was not straight.

How shelves are attached to upright ends depends on skill and equipment. In the simplest early assemblies, the ends of the shelves were nailed only (Fig. 2-1A). A better arrangement used securely clench nailed cleats under the shelves (Fig. 2-1B). Many early craftsmen could cut dadoes, although they would have called them "housing" joints (Fig. 2-1C) and cut them with saw and chisel. Now craftsmen use a router. The simplest were cut through, but a neater end is either stopped (Fig. 2-1D) or the shelf is cut to hide the end of the dado (Fig. 2-1E).

The wood-to-wood joint takes the downward thrust, but even with modern glues, the end grain surfaces do not make a good bond. Early assemblies had no glue and were nailed (Fig. 2-1F). It is neater to provide extra strength with nails or thin screws driven upwards inconspicuously through some joints (Fig. 2-1G). If you are making a faithful replica, end nailing into dadoes can be used. but otherwise it is better to add strength with this last method.

## BASIC SHELVES

Early light storage shelves were made with the required number of shelves between two uprights, with the back open to the wall, and all front edges curved, if the wood was not already straight. Rear

edges might have been shaped to fit an uneven wall, but a modern reproduction will have a flat back. The block of shelves in Fig. 2-2A is typical of the earliest shelves in New England and elsewhere. Sizes can be altered, but the assembly will always look best with shelf spacing narrower towards the top. Any wood can be used, but local hardwood with an oiled finish would be authentic.

Prepare the wood and draw a freehand outline that you like (Fig. 2-2B). The hollows should go in about as far as the 5-inch shelf width. Cut the pair of ends and mark the positions of the shelves.

The shelves could be parallel or the front edges might have shallower curves than the ends. Leave the last 1 inch of each shelf parallel to form the

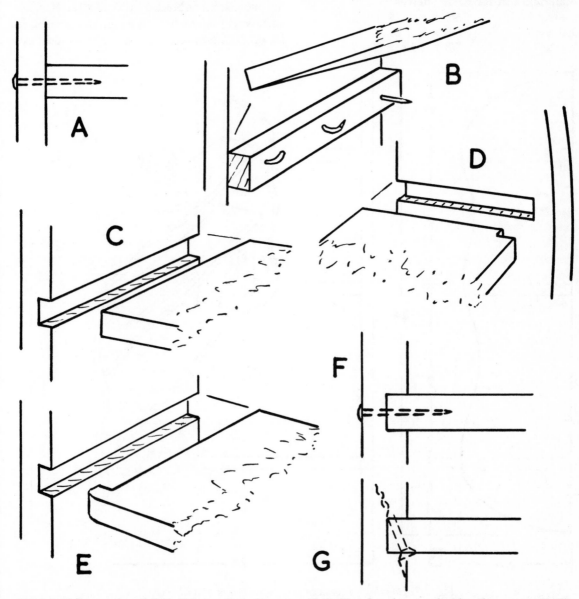

Fig. 2-1. Shelves can be nailed (A, B) but are better in grooves (C, D, E) and can be secured with nails or screws (F, G).

joints. Use any of the joints described (Fig. 2-1), but stopped dadoes are appropriate.

Assemble the parts on a flat surface. Check squareness by comparing diagonal measurements.

Put a strip (Fig. 2-2C) across under the top shelf for screws or nails into the wall. For a large assembly with a heavy load, you might need a strip under another shelf as well.

**Materials List for Basic Shelves**

| | |
|---|---|
| 2 ends | 5/8 × 6 × 25 |
| 3 shelves | 5/8 × 5 × 25 |
| 1 strip | 5/8 × 1 1/4 × 25 |

## SHELF WITH CLOTHES PEGS

A shelf with pegs for hanging clothes and other items has just as much use today as it did when the first settlers were making furniture. This shelf (Fig. 2-3A) could be made with straight boards and only the corners rounded, but wavy edges at the front would look better. Leave cross sections square, except for taking sharpness off edges.

The two main boards are the same, except for the peg holes. The brackets, (Fig. 2-3B) are 4 inches each way, preferably with the grain diagonal. In an original arrangement, the pegs would have

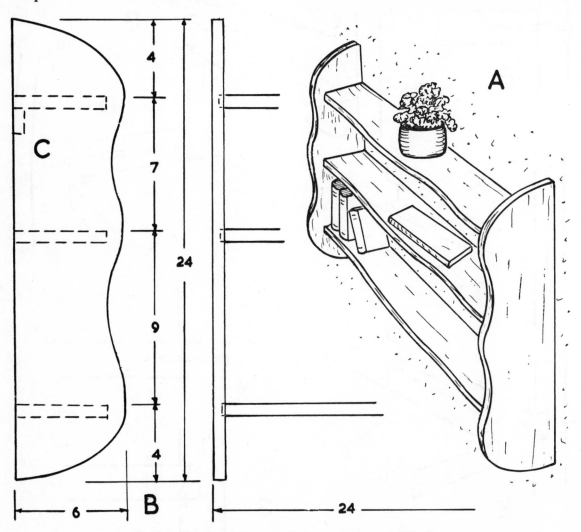

Fig. 2-2. Hanging shelves can display souvenirs or hold books.

been shaped by hand and would probably not be truly circular. You could make similar pegs by planing 3/4-inch square wood to an octagonal shape, then take the corners off and sand them round. Alternatively, you could use dowel rod. Drill a slight angle. The shakers used turned pegs. You can buy replicas or turn them yourself.

The top board can be joined to the back one with dowels or nails, punched and covered with stopping. The brackets could have screws through the back where they will not show. Glue alone might be sufficient under the top.

**Materials List for Shelf with Clothes Pegs**

| 2 boards | 3/4 × 6 × 21 |
| 2 brackets | 3/4 × 5 × 8 |
| 3 pegs | 5 × 3/4 diameter |

## SHAKER PEGBOARD

Although not exactly a shelf, the pegboard used by Shakers served a similar purpose and would hold shelves and many other things. The board carried pegs at convenient intervals, maybe 12 inches apart, and was arranged fairly high but within reach in a Shaker room. Almost anything,

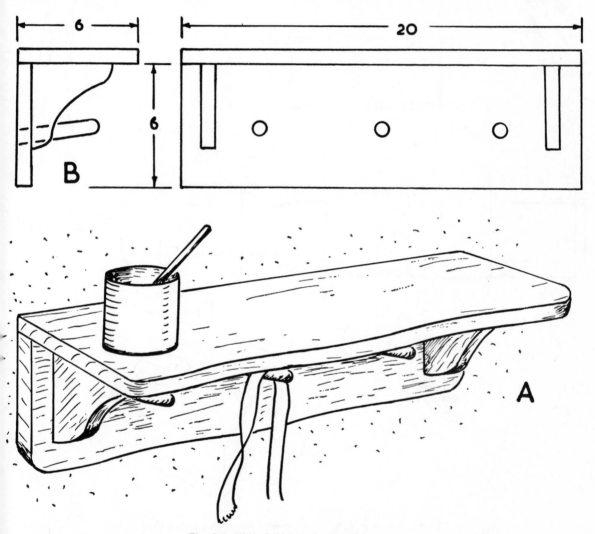

*Fig. 2-3. This shelf includes hanging pegs.*

including chairs, not needed for immediate use, would be hung on the wall to leave a clear area of floor. In a modern home a length of pegboard could be used in a similar way along a wall. Small furniture items could be made to hang on pegs, and these could also be used for coats, domestic cleaning tools, and anything else not in constant use that could be hung — thus carrying on one of the good ideas the Shakers have left us.

The board might be a piece of 1-inch-by-3-inch hardwood or softwood (Fig. 2-4A). The pegs could be whittled round or pieces of dowel rod, but Shaker pegboards had turned hardwood pegs to a fairly standard design. It is possible to buy them from woodwork supply stores, but you can turn your own (Fig. 2-4B). Have a hole made with the bit you will use in a piece of scrap wood to test the dowel end of each peg as it is turned. Make

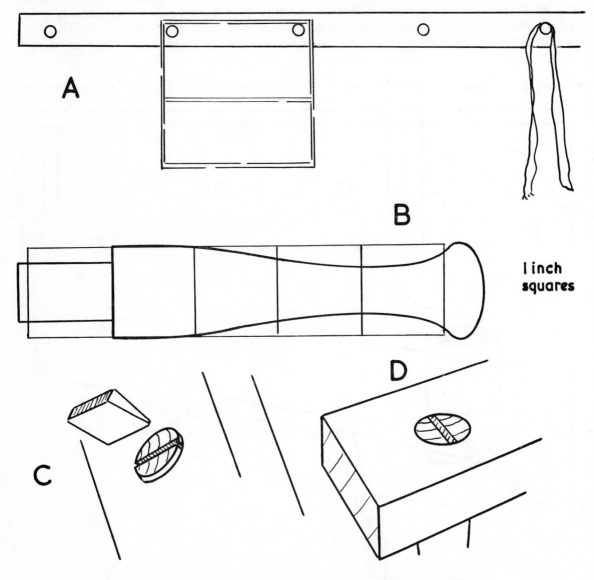

Fig. 2-4. Shakers devised a pegboard above head height that uses turned pegs.

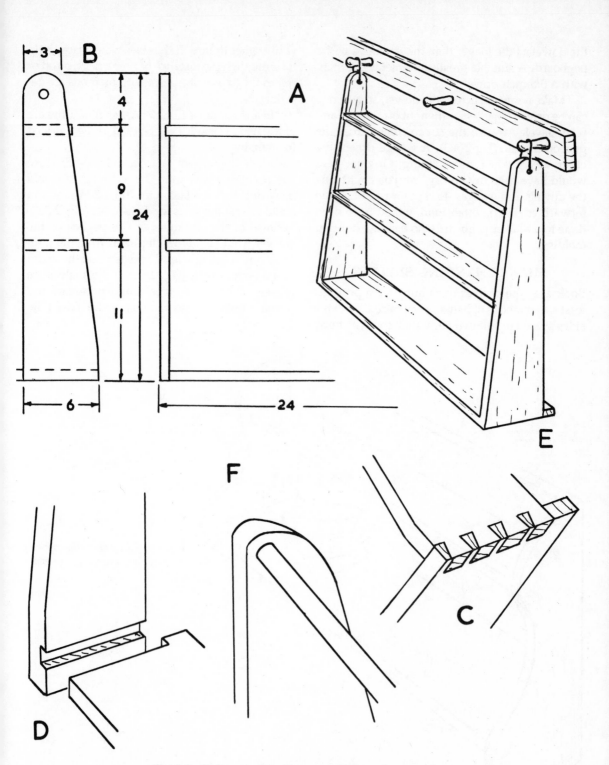

*Fig. 2-5. Shelves can hang from pegs with cords or a rod.*

the dowel a little longer than the thickness of the pegboard. A suitable greatest diameter is 1 inch, with a 5/8-inch dowel.

Make a saw cut across the dowel, so a wedge can be driven (Fig. 2-4C), then cut off the end and plane level. Arrange the cut to come across the pegboard grain (Fig 2-4D). A wedge driven the other way might cause splitting. Original pegs would have been driven dry, but you could glue the dowels and wedges. Except for rounding the forward edges, no other work would have been done to a Shaker pegboard—no beading or other molding.

## SHAKER HANGING SHELVES

Bookcase type shelves were hung from pegs. At least two methods of hanging were used. With the sides spaced to suit two pegs, they could be hung with leather thongs. If the sides were spaced a little more than the distance between pegs, a rod or rail could go over the pegs. Both methods are described here.

In the example (Fig. 2-5A), shelf widths are graduated. The sides are tapered and are drilled for hanging thongs.

Mark out a pair of sides (Fig. 2-5B). Two shelves have dado joints. The bottom shelf would be strong with dovetail joints (Fig. 2-5C), or you could extend the sides for dado joints (Fig. 2-5D). Because of the thickness of the pegboard, the shelves would tend to swing away from the wall. They can be brought level by extending the width of the bottom shelf (Fig. 2-5E). If the shelves are to hang from a rod, fit a round or square rod through holes toward the rear of the sides (Fig. 2-5F).

*Fig. 2-6. A strip above the top shelf improves appearance and provides stiffness.*

Assemble squarely. Check how the shelves hang. It might be necessary to plane the back edge of the bottom shelf to get a satisfactory fit.

### Materials List for Shaker Hanging Shelves

| | |
|---|---|
| 2 sides | 5/8 × 6 × 25 |
| 1 shelf | 5/8 × 4 × 25 |
| 1 shelf | 5/8 × 5 × 25 |
| 1 shelf | 5/8 × 7 × 25 |

## STIFFENED SHELVES

When a block of shelves is made with an open back, any twisting strains have to be taken by the joints at the ends of shelves. One way to provide extra strength is to add a back, which would usually be done today with plywood. As that was not available to early furniture makers, and solid wood cut thin and in sufficient width meant con-

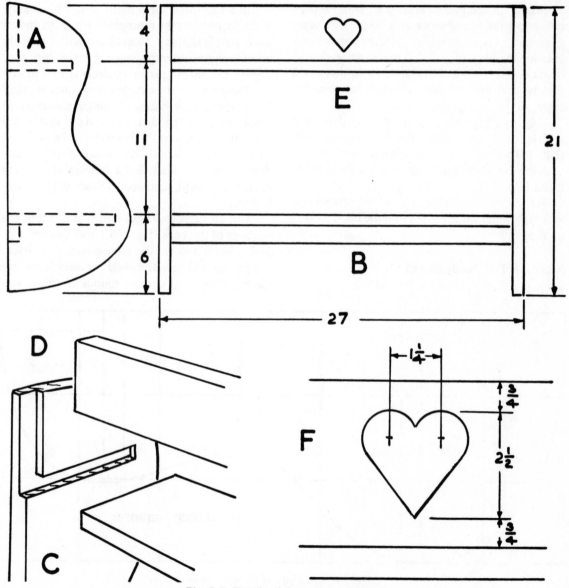

Fig. 2-7. Details of the stiffened shelves.

siderable extra work, they stiffened in other ways. A board above the top shelf provided rigidity and formed a back where it was wanted.

The example in Fig. 2-6 has a 5-inch and 8-inch shelf with shaped end pieces. There is a back at the top (Fig. 2-7A), and you can fit a strip below the lower shelf to take additional screws to the wall. If you want to keep things on that shelf away from the wall, arrange the strip above instead of below it.

Mark out the pair of ends (Fig. 2-8). Prepare the wood for the shelves and back. Cut dado grooves for the shelves (Fig. 2-7C) and make rabbets for the back (Fig. 2-7D) to the same depth. If you fit a strip against the lower shelf, that could also be rabbetted or just cut to fit between the ends.

Many early pieces of furniture were decorated with cutout hearts, and one is shown on the back (Fig. 2-7E). Drill two holes with sufficient overlap to make the top shape, then cut from them to the point (Fig. 2-7F).

When you assemble, use a few screws upwards through the top shelf into the back, as well as glue.

**Materials List for Stiffened Shelves**

| | |
|---|---|
| 2 ends | 3/4 × 9 × 22 |
| 1 shelf | 3/4 × 5 × 27 |
| 1 shelf | 3/4 × 8 × 27 |
| 1 back | 3/4 × 4 × 27 |
| 1 strip | 3/4 × 1 1/2 × 27 |

## SINGLE SHELF

A single shelf might have held a treasured ornament, possibly as one of a pair on each side of the fireplace. Such a shelf might now be used for a vase of flowers or a plant in a pot.

In its simplest form there would have been plain boards, but the example in Fig. 2-9A shows some simple shaping. Most of the outline is made up of straight cuts with sweeping curves between. Today, the shaping is easily done with a jigsaw or a band saw. In the simplest construction, all of the parts can be nailed. A better construction would be to fit the shelf into a dado slot in the back, then that and the bracket can be screwed from the rear where the screw heads will be hidden against the wall. For a bracket of the size shown (Fig. 2-9B), hardwood 5/8 inch thick is satisfactory.

Cut all parts to length and width. Mark the outlines of the back (Fig. 2-9C) and bracket (Fig. 2-9D). Mark and cut the groove across the back. Shape the outlines. The shelf is a simple rectangle with the front corners rounded, unless you

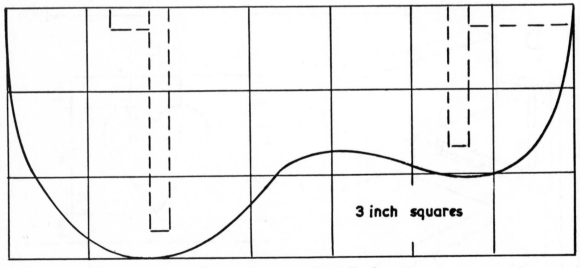

*Fig. 2-8. The shape of the shelf ends.*

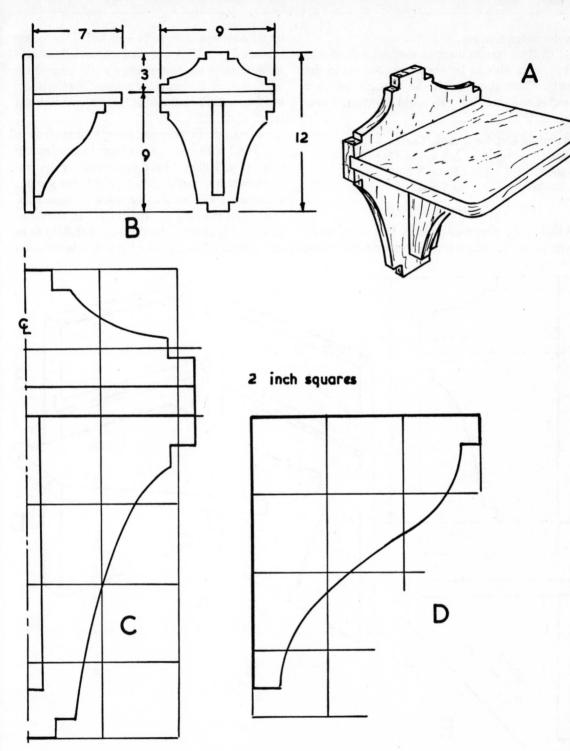

7

9

3

9

12

A

B

℄

2 inch squares

C

D

Fig. 2-9. A single shelf makes a good display point.

prefer more shaping.

Drill for screws through the back—three into each piece should be sufficient. Assemble the parts. Glue alone might be enough between bracket and shelf, but pins could be driven downwards, if necessary.

### Materials List for Simple Shelf

| | |
|---|---|
| 1 back | 5/8 × 9 × 13 |
| 1 shelf | 5/8 × 7 × 10 |
| 1 bracket | 5/8 × 6 × 8 |

## CORNER SHELF

A shelf in a corner uses up space that might otherwise be empty, and it is in a position where what it carries is less likely to be knocked. This corner bracket (Fig. 2-10) is intended to match the single shelf. Its sizes are comparable, and the edge shaping is similar. The parts are shown 5/8 inch thick, but they could be reduced to 1/2 inch with a strong hardwood.

Mark out the two wall boards (shaped as in Fig. 2-9C) with one wide enough to overlap the other (Fig. 2-10A). Check squareness of the corner where the bracket is to fit. If it is not square, set an adjustable bevel to the actual angle and use that when marking out the shelf. Cut the dado grooves (Fig. 2-10B), then make the shelf to fit in and project 1/2 inch to overlap and hide the ends

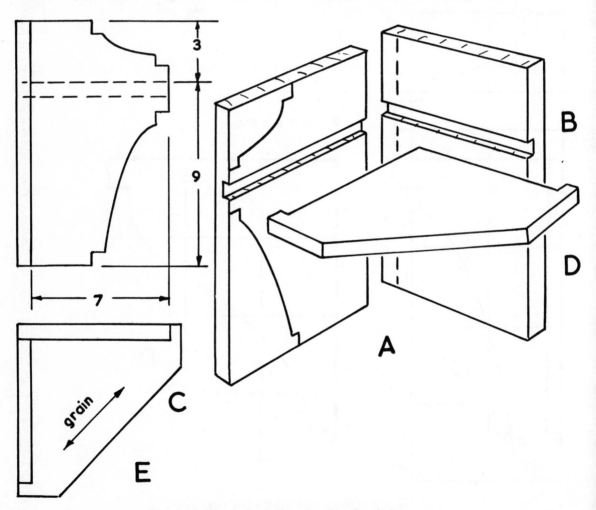

Fig. 2-10. The single shelf can be adapted to fit in a corner.

of the grooves (Fig. 2-10C and D).

A simple triangular shelf would not have much capacity, so square the front corners 2 inches from the wall (Fig. 2-10E) before cutting across. Cut the outlines. Glue and screw the corner overlap. Glue and screw in the shelf. Check the fit against the wall and drill for hanging screws.

**Materials List for Corner Shelf**

| 1 back | 5/8 × 7 × 13 |
| 1 back | 5/8 × 7 5/8 × 13 |
| 1 shelf | 5/8 × 7 × 13 |

## PLATE RACK

Some plate racks are for display, but the one in Fig. 2-11 is based on a Pennsylvania original that holds plates in regular use face downwards (Fig. 2-11). It is intended for plates from 11 inches down to 7 inches. A length of 36 inches allows a large number of plates to be stacked three or four deep. Pine or a light-colored hardwood looks hygienic.

The sides control other sizes. Mark out with the positions of the shelves and the rails (Fig. 2-12A). Back rails keep the plates away from the

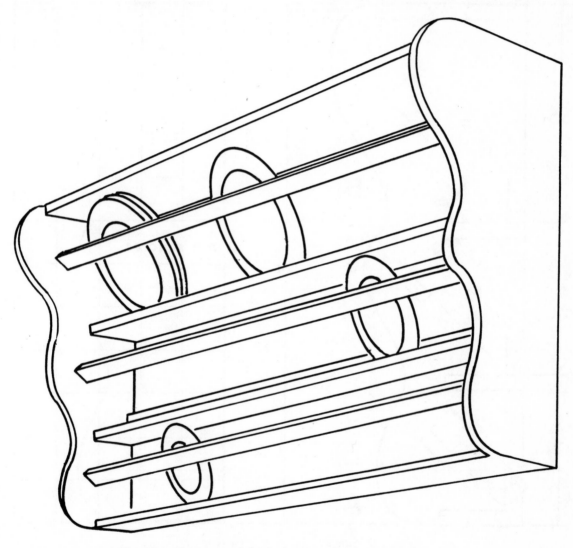

*Fig. 2-11. This plate rack holds the plates cleanly face downwards.*

wall (Fig. 2-13A). The rails that support the plates are on lines 45 degrees to the junction between each shelf and its rail (Fig. 2-12B). When you have marked the location of all lengthwise parts, draw the curved front edges (Fig. 2-12C) but do not shape them until after all joints have been cut.

Prepare the lengthwise parts. Dovetail the top and bottom (Fig. 2-13B). Make dado joints in the shelves (Fig. 2-13C). Nail or glue the back rails above the shelves and use one 1/4-inch dowel at each end (Fig. 2-13D). The sloping rails can also be dowelled.

Cut the outlines of the ends and well round these and other exposed edges. Check diagonal measurements at the back when you assemble. The rack can be hung with screws through the upper back rail.

**Materials List for Plate Rack**

| 2 ends | 5/8 × 9 × 26 |
| 1 top | 5/8 × 7 × 37 |
| 3 shelves | 5/8 × 3 1/2 × 37 |
| 3 rails | 5/8 × 2 × 37 |
| 3 rails | 5/8 × 1 1/2 × 37 |

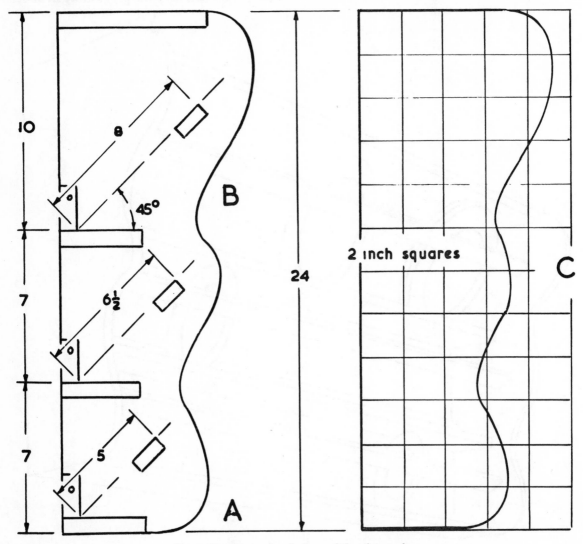

Fig. 2-12. Sizes and end shape of the plate rack.

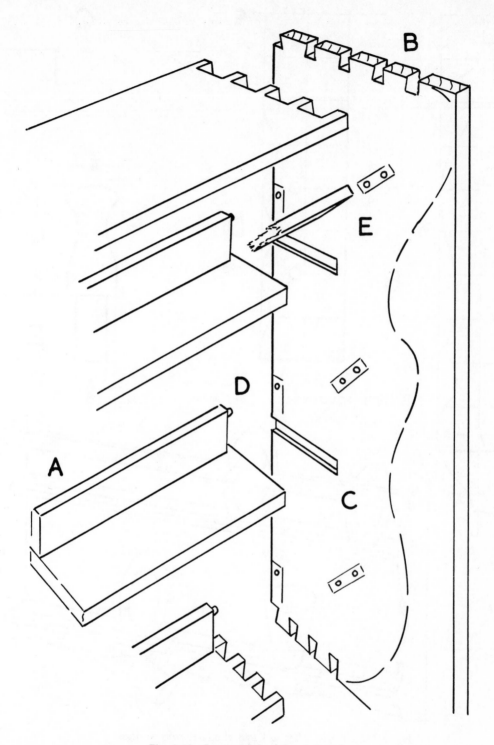

*Fig. 2-13. Construction of the plate rack.*

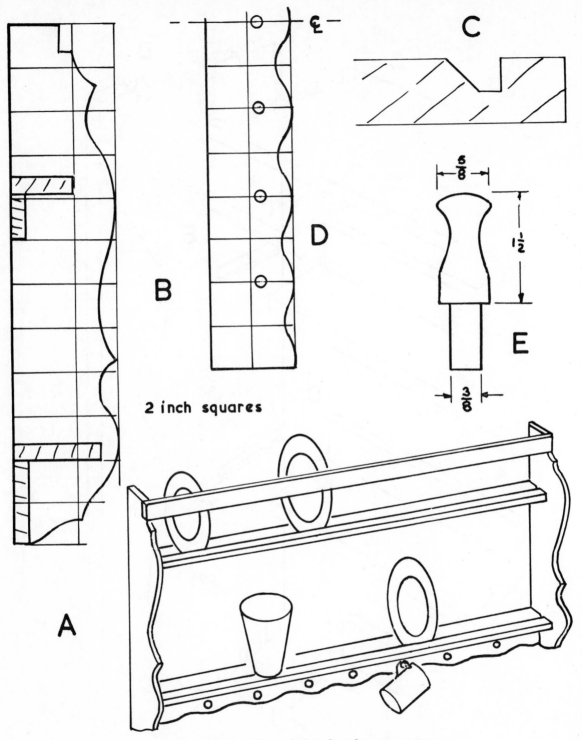

A

B

C

D

E

2 inch squares

$\frac{5}{8}$

$1\frac{1}{2}$

$\frac{3}{8}$

Fig. 2-14. A display plate rack that also takes cups on pegs.

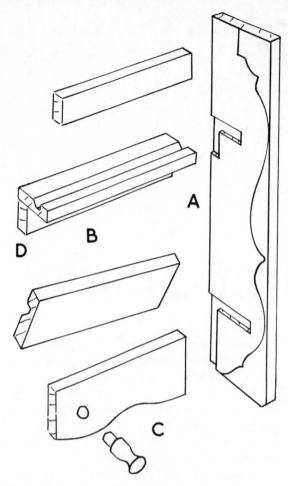

# DISPLAY PLATE RACK

There are still valued pieces of chinaware that have to be displayed rather than used. Earlier owners prized their plates and cups and made racks to display them. This project (Fig. 2-14A) is one of these racks. The squared drawings (Fig. 2-14B) show suggested sizes, but you might wish to gather the things to be displayed and make the rack to suit. A good hardwood, finished with stain and polish, will show off the chinaware.

Mark out the pair of sides. Cut the joints (Fig. 2-15A) before shaping the front outline. Cut grooves (Fig. 2-14C) near the fronts of the shelves (Fig. 2-15B) to steady plates stood on edge. Shape the lower edge of the cup rail (Fig. 2-14D) and drill it for the pegs (Fig. 2-15C). These could be turned like miniature Shaker pegs (Fig. 2-14E).

Make a strip to go under the top shelf (Fig. 2-15D) and take screws into the wall. Glue it to the shelf. Assemble the parts with glue and fine nails set below the surface and covered with stopping. Check squareness.

## Materials List for Display Plate Rack

| | |
|---|---|
| 2 ends | 3/4 × 5 × 26 |
| 1 top shelf | 3/4 × 3 × 34 |
| 1 bottom shelf | 3/4 × 4 × 34 |
| 1 top rail | 1/2 × 1 1/2 × 34 |
| 1 cup rail | 3/4 × 4 × 34 |
| 1 screw rail | 3/4 × 2 × 34 |
| Pegs from | 3/4 × 3/4 × 18 |

*Fig. 2-15. Constructional details of the display plate rack.*

# Three

# Benches and Stools

In the seventeenth and eighteenth century, it was usual for most families in Europe to sit on benches. Only the head of the household might have a chair. Immigrants making furniture would have made stools and benches, partly because of tradition, but also because they were simpler and could be arranged to push under a table when out of use. In the early days they could serve a dual purpose in supporting wood while being sawn.

Early benches were fairly heavy mainly because it was easier to prepare wood to thick sections than to reduce it to thinner pieces. Seasoning was probably inadequate, and thicker pieces were less likely to warp when they dried out after being made into furniture. This tendency to thick sections should be remembered, but with modern prepared wood, reproduction furniture can be made lighter.

Although some better benches had mortise and tenon joints, many assemblies used roughly rounded ends driven into holes. A leg would project through a seat, then a wedge was driven into a saw cut in its end (Fig. 3-1A) and the end cut off level. When cutting this joint, make a deep saw cut and arrange it so it is square to the grain of the part with the hole (Fig. 3-1B). Driving the wedge the other way might split the wood. Give

the wedge a moderate taper, so that it will drive deeply. Original joints would have been dry, but glue should be used in new work.

If the joint is not to go through, drill as deeply as possible. Using a shorter saw cut and a short wedge of wider angle (Fig. 3-1C) lets it hit the bottom of the hole and allows the joint to close up as it spreads wood (Fig. 3-1D).

It seems obvious to give a seat four legs, but if the floor is uneven, they might wobble. Three legs will stand fi m on any surface, and many early seats (and tables) had three legs.

For use away from a table, a seat height of 15 inches is reasonable. With a normal table, 17 inches would be better. For a bar stool you must increase to suit. A foot stool or child's seat can be 9 inches or 12 inches.

## MILKING STOOL

Milking stools were always three-legged because of the uneven floor of a cow shed. A reproduction of the fairly crude stool could be used in the yard or when gardening. In its simplest form, the top is a cross section of log and the legs are branches, all with the bark left on (Fig. 3-2A).

Make the top 9 inches to 12 inches in diameter

and 2 inches thick. The legs should be about 2 inches in diameter. Hardwood is preferable; it should have dried out to reduce the risk of later cracking.

Draw a circle on the top and step off the radius around it. The holes will come at alternate marks (Fig. 3-2B). For 2-inch legs, make the holes 1 1/4 inches. Drill them all at the same angle so that the feet will spread to a greater area than the top.

Pare or turn the leg ends with a parallel part to go through the holes (Fig. 3-2C). Saw across the ends, with wedges to match, and glue and drive in the joints. As the top is end grain, arrange the saw cuts radially. Drive in the wedges and level the tops of the legs.

Invert the stool and mark even lengths for the legs (Fig. 3-2D). Saw them off and bevel around the ends to reduce the risk of breaking out the edge grain.

## TURNED MILKING STOOL

Simple lathes were commonly used by early craftsmen. It was easier to produce an acceptable result from rough or unseasoned wood on a lathe than it was to attempt to get a good surface on squared stock.

The simple milking stool was too crude for use indoors as a home became established, and turned versions were made. This stool (Fig. 3-3) has a top about 10 inches in diameter and leg lengths to suit needs. The top could be one piece or several strips glued to make the width to reduce the risk of warping. Elaborate turning details would be inappropriate for this project.

Turn the top as a simple disc with a rounded edge and a line cut in where the holes will come (Fig. 3-3A). Turn one leg and use it as a pattern for the others (Fig. 3-3B). Use a hole in a piece of scrap wood to test the end before removing the wood from the lathe.

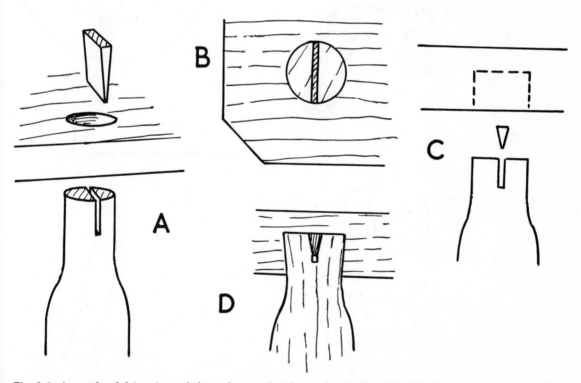

Fig. 3-1. A round end driven into a hole can be spread with a wedge (A, B). If the hole does not go through, a short thick wedge can be used inside.

Mark out and drill the holes. Glue and wedge the legs. Check that the stool top is parallel with the floor before leaving the glue to set, then level the ends of the legs.

**Materials List for Turned Milking Stool**

| | |
|---|---|
| 1 top | 1 1/8 × 10 × 10 |
| 3 legs | 1 1/2 × 1 1/2 × 20 |

## RUSTIC BENCH

A piece cut across a log, as in the first milking stool, does not stand up to the weather very well if left exposed outdoors for long periods. The end grain upwards will suffer from sun and rain. Having the grain across the top is more durable and suitable for a bench to be kept in the yard.

Some early benches and stools were made from logs split along the center and with three or four legs (Fig. 3-4A and B). A sawn piece could have some of the underside cut level for lightness (Fig. 3-4C). A very uneven outline might be partially straightened, but leave enough of the natural waney edge (Fig. 3-4D) to give the seat character.

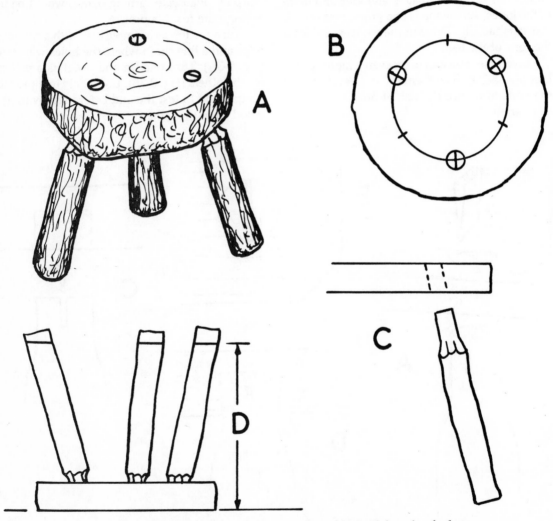

Fig. 3-2. This milking stool is made from a section of log with branches for legs.

Make the legs as already described. If the seat is for a single person, make three; for a long bench four would be better. Splay the legs well for stability.

## SLAB BENCH

Legs were cut into standard size boards of fairly large sections because that meant fewer cuts. If furniture could be made without further reduction of sections, the labor was reduced. Some benches were made with nearly all parts the same section.

The bench in Fig. 3-7 is made from wood 1-inch-by-12-inch sections. The sides are formed by cutting a board along its center. Other stock sizes could be used, and the bench made any length. The parts are nailed using 3-inch nails, preferably galvanized if the bench is for outdoor

use. Any wood could be used, but a durable hardwood is advised.

The important parts are the legs. Set out the angle (Fig. 3-6A). Set an adjustable bevel to this and use it when marking across each leg (Fig. 3-6B). Setting out the angle also gives you the length of a leg. Mark the recesses to suit the sides (Fig. 3-8C) and notch the bottom to make feet (Fig. 3-8D).

Make the two sides and mark on them the positions of the legs (Fig. 3-8E). Shape the ends.

Nail the sides to the legs and check squareness. Nail on the top.

**Materials List for Slab Bench**

| 1 top | 1 × 12 × 49 |
| 2 sides | 1 × 6 × 49 |
| 2 legs | 1 × 12 × 18 |

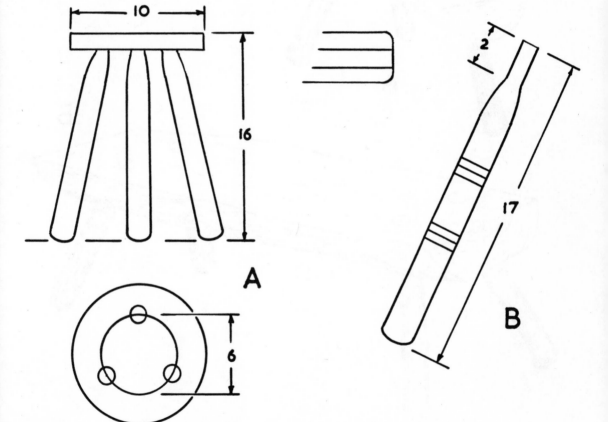

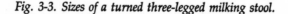

*Fig. 3-3. Sizes of a turned three-legged milking stool.*

## TEXAS STOOL

A scaled-down bench becomes a stool. A smaller version of the bench just described would make an excellent stool. It has the advantage of stability due to a good spread of its feet and a width on the floor as great as the top. Many early stools are smaller at floor level than on top, however. A small difference does not matter. Some early stools did not have legs notched for the sides and that made a less stable base due to the narrower legs. Maybe construction was hasty and unskilled, but in making a reproduction notching is advised.

Many early stools and benches had upright legs, as in this Texas stool (Fig. 3-7A). The legs are notched and have a semicircular cutout, when a V cut was more usual. There is a hand slot at the center of the top, which overhangs 1/2 inch all round.

Make the two legs (Fig. 3-7B) and notch them to suit the sides, which slope at the ends (Fig. 3-7C). Nail and glue these parts together. Make the top with rounded corners (Fig. 3-7D). Cut the

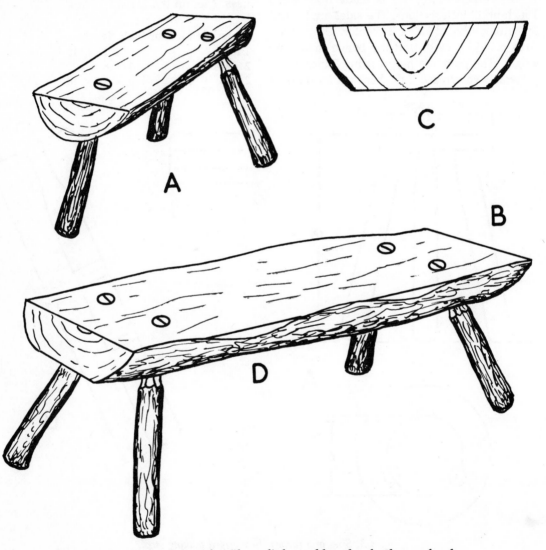

*Fig. 3-4. A rustic bench is made with a split log and branches for three or four legs.*

hand slot by drilling 1-inch holes at 4-inch centers and removing the waste between them. Well round all edges of the top, then nail and glue it on.

**Materials List for Texas Stool**

| | |
|---|---|
| 2 legs | 3/4 × 8 × 10 |
| 2 sides | 3/4 × 3 × 18 |
| 1 top | 3/4 × 9 × 19 |

## PRIMITIVE STOOL

If your interest is in reproducing early work of the most basic form, wood fashioned without the aid of a plane should be used, as in this stool found in Virginia (Fig. 3-8). The legs are branches and the top is a section across a log. The rails are split from branches and roughly flattened. Despite the crude construction, the stool should have a reasonable life. Because rusting of the nails might be the final weakening, choose nails protected by galvanizing or other coating.

The top determines general sizes—a 1 1/2-inch thickness of a 12-inch log would be suitable. Remove the bark. The legs should be about 2 inches in diameter and could be up to 24 inches long. Remove the bark and any projections, preferably with a drawknife. Prepare the rails with plenty of spare length.

It will help to draw a triangle with equal sides on the underside of the top as a guide to spacing. Spread the legs an amount that seems reasonable (Fig. 3-8A). If you start at one leg and let excess rail length extend at the next leg, you can work around in turn, cutting as you go. Check that the rails have reasonably matching lengths. Two nails at each crossing should be sufficient, but drill undersize holes to prevent splitting. Round the outer ends of the rails (Fig. 3-8B). Nail on the top, then invert the stool to mark equal lengths of legs.

## TENONED BENCH

A stool or bench made by a craftsman would have had something better than nails for joints. The usual choice was mortise and tenon that depended on wedges rather than glue. This bench (Fig. 3-9) is typical of the type of better benches made in many early settlements.

Use local hardwood. If it has been machine-planed, follow with a hand plane, rather than sanding, to give the traditional appearance on visible surfaces. The suggested sizes (Fig. 3-10A) can be modified without altering the method of construction.

Make the two legs (Fig. 3-10B) with tenons at the top (Fig. 3-10C). Make 45-degree cuts for the feet.

*Fig. 3-5. A slab bench is made with boards of stout section. It is strong and stable.*

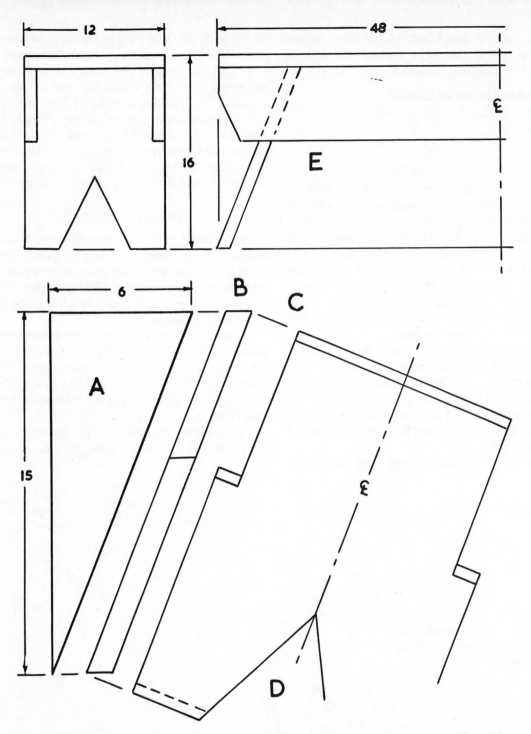

Fig. 3-6. Sizes and leg details of the slab bench. The legs extend as far as the top to provide stability.

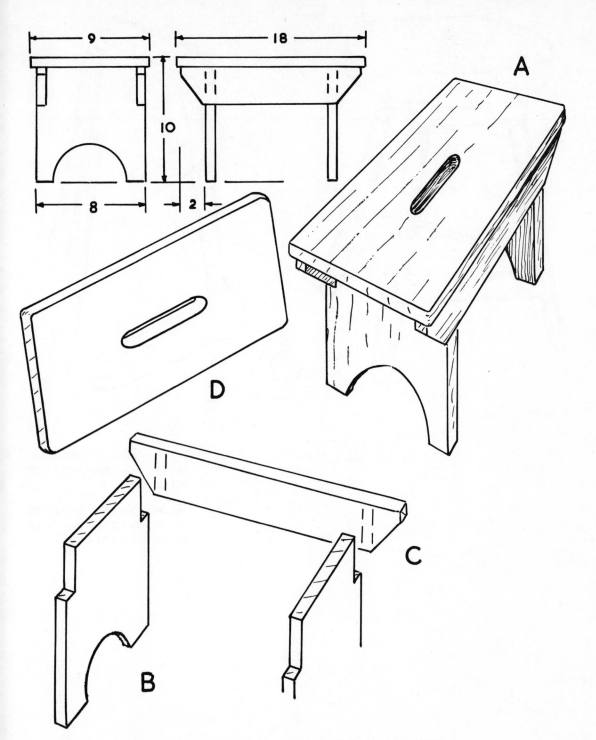

Fig. 3-7. *The Texas stool has upright legs and a hand hole for lifting.*

A

B

Fig. 3-8. (above) A primitive stool uses the simplest construction without cut joints.

Fig. 3-9. (left) A good-quality bench has the legs tenoned into the top and the rail tenons wedged.

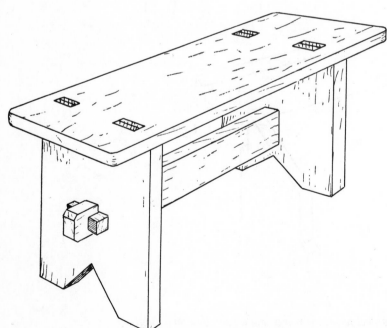

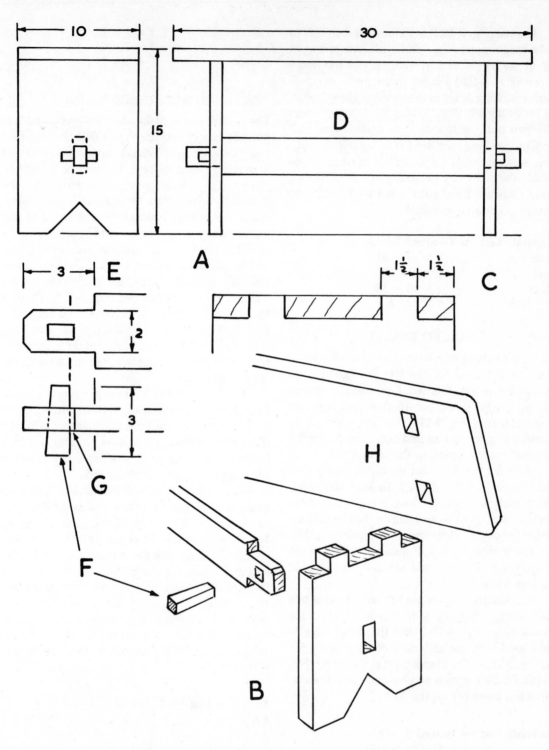

Fig. 3-10. Constructional details of the tenoned bench.

The rail (Fig. 3-10D) is reduced at the ends to make long tenons (Fig. 3-10E). Make mortises to suit in the legs. Cut two wedges with moderate slopes (Fig. 3-10F) longer than finally needed. Make matching holes in the tenon slightly undercut inside the legs (Fig. 3-10G); the driven wedges will then pull the tenons tight against the legs.

Cut matching mortises in the top (Fig. 3-10H). Have saw cuts ready for wedges in the tenons. Assemble the parts dry or with glue. Trim the leg tenon ends level and cut the rail wedge ends so they project equal amounts.

**Materials List for Tenoned Bench**

| | |
|---|---|
| 1 top | 1 × 10 × 31 |
| 1 rail | 1 × 3 × 30 |
| 2 legs | 1 × 10 × 15 |
| 2 wedges | 1 × 1 × 6 |

### BRACED BENCH

If a bench is long in relation to the cross section of the board used for the top, it might be too springy if it is not stiffened. One method of supporting is with sides, but another way is to use diagonal braces (Fig. 3-11). This bench is made in a similar way to the tenoned bench except for the diagonal braces replacing the central rail.

Make the two legs and the top with mortises and tenons (see Fig. 3-10C). To keep the crosspieces fairly low, make shallow cutouts to form feet (Fig. 3-11A). Glue and nail on the crosspieces. Attach the central strip under the top (Fig. 3-11B). Join the legs to the top. If necessary, put a temporary piece of scrap wood across the feet to hold the legs square.

The diagonal braces can be marked out at one side. Arrange one edge to fit into the corner of the central strip (Fig. 3-11C) and the other edge to come level with the underside of the strip on the leg (Fig. 3-11D). The braces meet at the center (Fig. 3-11E). Fit the braces with glue and nails, then remove the piece across the feet.

**Materials List for Braced Bench**

| | |
|---|---|
| 1 top | 1 × 10 × 46 |
| 2 legs | 1 × 10 × 16 |

| | |
|---|---|
| 1 central strip | 1 × 4 × 11 |
| 2 leg strips | 1 × 2 × 11 |
| 2 braces | 1 × 3 × 23 |

### UPHOLSTERED STOOL

The easiest way to make an upholstered seat is to put padding on a plain board. This was done for many early stools and chairs and is still a good way of making a softened seat. At one time the upholstery had to be built up with a variety of padding materials, which often settled and became hard. For a seat today, you can use rubber or plastic foam, which is easy to use and is resilient.

This stool is of straightforward construction and has a lift-out padded top (Fig. 3-12A). Lower rails are optional. Rails could be doweled to the legs but are shown tenoned (Fig. 3-12B). Prepare the rails with rabbets 1/2 inch wide and deep (Fig. 3-12C). Mark the tops of the legs for matching recesses (Fig. 3-12D) but do not cut these away until after you have cut the mortises and tenons. Assemble squarely.

The seat could be 1/2-inch plywood. It has to fit in the rabbets with the covering cloth wrapped over it. Get the size by experimenting with the cloth you will use. Drill a pattern of four, 1/2-inch holes in the wood to allow air in and out as the padding compresses and expands.

Foam 1-inch thick will be suitable. Cut it up to 1/2 inch bigger all around and bevel it underneath (Fig. 3-12E). Harder foam can be cut slightly less. Use 3/8-inch tacks as you pull the cloth over (Fig. 3-12F). Start near the centers of opposite sides and pull enough to compress the foam edges. Do the same the other way and work towards the corner. Space the tacks to get an even shape—probably 1 inch apart. At the corners, fold the cloth under. Cut a neat edge inside the line of tacks, which should be far enough in to clear the rail rabbets.

**Materials List for Upholstered Stool**

| | |
|---|---|
| 4 legs | 2 × 2 × 16 |
| 2 rails | 1 × 4 × 21 |
| 2 rails | 1 × 4 × 15 |
| 1 seat | 1/2 × 14 × 21 |

## BENCH WITH BACK

Benches have been made in many forms with legs extended to support a back, but the usual upright arrangement does not make for comfort. The bench in Fig. 3-13 is a modification of sawbuck legs. It has a moderately sloping seat with a back rail that gives support at a more correct angle. This type was used in churches as well as in home and yard.

Any reasonable length is possible, but the sizes suggested are for a seat 72 inches long. A stiff hardwood is advised. All the parts of the ends are 1 3/4 inches thick. There could be mortise and tenon joints, but it is simpler to use 3/4-inch or 1-inch dowels. Have three in each joint and take

them about 1 1/4 inches into each piece. Make all the dowel holes square to the meeting faces.

Draw a full-size end view on a grid of 2-inch squares, 20 inches by 30 inches (Fig. 3-14A). The main leg slopes 60 degrees to the base. Marking the main positions on this leg and the base will help in locating the other parts. Mark across the base the approximate positions of the edges of the legs (Fig. 3-14B). Mark the angle on the main leg and 7 inches to where the other leg joins (Fig. 3-14C), then mark the positions of the back and top rails. From these parts you can mark the shape of the short leg (Fig. 3-14D). Round the outer corners of the base and cut away the bottom to make feet.

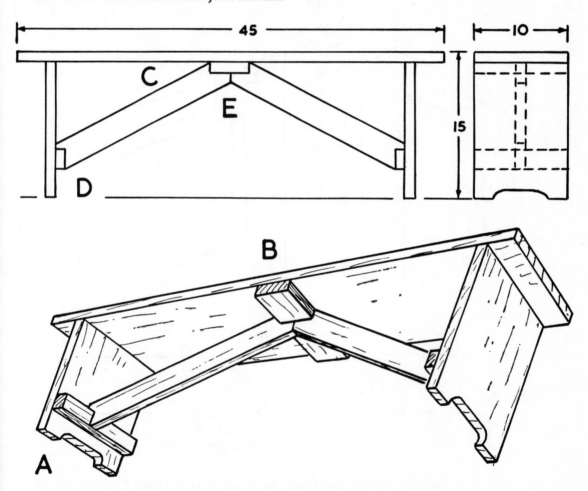

*Fig. 3-11. This bench is braced to give stiffness to a long top.*

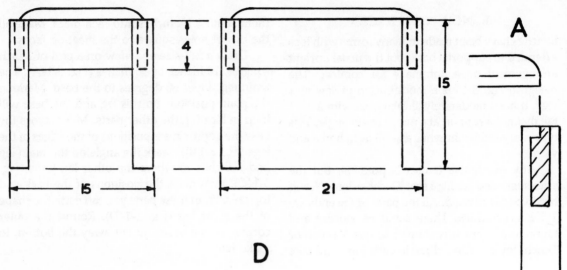

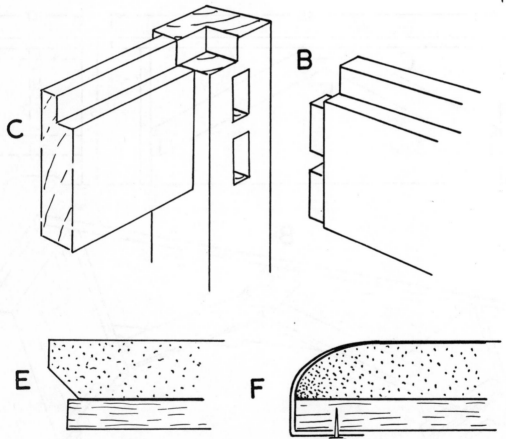

Fig. 3-12. Constructional details of an upholstered stool (A-E) and the method of fitting foam padding upholstery (E, F).

From the details on the squared drawing, make the seat bracket with grain lines diagonal (Fig. 3-14E). Prepare it for dowels to the leg. You could improve the appearance of the main parts by cutting stopped chamfers on the edges between joints. Assemble all parts made so far. Check that the opposite ends match and are flat.

The back rail (Fig. 3-14F) fits between the ends with dowels into them. The seat (Fig. 3-14G) is beveled against it and is notched to the same length but extends 2 inches past the ends. Make the seat rail (Fig. 3-14H) to extend 1 inch. The top rail (Fig. 3-14J) extends the same amount as the seat. Round the edges and corners of the seat and top rail. Drill for dowels between the notched parts of the seat and the legs.

Make a square bracket 6 inches each way for each end (Fig. 3-14K). Attach these to the ends with dowels, square to the seat. Join the back rail and seat together with glue and screws, then with

dowels to the ends. All other crossings should be screwed as well as glued, with the screw heads sunk and covered with plugs (Fig. 5-14D).

See that the ends are upright and square to the seat as you screw it down to the brackets. Screw and glue the seat rail to the brackets and seat.

Fit the top rail into its notches. If it lacks stiffness or you are making a very long bench, put a strip like the seat rail between the legs behind it.

## Materials List for Bench with Back

| | |
|---|---|
| 2 bases | 1 3/4 × 3 × 22 |
| 2 legs | 1 3/4 × 3 1/2 × 32 |
| 2 legs | 1 3/4 × 3 1/2 × 14 |
| 4 brackets | 1 3/4 × 6 × 10 |
| 1 top rail | 1 1/8 × 4 1/2 × 74 |
| 1 back rail | 1 1/8 × 4 × 70 |
| 1 seat | 1 1/8 × 14 × 74 |
| 1 seat rail | 1 1/8 × 2 1/2 × 72 |

Fig. 3-13. This bench with a back uses a modified form of sawbuck legs for the end supports.

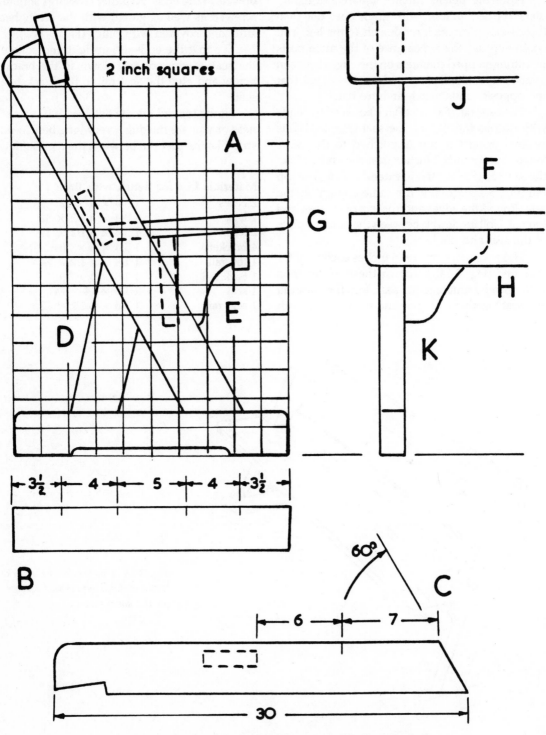

2 inch squares

A

G

E

D

B

3½  4  5  4  3½

J

F

H

K

60°

6  7

C

30

Fig. 3-14. Shapes and sizes for the parts of a bench with a back.

# *Four*

# *Tables*

Some sort of a working surface at a convenient height is a priority in any home. In the first homes this need for somewhere to prepare food and eat it, as well as for many other household tasks, would have been met by fashioning a table. Early tables might have been temporary assemblies of split logs, but something more like the usual table would soon have been produced.

Today, a table similar to that if made of split logs can still look attractive in a yard, but for indoor use, tables made from cut boards are more suitable. Besides the comparatively crude tables, there were others of better quality that would make attractive reproductions in a modern setting as well as in a room with a country theme. Most country tables were of rather heavy and robust construction with little decoration added, but it was not long before craftsmen started making tables and other furniture with traditional joints and a generally lighter and more attractive finish. The development of country table designs on the eastern coast was mostly from late seventeenth century to the late eighteenth century.

The obvious table design would seem to be a top on suitably framed four legs, but there are many other arrangements. In the New England states, a basic four-legged table might be called a *tavern table*. A *trestle table* is one where the top can be lifted off its end supports. This was common in medieval Europe, but the name might also be given to a table with a central pillar on spread feet at each end. A *refectory table* could be any table used for meals, but its name comes from the massive tables with rails near the floor that were used in medieval monasteries. A *sawbuck table* has crossed legs and is the American name for a form which goes back to earlier days in ecclesiastical furniture.

Tables could be made from any wood, and there are some attractive ones made of softwood. Both for appearance and the ability to stand up to hard used, however, it is better to use hardwood, preferably of a local variety.

## RUSTIC TABLE

For use outdoors with rustic benches, as described in Chapter 3, a table made from natural wood with the minimum of finishing work would have a country look. It would be an interesting change from the almost universal picnic table design.

Sizes will depend on available wood, but reasonable size would have three, 10-inch wide boards in the top, each about 2 inches thick and any length you require. The supports could be 2

inches by 4 inches and the legs about 3 inches in diameter, long enough to lift the table to 30 inches high (Fig. 4-1).

The top boards should be sawn with straight meeting edges on top, but any waney edges can be left underneath (Fig. 4-1A). Leave outer edges as they come, if not too winding, or trim off the worst lumps.

To keep the top surfaces level and the boards close, glue in dowels (Fig. 4-1B). For 2-inch wood make them 1 inch in diameter.

Prepare the supports with flat top surfaces (Fig. 4-1C). Drill holes that will splay the legs outwards, preferably at least 1 1/2 inches in diameter. Make the legs too long at first. Taper the tops to drive in the holes (Fig. 4-1D). Use wedges, if necessary, and glue the joints.

The top might be nailed to the supports, but it would be better to use dowels. Space them two to each board at each place and take them right through both thicknesses.

Invert the table and trim all legs to the same length. It is advisable to treat most woods with a preservative, if the table is to remain outside, but some woods will weather to an attractive appearance without a tendency to rot if left untreated. Take local advice.

## JOINTLESS TABLE

If you are furnishing a room according to the earliest settlers' pattern, or want a table quickly for use in a shed, shop or summerhouse, just nail the parts together. Some primitive tables made in this way have survived a long time, so the method is stronger than you might have thought.

Sizes may be almost anything, but rigidity depends on deep rails secured to the legs. Whatever the size, for a table 30 inches high the rails should be at least 6 inches. Use plenty of nails, which should enter at least 1 inch into the leg.

The table shown in Fig. 4-2A has three, 8-inch boards making up the width of the top. Though it isn't necessary, you might prefer to glue these and all other joints. If the wood has been machine-planed, go over visible surfaces with a hand plane. Slight flaws will add to an authentic appearance.

The four legs are 2 1/2 inches square. Allow for rails being 1 inch in from the edges of the top (Fig. 4-2B). Nail and glue the short rails to the legs (Fig. 4-2C) using five long nails in drilled holes at each joint. Check squareness. Join with the long rails with the nails pattern the opposite way and more nails into the end grain of the end rails. Check squareness all around and nail on the top.

**Materials List for Jointless Table**

| | |
|---|---|
| 3 top boards | 1 × 8 × 49 |
| 4 legs | 2 1/2 × 2 1/2 × 27 |
| 2 end rails | 1 × 6 × 22 |
| 2 side rails | 1 × 6 × 48 |

## TENONED TABLE

The basic, well-made tavern table had the rails joined to the legs with mortise and tenon joints. In a similar table today you might use dowels, but they were never used two centuries ago. You should make the traditional joints, even if you cut them with a router.

This project (Fig. 4-3) is shown the same size as the previous table for comparison, but it could be made any size. A wide top will expand and contract, so rigid nailing or screwing could lead to cracking or warping. This table allows for movement of the top by using buttons that slide in grooves.

Prepare wood for the rails with 1/4-inch grooves, 1/4 inch from the top (Fig. 4-3A). Cut the wood for the legs with a little excess length at the tops. They will be trimmed after the joints have been cut.

Mark the joints (Fig. 4-3B) with tenons 1/2 inch wide and penetrating the legs until they meet (Fig. 4-3C). Cut and glue the joints, then clamp tightly one way. When the glue that way has set, join rails the other way.

Glue boards to overlap the top 1 inch outside the legs. Make buttons (Fig. 4-3D) that will pull tight on a groove when screwed to the top. It should be sufficient to have three buttons each side and two at each end. After a trial assembly, the top may be removed for convenience in finishing the wood with stain and polish.

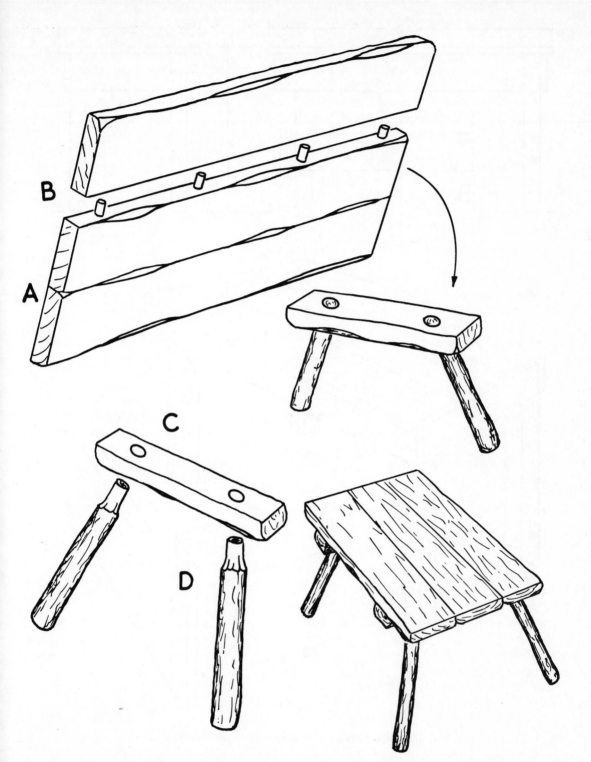

Fig. 4-1. For outdoor use, this rustic table has a top made of roughly shaped boards and legs of natural wood.

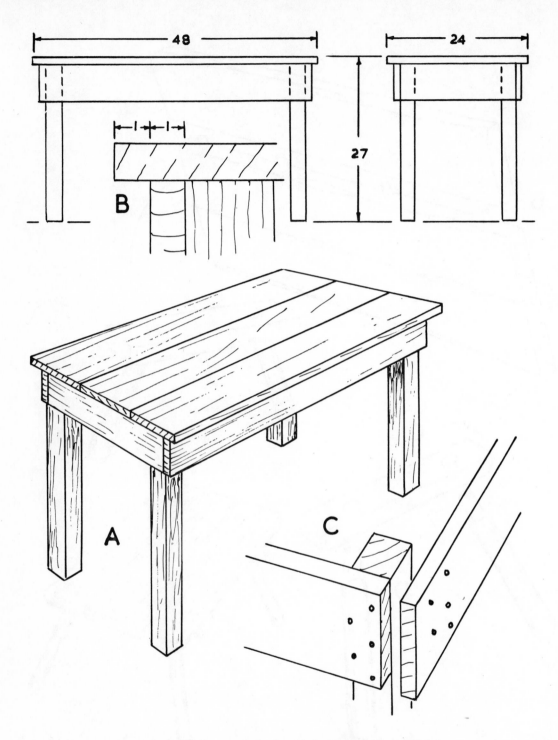

Fig. 4-2. *This table is made in the simplest way without cut joints.*

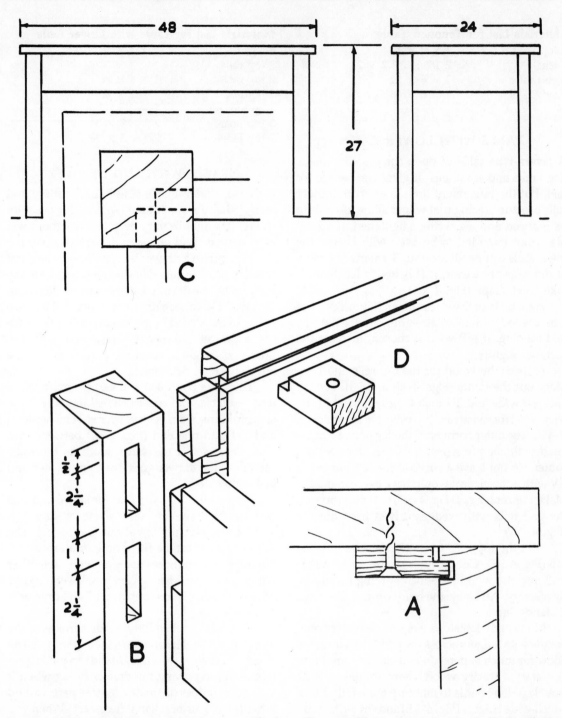

Fig. 4-3. *A basic table, known earlier as a tavern table, has stiffness provided by deep tenoned rails (B, C). The top is held by buttons in grooved rails to allow for expansion and contraction (A, D).*

**Materials List for Tenoned Table**

| | |
|---|---|
| 3 top boards | 1 × 8 × 49 |
| 4 legs | 2 1/2 × 2 1/2 × 27 |
| 2 end rails | 1 × 6 × 22 |
| 2 side rails | 1 × 6 × 46 |

## TABLE WITH LOWER RAILS

A tavern-type table of open construction needs deep rails and stout legs. It gives clear space for feet, but the rails might limit knee room. Lower rails provide bracing that would allow top rails to be reduced and leg sections lightened. If the table is not intended to be used with chairs, the lower rails can go all around. To allow leg room at the sides, however, it is better to let the rails take an H-shape (Fig. 4-4A).

For a table of the sizes shown (Fig. 4-5A), use a hardwood with fairly straight grain for the legs and framing. If softwood is chosen, increase the sections slightly.

Prepare the wood for the top rails and legs. Mark out the joints (Figs. 4-4B and 5B). Tenons 1/2 inch wide and 3/4 inch long will meet in the legs. The crosswise rails have simple tenons (Fig. 4-4C). The outer corners of the legs can be lightened with chamfers (Fig. 4-5C). If done with a router, do not leave a curve at the top but cut to a V with a chisel, as it would have been originally. Make the center rail (Fig. 4-5D) to tenon through the end rails with wedges driven from outside (Fig. 4-4D).

Drill the top rails for pocket screws into the top (Fig. 4-5E). Cut recesses so the screw heads pull into the wood. A 9-inch spacing should be satisfactory. Assemble the framework and see that it stands square.

Many early tabletops were made with several boards with ledgers across the ends. This does not allow for much expansion and contraction, but if you start with dry wood, there should be little trouble. Glue boards to make up the width. Make 3-inch-wide ledgers (Fig. 4-4E) and cut tongue and groove joints, with the tongue one-third the thickness of the wood and extending about 3/4 inch. Invert the table and screw through the top rails.

**Materials List for Table with Lower Rails**

| | |
|---|---|
| 4 legs | 2 × 2 × 30 |
| 2 top rails | 1 × 4 × 50 |
| 2 top rails | 1 × 4 × 23 |
| 2 bottom rails | 1 × 2 × 23 |
| 1 bottom rail | 1 × 2 × 50 |
| 3 top boards | 7/8 × 9 × 54 |
| 2 top ledgers | 7/8 × 3 × 28 |

## TABLE WITH END DRAWER

A drawer under a table is useful for cutlery and many other things, but if it is a table for use with chairs, it cannot be very deep or knee room will be restricted. With a tavern or similar table, the useful depth in a drawer is only a few inches, but that can provide valuable storage space. In many early tables the drawer is in the narrow direction. This might have been for convenience, but it is also easier to get a good fit and action that way. Adding a drawer reduces the transverse stiffness. Lower rails might be advisable, particularly if there are drawers at both ends.

This table (Figs. 4-6 and 4-7) is similar to the tenoned table, and constructional details are the same for three sides. The drawer is 24 inches long and fits into one end (Fig. 4-7A) between two crosspieces set at the same depth as the rails; therefore, the drawer goes between the legs and is 4 inches deep.

Prepare the legs, the rails for sides, and one end. For the drawer end dovetail the top strip (Fig. 4-7B) and tenon the lower rail (Fig. 4-7C). The drawer guides can be fitted now or after assembly. Make sure surfaces are level with each other where they meet. Making parts parallel and square with each other is also important if the drawer is to slide easily.

Fit guides level with the inside surfaces of the legs (Fig. 4-7D). Fit runners to them (Fig. 4-7E) on which the drawer will slide. At the top put kickers (Fig. 4-7F) to prevent the drawer tilting when it slides out. It does not matter if these parts extend into the table further than is necessary. When you have made and tried the drawer, put stops under the kickers (Fig. 4-7G) to limit movement and leave the drawer front level with the legs.

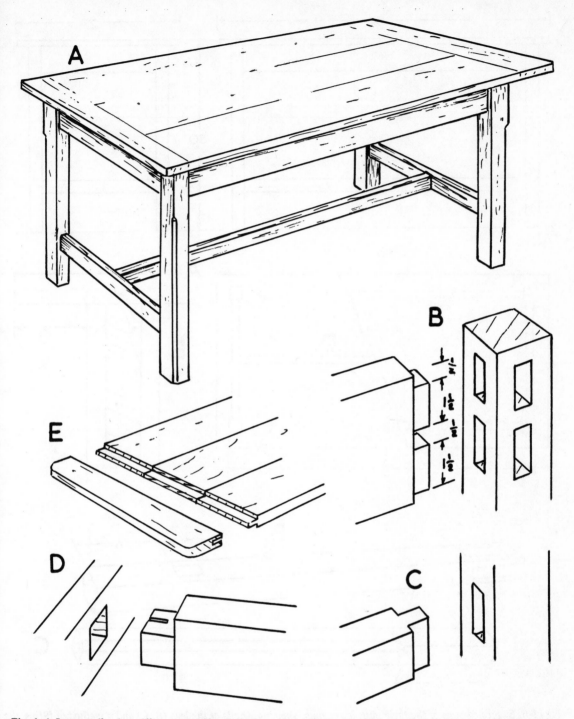

Fig. 4-4. Lower rails give stiffness to a table. A single central rail gives good leg room. A flat top is ensured by ledgers across the ends (E).

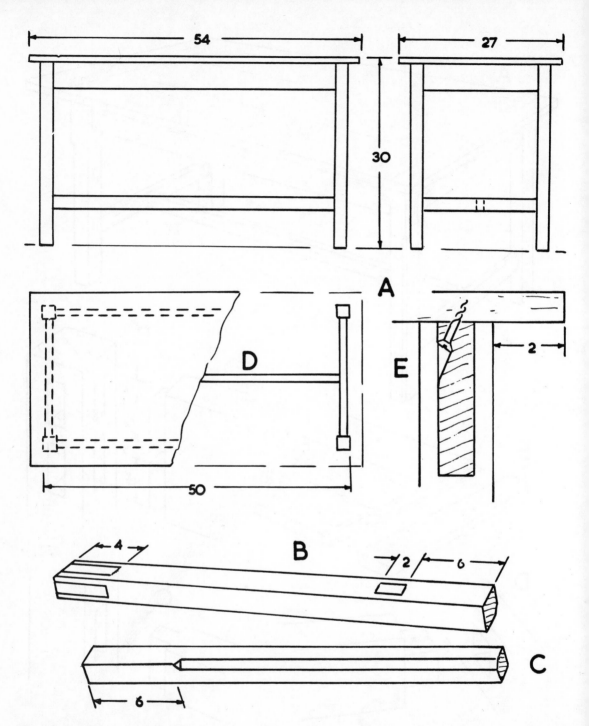

Fig. 4-5. Suggested sizes of the table with lower rails, showing details of the legs (B, C) and a method of fitting the top with pocket screws.

The drawer could have been a nailed box, but anyone with the skill to make this table would almost certainly have made a drawer with a dovetailed front. Prepare the front to fit the opening (Fig. 4-8A). Make the sides (Fig. 4-8B) to slide in their guides. Cut grooves for the bottom (Fig. 4-8C). It would be wrong to use plywood for the bottom. An original table would have had thicker wood thinned at the edges to fit in the grooves. An alternative to grooves would have been strips to which the bottom would have been nailed (Fig. 4-8D).

Cut the front dovetails. Either cut dovetails for the back or groove the sides (F g. 4-8E). Make a dry assembly and try the drawer in the table. Glue

Glue the parts. A simple wood handle (Fig. 4-8F) would be more appropriate than a metal one.

### Materials List for Table with End Drawer

| | |
|---|---|
| 4 legs | 2 1/2 × 2 1/2 × 30 |
| 2 rails | 1 × 6 × 50 |
| 1 rail | 1 × 6 × 24 |
| 2 rails | 1 × 2 × 24 |
| 2 kickers | 1 × 1 1/4 × 27 |
| 2 runners | 1 × 1 × 27 |
| 2 guides | 2 × 3/4 × 27 |
| 1 drawer front | 7/8 × 4 × 21 |
| 1 drawer back | 5/8 × 3 1/2 × 21 |
| 2 drawer sides | 5/8 × 4 × 25 |
| 1 drawer bottom | 1/2 × 19 × 24 |

*Fig. 4-6. A drawer under a table is useful, but it has to be kept within the rail depth.*

## TABLE WITH SPLAYED TAPERED LEGS

Tapered legs give a lighter appearance and splaying the legs adds to the effect. In better early furniture these were design features. The example in Fig. 4-9 is a square occasional table, but the method could be used for tables of other sizes. If legs are splayed both ways very much, there are complications in the joints; but with these moderate angles, the joints can be cut as if square in section. A good quality hardwood is advised. The top

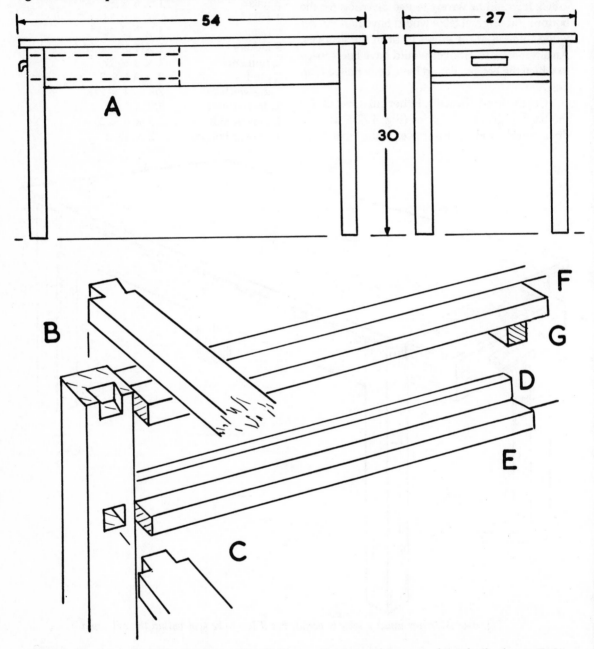

Fig. 4-7. Sizes of a table with end drawer (A) and the way the open end is arranged to take the drawer (B-G).

could be different wood from the other parts.

Draw a full-size side view (Fig. 4-10). This gives the leg angles and the size of rails. The legs are tapered on the inner edges only. Do all marking out of them from the outer straight edges using an adjustable bevel set to the correct angle (Fig. 4-10A). Mark where the rails come and start tapering 1 inch below.

Mark the rails, allowing for 1/2 inch thick tenons entering far enough to meet in the legs (Fig. 4-10B). Dowels could be used, but they would not be authentic for a reproduction. Plane the top edges of the rails to the correct angle and groove them for buttons (Fig. 4-10C). The lower edges are improved by shaping (Fig. 4-10D). Make a half template and use it to mark all rails the same.

Assemble opposite parts of legs, then join them. See that the legs stand level and the framework is symmetrical and square.

Join boards to make up the top width. Edges could be square, rounded, or molded, but keep the molding narrow and simple. Invert the frame

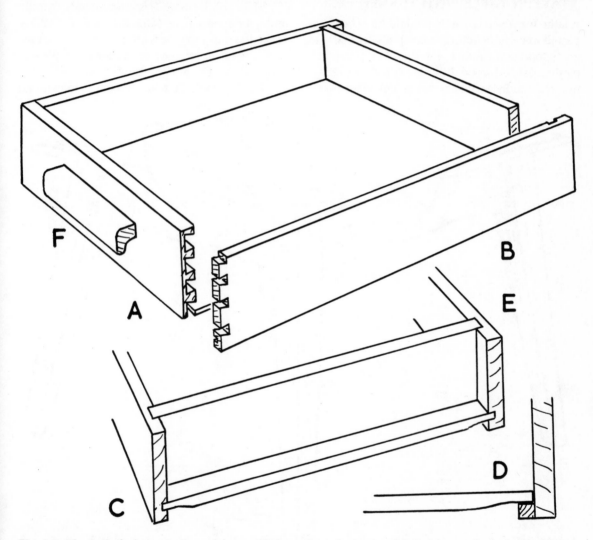

Fig. 4-8. *The method of constructing a drawer with dovetails at the front and dado joints at the back. The bottom can fit into grooves (C) or be supported by strips (D).*

work on the underside of the top and center it. Eight buttons, arranged fairly close to the legs, will hold the top on.

**Materials List for Table with Splayed Tapered Legs**

| | |
|---|---|
| 4 legs | 1 3/4 × 1 3/4 × 25 |
| 4 rails | 1 × 5 × 19 |
| 1 top | 7/8 × 24 × 26 |
| 8 buttons | 3/4 × 1 1/2 × 3 |

## TAVERN TABLE WITH TURNED LEGS

A lathe was used more than might have been expected in early furniture. Mainly it was easier to get a good surface that way than to try to plane partly seasoned wood, but it also produced attractive results. In particular, table legs were partly or completely turned. The example in Fig. 4-11 is a type of tavern table from New England and elsewhere. The top has a wide overhang at the ends to compensate for the restriction of foot space due to the rails. The sizes shown (Fig. 4-12A) are for a table suitable for use with chairs when working or eating.

Make the four legs (Fig. 4-12B) with the square parts extending 1 inch past the rail positions. Choose your own pattern but avoid excessive detail. Leave a little extra length at the top until after the joints have been cut.

Mark out the mortise and tenon joints for top and bottom rails in the same way as earlier tables. Make the four top rails with grooves for buttons. The long lower rail tenons into the end rails (see Fig. 4-4B, C, D). Join all framing parts.

The top could be made of boards joined and

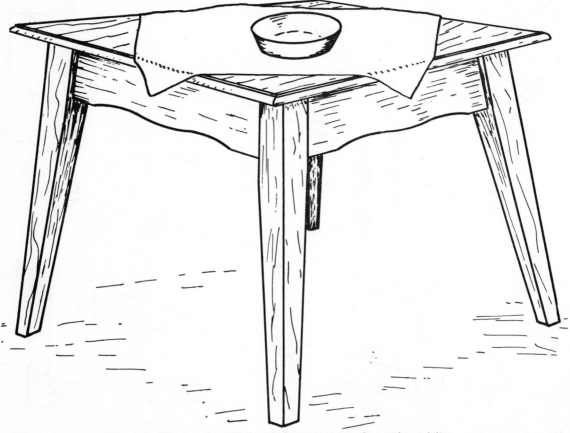

*Fig. 4-9. Splaying the table legs looks attractive and provides stability.*

the ends left open, or there could be ledgers (see Fig. 4-4E). Leave the edges square or moderately rounded. Join the framing to the top with buttons (see Fig. 4-3A and D)—two at the ends and three each side should be enough. Early tavern tables often had the lower parts painted and the top left bare, for washing occasionally.

**Materials List for Tavern Table with Turned Legs**

| | |
|---|---|
| 4 legs | 2 1/2 × 2 1/2 × 30 |
| 2 rails | 1 × 5 × 38 |
| 2 rails | 1 × 5 × 23 |
| 2 rails | 1 × 3 × 23 |
| 1 rail | 1 × 3 × 38 |
| 10 buttons | 3/4 × 2 × 4 |

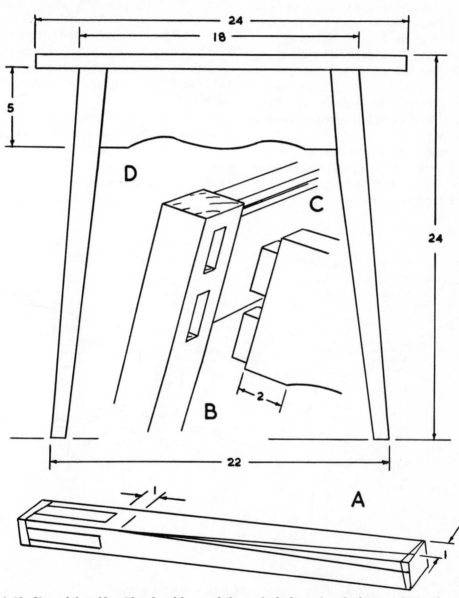

Fig. 4-10. Sizes of the table with splayed legs and the method of tapering the legs on the inside surfaces.

## TABLE WITH CABRIOLE LEGS

The name *cabriole* can refer to a variety of legs formed after the manner of an animal's leg and paw or claw. A simplified version can be turned; the result is an attractive leg for a light coffee or side table. Such tables were made with round and octagonal tops. Either can be used without affecting construction. This table (Figs. 4-13 and 4-14) has the legs slightly splayed. If this type of leg is made upright, it might appear to slope inwards. Draw a full-size view (Fig. 4-14A), either complete or to the centerline, to obtain sizes and angles.

Carefully mark the center of the square leg wood. At the foot mark a second position diagonally from the first (Fig. 4-14B). The further the second center is moved, the more slender will be the leg, but 3/8 inch should be satisfactory on a 2-inch square leg.

With the true center at the tailstock, turn a bead under the square top (Fig. 4-14C) and short distance down the leg. At the bottom turn a small parallel circle topped by the foot (Fig. 4-14D).

Change to the offset center and turn the tapered part of the leg. You might have to return to the true center to blend in the foot and leg, followed by a little work with file and abrasive paper.

Make the four rails (Figs. 4-13A and 4-14E). They are shown finishing level with the outsides of the legs (Fig. 4-13B). There could be dowels, but the traditional joint is a *barefaced* mortise and tenon, with the tenons level with the inside surfaces of the rail (Fig. 4-14F). Groove the insides of the rails for buttons. Assemble the framework.

Join boards sufficient for the top and cut it circular or octagonal (Fig. 4-14G). Edges could be molded, but an original table would probably have had a simple rounding. Join the framework to the top with buttons.

### Materials List for Table with Cabriole Legs

| | |
|---|---|
| 4 legs | 2 × 2 × 28 |
| 4 rails | 1 × 6 × 16 |
| 1 top | 7/8 × 24 × 24 |

*Fig. 4-11. Turned legs give a table a distinctive appearance.*

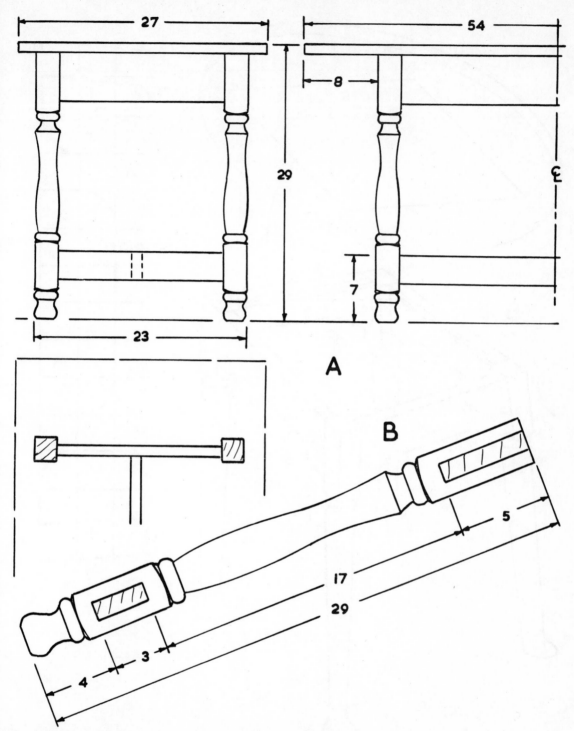

Fig. 4-12. Constructional details are similar to earlier tables. The top is shown with a long end overhang that gives leg room there (A). The legs are left square where the mortises are to be cut (B).

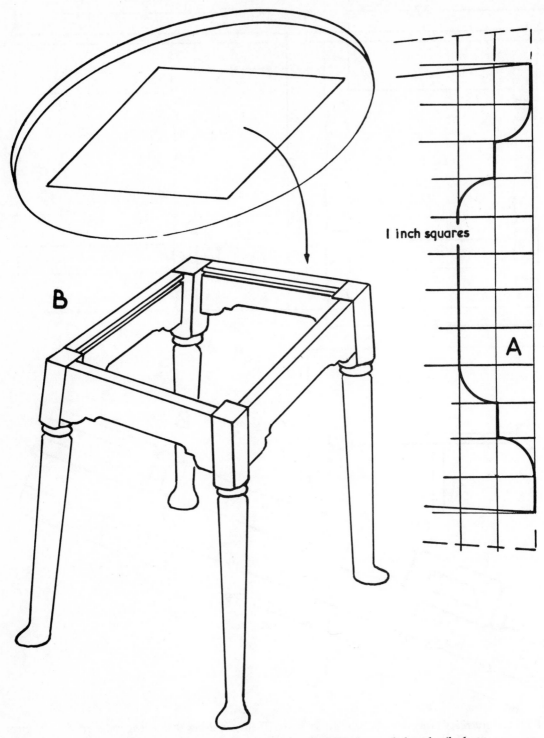

I inch squares

A

B

Fig. 4-13. This round-topped table has a form of cabriole legs and shaped rail edges.

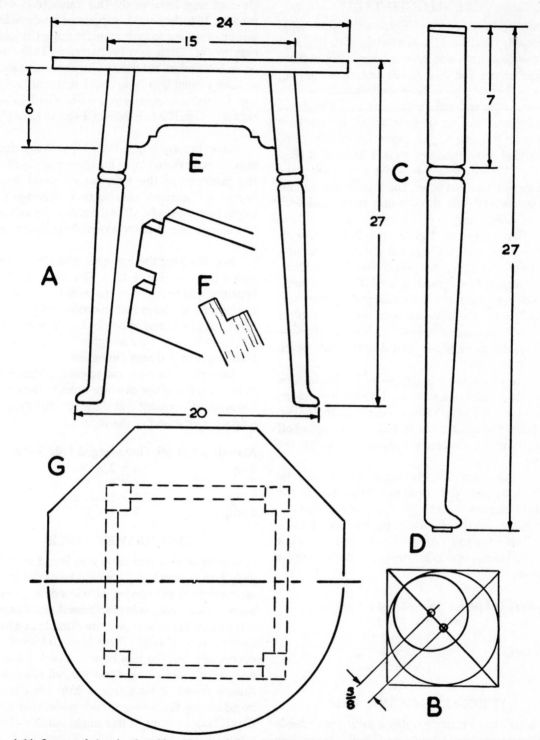

Fig. 4-14. *Suggested sizes for the table with cabriole legs. The legs are formed by turning with the lathe center in two positions (B, D). An octagonal top (G) could be substituted for a round one.*

## THREE-LEGGED TABLE

Some early tables were made with three legs, probably because of the advantage over four legs of standing firm on an uneven floor. Some of these were simple and crude, like oversized milking stools, but they later developed into tables with turned legs and rails with round or hexagonal tops. Some had square tops, which did not look right on three legs. This example is a light table intended to be made in a good hardwood (Fig. 4-15A). The suggested sizes (Fig. 4-15B) will make a useful occasional table. The legs fit into a triangular frame under the top and are braced with three lower rails.

To obtain sizes, draw a circle 28 inches in diameter and step off the radius around the circumference, then join these points (Fig. 4-16A). Draw a 10-inch radius circle and mark the leg centers. Make the three parts of the triangular frame (Fig. 4-16B) with the distance between hole centers taken from your drawing. Halve the corners, round the outer edges, and drill through 1-inch holes.

Turn the three legs (Fig. 4-16C), with the tops to fit the frame holes. At the lower rail positions drill two, 5/8-inch holes 60 degrees apart (Fig. 4-16D). The spacing can be found by stepping off half the diameter of the wood from one hole to the next.

Make the three rails (Fig. 4-16E). Check the length against your drawing. Miter where the ends will meet in the legs. Assemble all parts. If necessary, wedge the top of the legs (Fig. 4-15C).

Make the top with rounded edges. Attach it by screwing upwards through the triangular frame.

### Materials List for Three-legged Table

| | |
|---|---|
| 3 legs | 2 × 2 × 27 |
| 3 rails | 1 1/4 × 1 1/4 × 20 |
| 3 frames | 1 1/2 × 4 × 24 |
| 1 top | 1 × 25 × 28 |

## THREE-LEGGED SIDE TABLE

A table for an entrance hall or a passageway needs to be narrow and fit against a wall with its legs clear of any baseboard. This table (Fig. 4-17) projects 15 inches and is supported by three legs arranged square to each other, making the joints easy to cut. There is a Pennsylvania Dutch feel about the design, but their tables were more likely to have turned legs. You could substitute round legs for those shown, if you wish. The legs and rails are made like two sides of a square table (Fig. 4-18A).

Make the legs (Fig. 4-18B). Taper in one direction, then mark and taper the other way. Mark on the positions of the rails, which could be tenoned in traditional construction, although you might prefer dowels. Make the rails and join them to the legs. See that the assembly is square and level.

For attaching the top, glue and screw strips inside the rails (Fig. 4-18C). The top is made of boards glued to make up the width. The outline can be semicircular or half an octagon (Fig. 4-18D). Edges can be rounded or molded. You could fit a strip on the top of the straightedge to protect the wall or prevent things falling off.

Invert the assembly and screw the framework to the top. If you use oversize holes in the strips, the screw movement will allow for slight expansion or contraction of the top.

### Materials List for Three-legged Side Table

| | |
|---|---|
| 3 legs | 2 × 2 × 28 |
| 2 rails | 1 × 6 × 15 |
| 1 top | 1 × 15 × 32 |
| 2 strips | 1 × 1 × 15 |

## TWO-DRAWER TABLE

A narrow side or sofa table was found in many early homes, and today it would be useful inside an entrance or as a serving table in a dining room. Some tables were made of softwood, but this one would look better and be more durable in a local hardwood (Fig. 4-19). There is the minimum of decoration, but the legs have stopped chamfers and there could be beads on the rail edges and drawer fronts. If sizes (Fig. 4-20A) are altered, avoid having the drawers much wider than their depth back to front as this might cause difficult action.

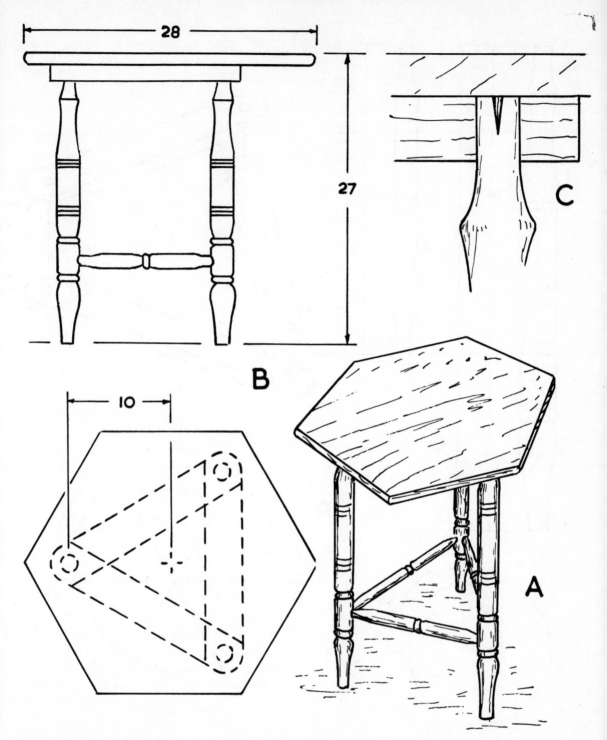

Fig. 4-15. Three legs will stand level on any surface. This table is shown with a hexagonal top over turned legs and lower rails.

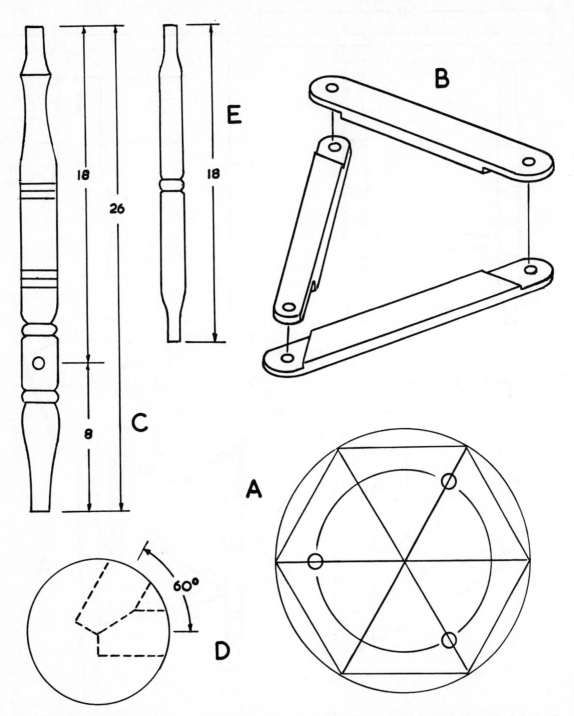

Fig. 4-16. Leg positions are spaced equally around a circle (A). Three halved rails (B) locate the legs. The holes in the legs (C) are spaced (D) to suit the rails (E).

The legs (Fig. 4-20B) are shown with mortises, as in earlier tables, but the rails could be dowelled. The chamfers are 2 inches below and above the rails. Cut V ends to them.

The rails are made as for other tables, with grooves for buttons and a bead on the outside of the top rails, if you wish (Fig. 4-21A). Cut drawer openings in the long front rail (Fig. 4-20C), leaving 1 inch above and below. In an earlier table, the drawer guide assemblies would have been tenoned, or just nailed in simpler work, but dowels are suggested. The parts are the same at top and bottom. At the center make boards wide enough to go 1 inch under each opening and set strips level with the edges of the openings (Fig. 4-20D). There are similar guides at the outer edges, but

*Fig. 4-17. This table fits against a wall and is supported by three legs.*

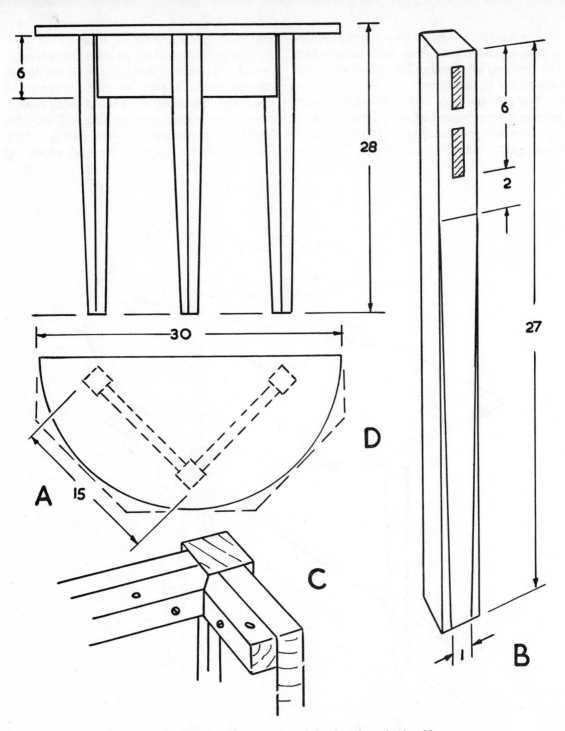

Fig. 4-18. Details of construction of the three-legged side table.

they are narrower (Fig. 4-20E). Drill for 3/8-inch dowels. Be careful that the edges that will guide the drawers come level with the openings.

Assemble the parts made so far, being careful with squareness, particularly across the drawer guides. Sight across to see that there is no twist.

Make the drawer fronts to fit the openings. Bead the top and bottom edges (Fig. 4-21B). Cut strips a little too long for the sides, to slide in the guides. Drawer parts could be joined in several ways, but if you want to follow the original design, use dovetails stopped at the front (Fig. 4-21C) and through at the back (Fig. 4-21D). Groove the front and sides for the bottom, which could be ply-

wood, or use pieces of thicker wood thinned at the edges if you want to copy original construction (Fig. 4-21E). Let the rear side dovetails extend a little at first, then plane them off to stop against the back rail when the drawer front is level. The drawer back goes above the bottom (Fig. 4-21G), and nails or screws are driven up into it. The edge of the bottom can also extend to be planed to serve as a stop against the back rail.

Drawer knobs should be turned wood with glued dowel ends (Fig. 4-21F). See that drawer action is satisfactory before working on the tabletop. Wax will ease movement.

Glue boards to make up the top and attach it

*Fig. 4-19. Drawers in the side of the table are always useful. This example has stopped chamfer decoration on the legs.*

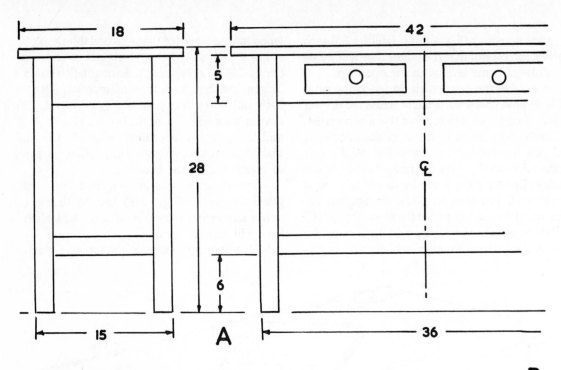

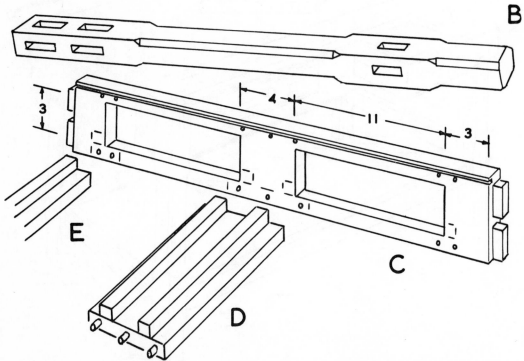

Fig. 4-20. Sizes of the two-drawer table (A), its legs (B), and the front rail (C) to take the drawer runners (D, E).

with buttons. Two on each rail should be sufficient.

## Materials List for Two-Drawer Table

| | |
|---|---|
| 4 legs | 2 × 2 × 28 |
| 2 rails | 1 × 6 × 36 |
| 2 rails | 1 × 6 × 15 |
| 2 rails | 1 × 2 × 36 |
| 2 rails | 1 × 2 × 15 |
| 1 top | 1 × 18 × 44 |
| 2 drawer guides | 1 × 6 × 15 |
| 4 drawer guides | 1 × 2 × 15 |
| 8 drawer guides | 1 × 1 × 15 |
| 2 drawer fronts | 1 × 3 × 12 |
| 4 drawer sides | 5/8 × 3 × 15 |
| 2 drawer backs | 5/8 × 2 1/2 × 12 |
| 2 drawer bottoms | 1/4 × 11 × 14 |

## BASIC TRESTLE TABLE

A trestle table has two supports separated by stretchers; and it is found in many variations in modern furniture as well as examples of early craftsmanship. This example (Fig. 4-22A) is intended to have a top 30 inches wide and 60 inches long, standing 29 inches high. It would have been the general-purpose table in an early home, and it still makes an attractive piece of furniture if you are looking for something more advanced than the tavern type. A good hardwood is preferable to softwood, although a softwood top could be put over a hardwood framework.

Start with the tops and bottoms of the trestles (Fig. 4-22B and C). They have the same general shapes, except the bottoms are cut away to make

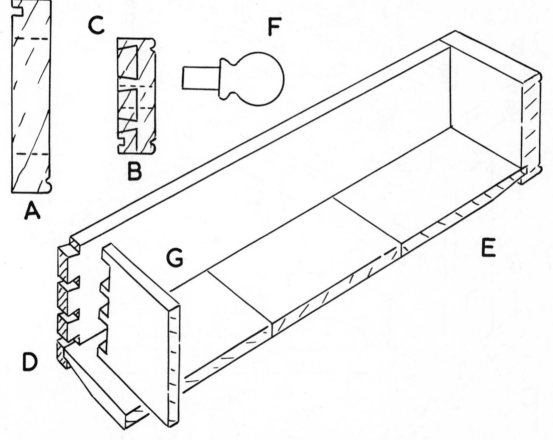

Fig. 4-21. Rail and drawer parts and a section showing how the drawer is made.

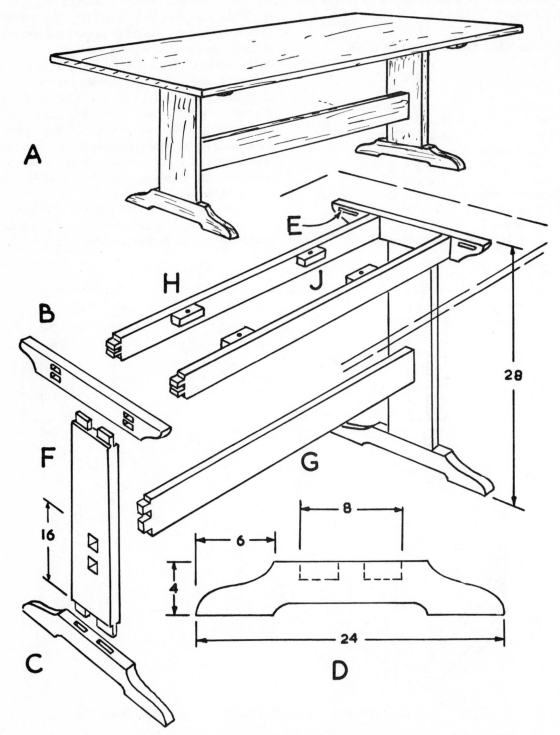

A

E

H        J

B

F

G

16

C        D

4

6

8

24

28

Fig. 4-22. A trestle table of basic form has built-up ends and lengthwise stretchers between them.

feet (Fig. 4-22D) and the tops are given mortises for stretchers and short slots for buttons (Fig. 4-22E). The uprights (Fig. 4-22F) have tenons into them and mortises for the bottom stretcher (Fig. 4-22G). Make the top stretchers (Fig. 4-22H) the same length as the bottom one. All tenons are double and should be wedged from outside. Put blocks inside the top stretchers (Fig. 4-22J) to take screws upwards into the top.

Assemble the trestles and check that they match. Join them with the three stretchers.

The top can be several boards glued to make up the width. Fit ledgers at the ends, if you wish, but it might be better not to restrict the wood so that it can expand and contract. Have buttons ready. Center the framework on the inverted top. Screw through the blocks (Fig. 4-22J) and add the buttons.

## Materials List for Basic Trestle Table

| | |
|---|---|
| 2 trestle tops | 1 1/2 × 4 × 25 |
| 2 trestle bottoms | 1 1/2 × 4 × 25 |

| | |
|---|---|
| 2 trestle legs | 1 1/2 × 8 × 28 |
| 1 bottom stretcher | 1 1/2 × 6 × 50 |
| 2 top stretchers | 1 1/2 × 4 × 50 |
| 1 top | 1 × 30 × 61 |

## SHAKER TRESTLE TABLE

The Shaker characteristics of simplicity and fitness for purpose is seen in their trestle tables, which top stringer to keep the parts from loosening up during use.

In this typical table (Fig. 4-23), because it is essential that all joints are strong, and only wedged followed very similar patterns in different communities. A lower stretcher was avoided to give maximum leg room and to allow chairs to be pushed under. That meant adding a strengthened deep mortises and tenons are suitable. Use a close-grained hardwood for the framing.

Prepare the two trestles (Fig. 4-24A). Because the base is tapered and reduced to a 3-inch depth to form feet, the upright has tenons to go through

*Fig. 4-23. This trestle table is based on Shaker designs and has a single deep stretcher to provide lengthwise stiffness.*

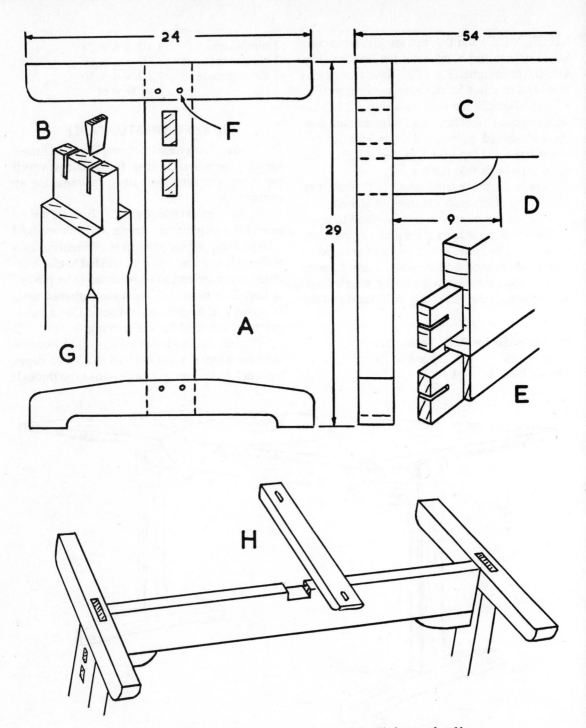

Fig. 4-24. Sizes and method of construction of the Shaker trestle table.

the same amount at each end (Fig. 4-24B). Put grooves for buttons near the ends of the top pieces as in the previous table (Fig. 4-22E).

The stretcher (Fig. 4-24C) is deepened at the ends with pieces glued on (Fig. 4-24D), then tenons are cut to go into the leg below the top piece (Fig. 4-24E). In the days when the original tables were made, glues were not as reliable as now, and it was usual to put dowels through the joints for extra strength. When you assemble the trestles you could add 3/8-inch dowels (Fig. 4-24F) after the joints have been tightened. Exposed edges of trestle parts could be chamfered (Fig. 4-24G). Assemble the trestles with wedges in the joints.

For a table with only a single stretcher, it is advisable to glue and screw a crosspiece (Fig. 4-24H) in a notch. Make slot holes for screws into the top to allow for expansion and contraction. Join the trestles with the other parts.

In a Shaker table the top was made of pieces glued together without ledgers at the ends. Join the framing to the top with buttons and screws through the slots.

### Materials List for Shaker Trestle Table

| | |
|---|---|
| 2 trestle tops | 3 × 3 × 25 |
| 2 trestle bottoms | 3 × 4 × 25 |
| 2 trestle legs | 3 × 4 × 30 |
| 1 stretcher | 1 1/2 × 8 × 56 |
| 2 stretcher stiffeners | 1 1/2 × 3 × 14 |
| 1 top | 1 × 30 × 66 |
| 1 top crosspiece | 1 × 3 × 25 |

### FOUR-LEGGED CANDLE STAND

When candles were the main source of illumination, there had to be places to put them at strategic points. If a candle was carried, the user needed to put it down where it would shed the most light. Besides wall sconces there were many tablelike stands made in various ways. Today, they make good stands for electric table lamps or for displaying flowers or plants.

This stand (Fig. 4-25A) is of light construction but made in the same way as a standard table. Polished hardwood would look good, but you could use softwood and paint it.

The legs are parallel, although you could chamfer the outer corners. Top rails would have had tenons (Fig. 4-25B), but you could use dowels (Fig. 4-25C). The lower rails are too small a section for satisfactory dowelling; tenons are better. Drill the top rails for pocket screws into the top (Fig. 4-5E). Two each way should be satisfactory.

Assemble opposite sides first, then add the rails the other way to ensure squareness. The lower shelf is octagon and rests on the lower rails (Fig. 4-25D). Either make an octagonal with equal sides or just cut away enough from a square to miss the legs.

The top can be left with square edges or can be molded or rounded. Invert the assembly and screw it on.

### Materials List for Four-legged Candle Stand

| | |
|---|---|
| 4 legs | 1 1/8 × 1 1/8 × 36 |
| 4 rails | 5/8 × 3 × 12 |
| 4 rails | 5/8 × 1 × 12 |
| 1 shelf | 1/2 × 12 × 12 |
| 1 top | 1/2 × 14 × 14 |

### PEDESTAL CANDLE STAND

Some attractive candle stands were made with a central pillar (Fig. 4-26A) and four feet instead of four legs. A reproduction would have similar modern uses to the last project. Hardwood is advisable. Overall sizes are the same as the four-legged candle stand. If they are altered, let the feet spread to greater width than the top. In this example, with a 14-inch top, the feet spread to 16 inches.

The pillar will go 1 inch below the joints with the feet. At the top, make two halved supports (Fig. 4-26B) and cut a square tenon on the pillar to go through them (Fig. 4-26C).

Make sure the four feet match (Fig. 4-26D). Position the grain diagonally. Drill for dowels in the pillar. So the joints can be closed tightly, leave

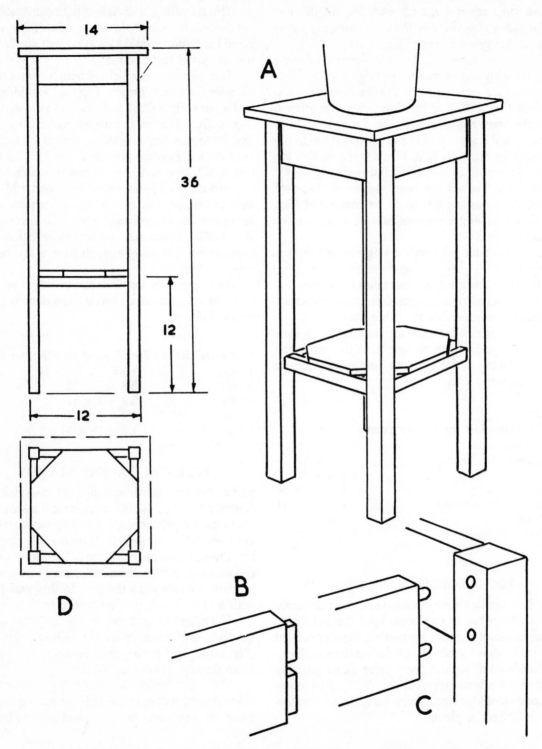

Fig. 4-25. *What was a four-legged candle stand can be used today for a table lamp or a flower display.*

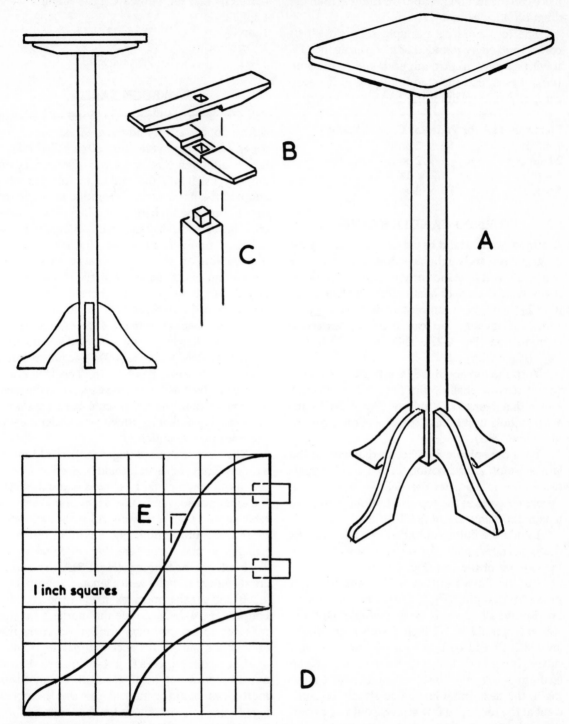

B

C

A

E

I inch squares

D

Fig. 4-26. This variation on the candle stand has a central pillar instead of four legs. At the top there is a tenon through a halved joint; the feet are dowelled to the pillar.

pieces on the feet (Fig. 4-26E) for clamps, then cut them off after assembly.

The top could be a simple square with its corners and edges rounded or made octagonal. Fix it with a screw up through each end of the supports. Check that the stand in upright. If necessary, adjust by planing the bottom of a foot.

**Materials List for Pedestal Candle Stand**

| | |
|---|---|
| 1 pillar | 2 × 2 × 36 |
| 2 supports | 1 × 2 × 13 |
| 1 top | 1/2 × 14 × 14 |
| 4 feet | 1 × 4 × 12 |

## TURNED CANDLE STAND

A turned candle stand based on a central spindle looks graceful and might have three instead of four feet to allow it to stand firm on an uneven floor. If you have the use of a lathe that will take more than 24 inches between centers and can swing a 13-inch diameter, you can make an attractive reproduction (Fig. 4-27). This stands 30 inches high (Fig. 4-27A).

Turn the top about 7/8 inch thick, preferably with a narrow shallow rim (Fig. 4-27B). Place a 6-inch diameter block under it (Fig. 4-27C) with a 1-inch hole in it to take the dowel on the spindle (Fig. 4-28D).

Turn the spindle 3-inches in diameter at the largest point. At the bottom turn a 4-inch length to 2 inches in diameter parallel (Fig. 4-27E). The decorated parts at the top and bottom then have maximum diameters of 2 1/2 inches.

Divide the bottom into three equal parts. At those positions, make flat surfaces as wide as the thicknesses of the feet (Fig. 4-27F).

Cut the three feet (Fig. 4-28A) and leave on pieces for clamping (Fig. 4-28B) until after assembly. Round all edges as far as possible. Drill the legs and spindle for 1/2-inch dowels (Figs. 4-27G and 28C). It will be best to fit the feet one at a time—gluing and clamping, then cutting off the clamping piece after the glue has set before moving to the next one. Glue alone should be sufficient at the top, but a few screws could be driven upwards, if necessary.

**Materials List for Turned Candle Stand**

| | |
|---|---|
| 1 spindle | 3 × 3 × 26 |
| 1 top | 7/8 × 13 × 14 |
| 1 top block | 1 × 6 × 7 |
| 3 feet | 7/8 × 4 × 13 |

## SAWBUCK TABLE

Tables with crossed legs were found in medieval castles, monasteries, and the great homes of Europe, where they were more often called trestle tables, although that name was also applied to other types. It was the settlers in America who adopted the name *sawbuck* from the similarity to the support used when sawing logs. Many sawbuck tables had fairly massive sections, particularly if a lengthwise stiffening rail was joined into the crossing of the legs. Because this had a weakening effect, sections of wood had to be larger than they need have been elsewhere to stand up to the reductions at the joint.

The sawbuck table in Fig. 4-29 is not so heavy and has two lengthwise rails tenoned into the legs above the halved joint (Fig. 4-30A), so not so much wood has to be cut out there. The legs cross squarely, which makes cutting easier, and the joint is stronger than the more acute crossing sometimes used. Another lengthwise rail under the top provides further stiffening.

The sizes suggested (Fig. 4-30B) would make a roomy dining table, or it could be used on a deck or patio. Length could be altered without affecting other sizes, even to the extent of making the table shorter than it is wide. All sizes could also be reduced proportionately, anything down to half-size to make an interesting coffee table.

Mark out the four legs (Fig. 4-31A). The ends are at 45-degree angles with a tenon at the top (Fig. 4-30B) and the sharpness taken off the point at the bottom (Fig. 4-30C). Locate the mortises for the rails but do not cut them until you prepare the ends of the rails. Cut the central halving joints.

The two top pieces (Fig. 4-30D) have central mortises for the top rail (Fig. 4-31B). The mortises for the legs should be marked from the assembled legs to get an exact match for the tenons.

Cut the tenons on the top rail to go through

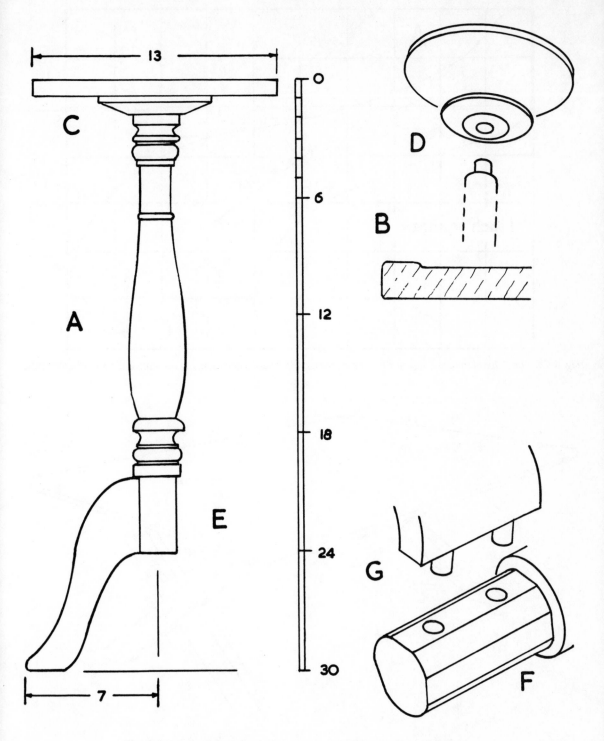

Fig. 4-27. Sizes and method of construction of the turned candle stand.

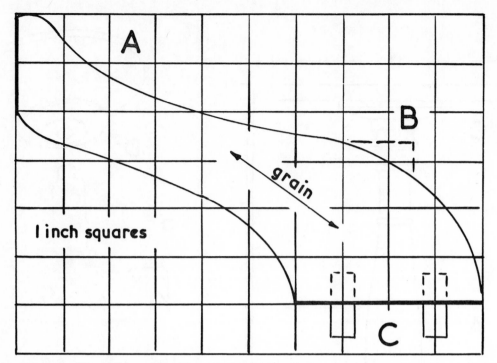

Fig. 4-28. The shape of the candle stand feet. The projection (B) is used when clamping the joint and is cut off afterwards.

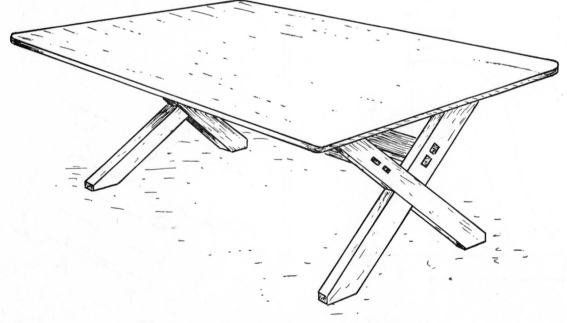

Fig. 4-29. Crossed legs give this the name of sawbuck table.

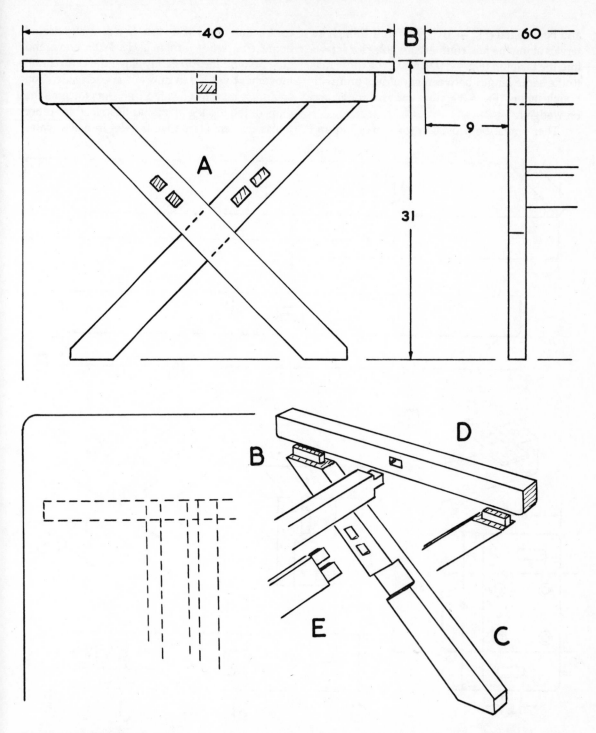

Fig. 4-30. *The legs of the sawbuck table are halved together and tenoned into top pieces across. The ends are joined with three lengthwise rails.*

and be wedged (Fig. 4-31C). At about 10-inch intervals along the rail, counterbore holes for screws into the tabletop (Fig. 4-31D). Make the other rails to the same length between shoulders and with double tenons (Fig. 4-30E) that will go through and be wedged.

There must be provision for expansion and contraction of the wide top. In a centrally heated home, contraction is more likely. With screws and glue holding the top firmly along the central rail, movement will be in and out at each side. You could use buttons engaged with slots towards the ends of the top leg pieces, as described for other tables, but an alternative is to let in metal plates

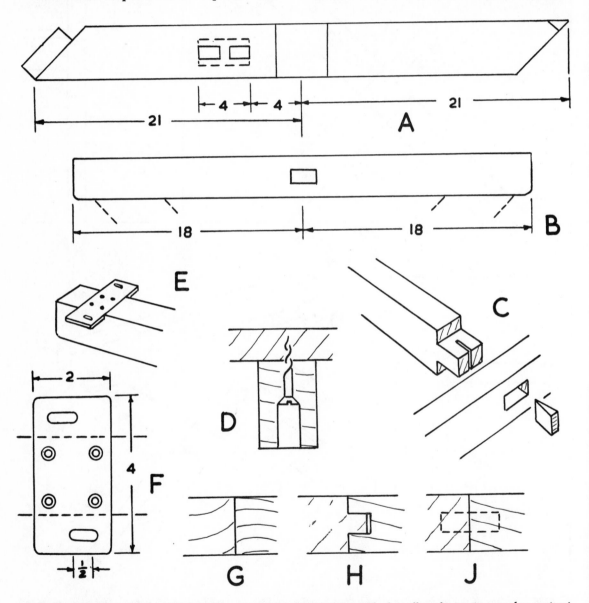

Fig. 4-31. Sizes and methods of joining table parts (A-D). Metal plates with slots allow the top to expand or contract (E,F). Boards used for the top can be glued directly (G), cut with tongues and grooves (H), or dowelled (J).

with slots for screws (Fig. 4-31E). Any sheet metal under 1/8 inch thick can be used (Fig. 4-31F). The screws downward should have countersunk heads, while roundhead screws can be used up through the slots, which are staggered to keep the holes in different grain lines.

Assemble the leg parts and check that opposite ends match. Join in the rails, working on a level surface. Compare diagonals to check squareness and sight along the top edges to make sure there is no twist.

The top can be made of several boards, not necessarily all the same width. As far as possible, alternating end grain pattern (Fig. 4-31G) will minimize any overall tendency to cup or warp. Edges could be glued with no reinforcement, but you might prefer to make tongue and groove joints (Fig. 4-31H) or drill for dowels at about 10-inch intervals along each joint (Fig. 4-31J). Finish the top with rounded corners and mark on its underside where the framework parts will come.

Invert the table. Use glue only along the center rail. Screw that first, then put screws through the metal plates.

**Materials List for Sawbuck Table**

| | |
|---|---|
| 4 legs | 2 × 4 × 45 |
| 2 leg tops | 2 × 3 × 38 |
| 1 top rail | 2 × 3 × 45 |
| 2 rails | 2 × 4 × 45 |
| 1 top, boards to make | 1 × 40 × 62 |

# Five

# Chests and Boxes

The basic item of furniture in many poorer homes in Europe was a chest in which nearly all their few possessions were stored. Immigrants brought their belongings across the Atlantic in chests and boxes, so these formed the basis of furnishing when they set up new homes. Their usefulness continued, and chests were included in the furniture of a home long after other things were made or acquired.

Chests have uses as well today—from tool to blanket storage. If a chest is made at a suitable height it can also be used as a seat. Some early examples were made as combination pieces to the extent where they became seats with storage, rather than chests for sitting on.

Smaller boxes were used for many purposes. They stood on tables and shelves and protected their contents from often dusty and dirty surroundings. Similar boxes today might keep together small items and add to the country look of a room.

Chests and boxes can be made from any wood, which might not even be planed, if the purpose is storing garden tools or logs outside. If you want to reproduce an early chest, you might wish to use rough wood, even if it is to be placed indoors. For a blanket box or other better-quality

chest, you might prefer good quality wood and cabinetmaking joints. Smaller boxes may also vary and could even be carved or inlaid.

## PLAIN CHEST

A plain box was sometimes called a *six-board* chest, although it might be necessary to use more boards to make up widths. This chest (Fig. 5-1A) could be any size, but as an example, it is 15 inches wide and deep, 36 inches long, and made of 1-inch boards. The grain of the ends is upright, but the grain of all other main boards runs lengthwise. The bottom comes inside the other parts (Fig. 5-1B) for strength, and the ends project below (Fig. 5-1C) to keep it above damp ground.

Make the two ends and put strips across the tops (Fig. 5-1D) for strength and to prevent warping. Prepare the bottom to the same width and nail on this and the sides.

Make the top overhang a small amount. Use T hinges (Fig. 5-1E) on the surface of the top and let it into the back so the lid closes flat. If there is to be a fastener, you could use a hasp and staple to take a lock.

For lifting, put blocks on the ends (Fig. 5-1F). They might serve as handles themselves, but if the

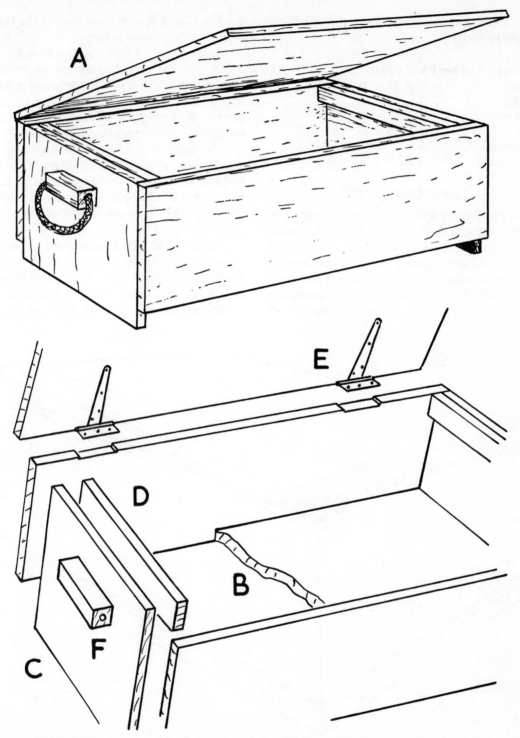

Fig. 5-1. This is an example of the early "six-board" chest with the parts nailed together.

chest is heavily loaded, rope loops through them would be better.

## Materials List for Plain Chest

| | |
|---|---|
| 2 ends | 1 × 15 × 15 |
| 2 sides | 1 × 13 × 36 |
| 1 bottom | 1 × 15 × 36 |
| 1 lid | 1 × 18 × 37 |
| 2 stiffeners | 1 × 2 × 16 |
| 2 handles | 1 1/2 × 1 1/2 × 6 |

### TRAVELING CHEST

For transporting goods a chest has to stand up to rough treatment and be reasonably weatherproof. You might not want to travel with a chest, but such a chest with a painted finish might be used for general storage with other painted furniture. If it's made of good quality wood with a clear finish, it would be attractive anywhere. Basically it is a box (Fig. 5-2) reinforced around the bottom and lid with a raised bottom.

The boards for the sides and ends are the same width. For the best construction, dovetail the corners (Fig. 5-3A). If you decide to nail or screw, strengthen the corners with sheet metal pieces (Fig. 5-3B). If they are painted in a contrasting color, they will increase the traveling look.

The bottom could be made up of random width pieces across (Fig. 5-3C) that are glued together and nailed on. Put strips across under the ends (Fig. 5-3D). Put plinth strips around the outside (Fig. 5-3E). They could be lapped or mitered at the corners.

Make the lid with boards glued to make up the width that are large enough to allow about 1/4-inch clearance at ends and front. Make framing strips for these edges, preferably with dovetailed corners (Fig. 5-3F). Screw and glue to

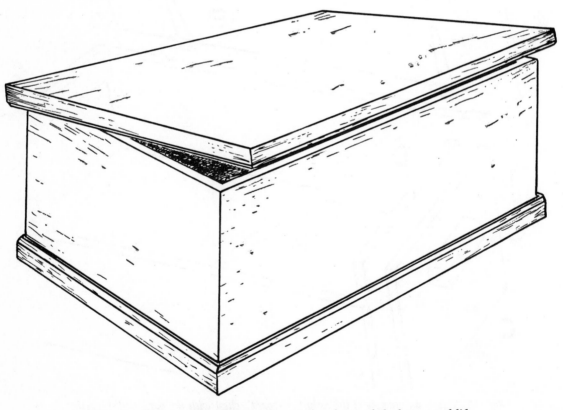

*Fig. 5-2. This travelling chest is a box reinforced around the bottom and lid.*

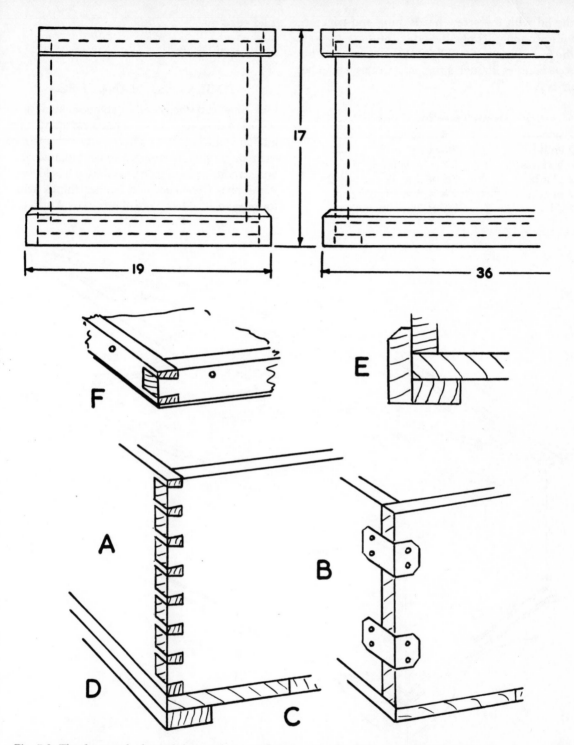

Fig. 5-3. The chest can be dovetailed (A) or have metal straps around nailed corners (B). The bottom boards are raised (C, D), and a plinth goes around the outside (E). The lid frame can be dovetailed (F).

the lid with the screw heads sunk and covered with stopping. Hinge the lid in the same way as the previous chest (see Fig. 5-1E). There could be rope handles, though strong metal ones would be suitable.

**Materials List for Traveling Chest**

| | |
|---|---|
| 2 sides | 7/8 × 14 × 36 |
| 2 ends | 7/8 × 14 × 18 |
| 6 bottoms | 7/8 × 6 × 18 |
| 2 plinths | 7/8 × 3 × 38 |
| 2 plinths | 7/8 × 3 × 20 |
| 1 lid | 7/8 × 18 × 36 |

| | |
|---|---|
| 1 lid edge | 7/8 × 2 × 38 |
| 2 lid edges | 7/8 × 2 × 19 |
| 2 bottom strips | 7/8 × 2 × 18 |

## TOOL CHEST/BLANKET BOX

Old time carpenters and cabinetmakers were proud of their tool chests containing many trays and compartments as it was an advertisement of their skills. This chest (Fig. 5-4) has just two trays and stands on raised feet. The trays will hold small items above blankets and similar things while forming an attractive piece of furniture. Any wood

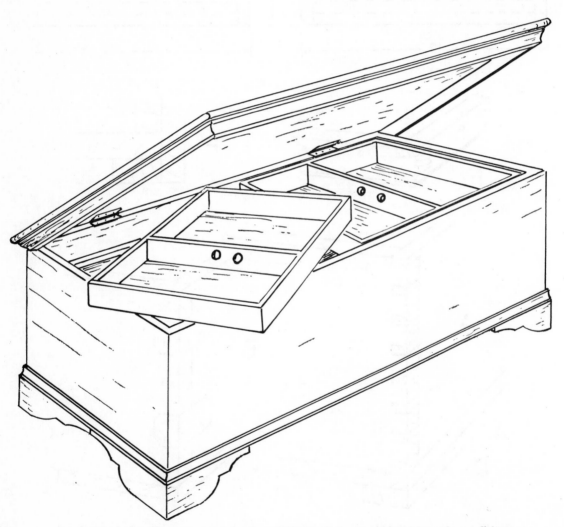

Fig. 5-4. This chest could be used for tools or blankets. It has two lift-out trays for small items.

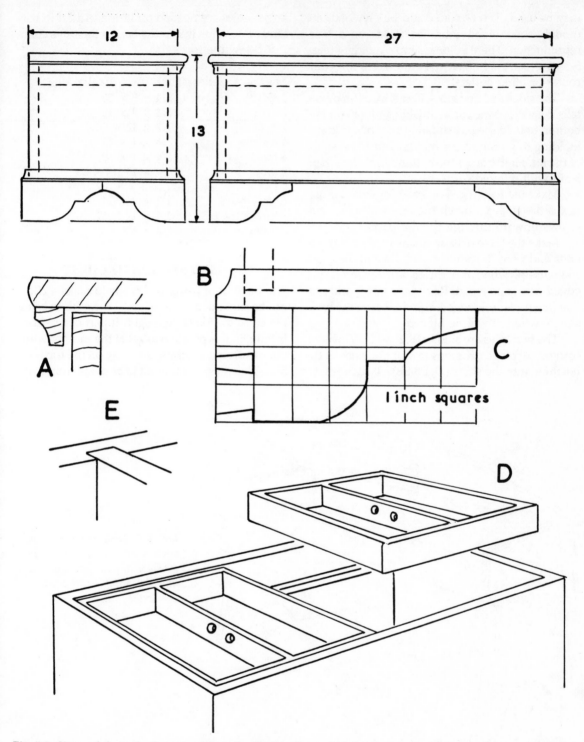

Fig. 5-5. Sizes and shapes for the parts of the tool or blanket chest, which is raised on shaped feet (C). There is a molded edge to the lid (A).

may be used. The bottom could be plywood, although solid wood must be used for a true reproduction. There is some simple molding (Fig. 5-5A), which might have to be altered to suit your router or other cutters.

The sides and ends look best if through dovetails are used at the corners. Glue and nail on the bottom to hold the box square. Prepare sufficient molding to go round the bottom and three sides of the lid. Fit it around the bottom of the box (Fig. 5-5B) with mitered corners.

Make the feet (Fig. 5-5C) with dovetails if the box is dovetailed. Attach the feet with glue and screws upward through the flat parts.

Make the lid to overlap about 1 1/4 inch at the ends and front. It should be solid wood, but you could use plywood or particleboard veneered and edged with solid wood. Round the edges and put molding under the front and ends. Leave the back square where it will be hinged.

The two trays are similar (Fig. 5-5D). Dovetail corners. Arrange divisions to suit your needs by notching into the sides (Fig. 5-5E). Two 3/4-inch

finger holes are needed for lifting. Add thin bottoms. Put strips inside the box so the trays come just below the top.

### Materials List for Tool Chest/Blanket Box

| | |
|---|---|
| 2 sides | 3/4 × 9 × 28 |
| 2 ends | 3/4 × 9 × 13 |
| 1 bottom | 1/2 × 12 × 28 |
| 4 moldings | 3/4 × 1 × 15 |
| 3 moldings | 3/4 × 1 × 30 |
| 1 top | 3/4 × 13 1/2 × 30 |
| 8 feet | 1 × 3 × 8 |
| 10 tray parts | 1/2 × 2 × 14 |
| 2 tray bottoms | 1/4 × 11 × 13 |
| 2 tray runners | 1/2 × 1/2 × 27 |

### RAISED SIX-BOARD CHEST

The method of using six boards to make a chest can be expanded to have legs at the ends to bring the chest to side table height. If part of the front is hinged, it is possible to get at the interior without disturbing anything standing on the top (Fig. 5-6). This chest is intended to be made from wide

Fig. 5-6. Six-board chests were often raised. This one has its ends extended to form feet. There is a hinged flap at the front for easy access to the inside.

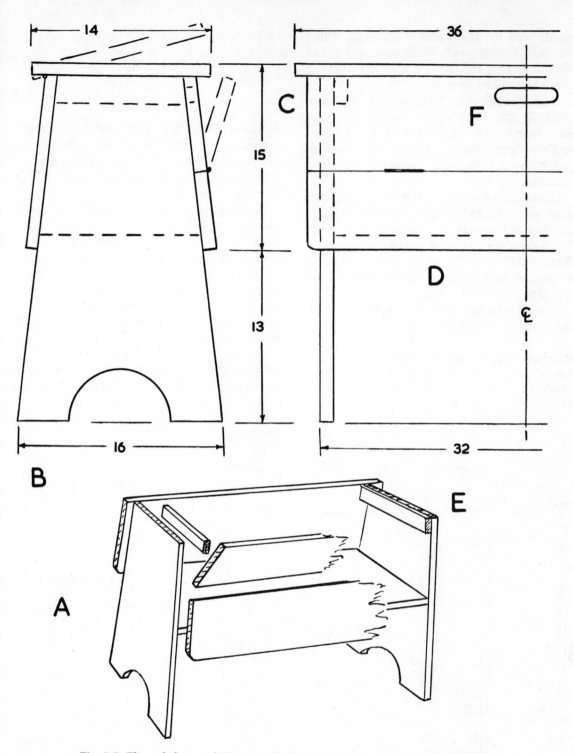

Fig. 5-7. The ends have a slight taper (A, B), and the outer parts extend past them.

boards with the traditional nailed construction (Fig. 5-7). The top holds the hinged front closed without a catch, but lifting it slightly allows the front to be pulled forward.

Make the pair of ends (Fig. 5-7B) tapering symmetrically from 16 inches to 10 inches. Cut away the bottom to make feet. The back and front extend at each end, then the top extends 1 inch over them both ways (Fig. 5-7C). Divide the front along its center.

Make the bottom (Fig. 5-7D) to fit between the sides, beveling it and the tops of the sides to match the slope of the ends. Put strips inside the ends (Fig. 5-7E). Glue and nail the main parts together. There could be a handle on the opening front, but an original chest was more likely to have a hand hole (Fig. 5-7F). Cut it 1 inch by 5 inches.

Round the edges and corners of the top. Four-inch hinges will suit both opening parts.

## Materials List for Raised Six-Board Chest

| | |
|---|---|
| 2 ends | 1 × 16 × 29 |
| 1 back | 1 × 15 × 36 |
| 1 front | 1 × 8 × 36 |
| 1 front | 1 × 7 × 36 |
| 1 bottom | 1 × 14 × 32 |
| 1 top | 1 × 14 × 37 |
| 2 strips | 1 × 2 × 13 |

## DRAWER CHEST

A drawer is an obvious useful addition to a chest, and many were made with one or two drawers under the chest, which still had an opening top. Front doors came later. The design in Fig. 5-8 has a Pennsylvania influence and comes from the period when chests were made of broad boards nailed or screwed together. Most parts are 3/4-inch solid wood. You could substitute plywood for some parts if authenticity is not very important.

Make the two ends (Fig. 5-9A). The cutout suggested will also be the shape of the front brackets (Fig. 5-9B). So there will be no risk of wood warping and spoiling the action of the drawer, the bottom of the chest is held by shallow grooves (Fig. 5-9C). There is no need for a broad solid piece under the drawer. A strip goes across the front, and this and the drawer runners fit into more grooves (Fig. 5-9D).

Fig. 5-8. This development of the six-board chest has a drawer fitted between the end legs below the chest bottom.

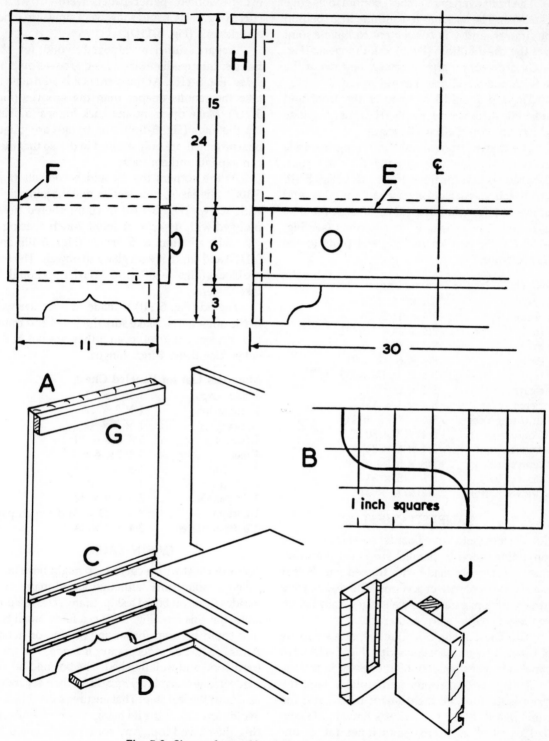

Fig. 5-9. Sizes and assembly of the chest and its drawer.

The front overlaps the chest bottom to its edge (Fig. 5-9E). The back has to continue to go behind the drawer, and it is convenient to have a joint over the chest bottom (Fig. 5-9F). Put cleats (Fig. 5-9G) to prevent warping across the tops of the ends. Assemble all parts made so far.

The top should overhang at the front and ends. Put strips across (Fig. 5-9H) under the ends of the top. Use plain or T hinges.

The drawer front should overhang the ends and the lower front strip to match the chest front. Cut grooves in it for the drawer sides (Fig. 5-9J), which can have blocks attached for glue and screws to strengthen the joints. Except for this, make the drawer as already described (see Fig. 4-21D-G). Fit two knobs or metal pulls to the drawer front.

## Materials List for Drawer Chest

| | |
|---|---|
| 2 ends | 3/4 × 11 × 24 |
| 1 bottom | 3/4 × 11 × 30 |
| 1 front | 3/4 × 14 1/4 × 31 |
| 1 back | 3/4 × 14 × 31 |
| 1 back | 3/4 × 6 1/2 × 31 |
| 1 top | 3/4 × 14 1/4 × 35 |
| 2 cleats | 3/4 × 2 × 12 |
| 2 cleats | 3/4 × 1 × 15 |
| 2 drawer guides | 3/4 × 1 1/2 × 11 |
| 1 front strip | 3/4 × 3 × 30 |
| 1 drawer front | 3/4 × 6 × 31 |
| 2 drawer sides | 5/8 × 5 1/4 × 12 |
| 1 drawer back | 5/8 × 5 × 31 |
| 1 drawer bottom | 1/2 × 11 × 31 |

## PANELED CHEST

Not all trees yield wide boards, so as facilities for converting wood to parallel strips became common, chests were made with framed panels that used wood of narrower sections. The results were attractive in appearance as well as generally lighter and less liable to warp and crack.

This chest's (Fig. 5-10A) main parts are made of 1-inch-by-3-inch section strips (Fig. 5-11A). No panel is bigger than about 9 inches by 12 inches.

Today, with a router and suitable bits, the grooves (5/16 or 3/8 inch) might be cut and the panel raised. Many early chests had simple beveled panels (Fig. 5-11B), sometimes rather unevenly worked. Better panels were cut with a curve (Fig. 5-11C), and some were similar to modern designs (Fig. 5-11D).

Prepare sufficient grooved wood for the frames. Intermediate strips need grooves on both sides (Fig. 5-11E). At the corners it is advisable to take the tenons deeper than the grooves (Fig. 5-11F). Make the front and back frames to overlap the ends (Fig. 5-10B). The frames are glued, but the panels are only pressed in dry so that they can expand and contract.

At the corners there could be dowels (Fig. 5-10C). It is easier, however, to pull the joints tight with screws (Fig. 5-10D) in counterbored holes plugged with dowels, at about 2-inch spacing.

Make a bottom to fit inside (Figs. 5-10E and 5-11G) and attach it with glue and dowels. The feet are blocks (Figs. 5-10F and 5-11H) large enough to take casters.

The lid (Fig. 5-11J) is made in a similar way to the other parts. Make sure the panel and frame top surfaces are level, even if they are not in the sides. Use three 4-inch hinges.

## Materials List for Paneled Chest

| | |
|---|---|
| 4 side strips | 1 × 3 × 35 |
| 4 end strips | 1 × 3 × 17 |
| 12 uprights | 1 × 3 × 12 |
| 8 panels | 5/8 × 8 × 10 |
| 4 feet | 1 1/2 × 4 × 5 |
| 2 lid strips | 1 × 3 × 38 |
| 4 lid strips | 1 × 3 × 16 |
| 3 lid panels | 5/8 × 9 × 12 |
| 1 bottom | 3/4 × 13 × 33 (from strips) |
| 2 bottom pieces | 3/4 × 3 × 14 |

## CABIN TRUNK

A box or chest with a curved top might have been called a cabin trunk, although it had many uses besides those on board a ship. Many sizes are possible, but this one (Fig. 5-12) is a fairly small box that could be used for storing sewing or hobby items, or just as a decoration if made of a good hardwood and well finished. The box and lid are made in one assembly (Fig. 5-13A), then separated as almost the last step. That ensures a good fit and avoids any risk of the lid being distorted while fitting the curved top. Any corner joints could be

used, but dovetails look best.

Draw half an end view (Fig. 5-13B). The top curve has its center at the bottom edges (Fig. 5-13C). Cut the wood for the ends and sides. Mark the cut between the lid and box with lines 1/8 inch apart (Fig. 5-13D). Mark dovetails, with an extra wide pin where the cut will come. Cut and assemble the corner joints. Make the bottom. It is shown

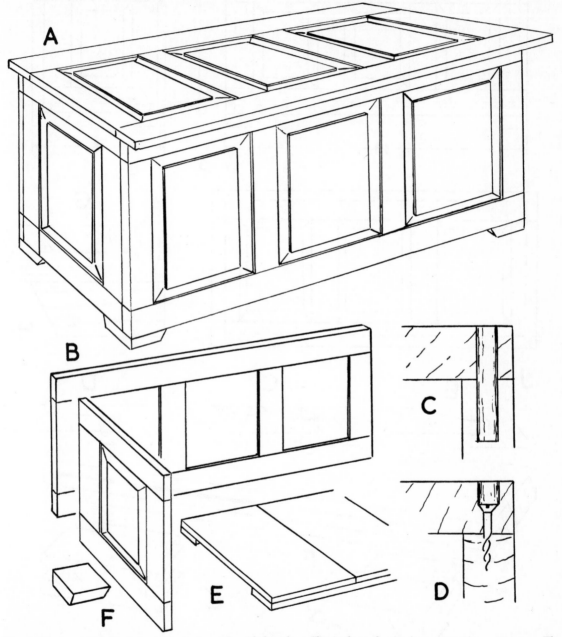

Fig. 5-10. A paneled chest does not require such wide boards, and raised panels give it an attractive appearance. The paneled parts are assembled with dowels (C) or counterbored and plugged screws (D).

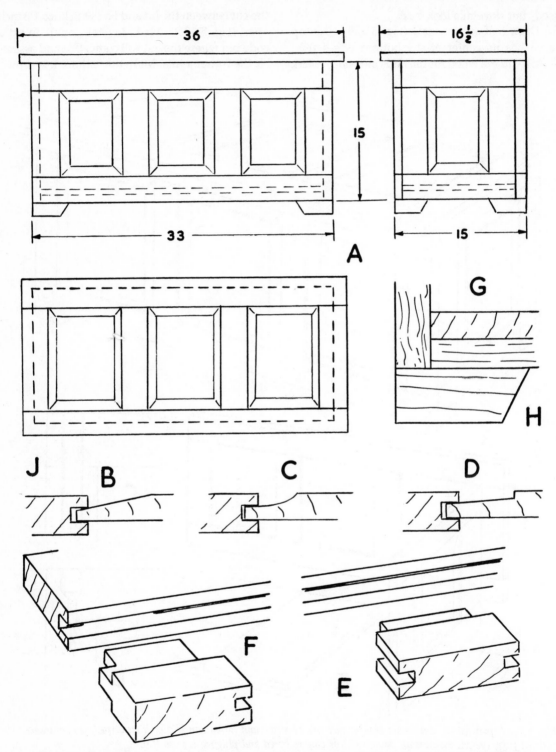

Fig. 5-11. Sizes (A), panel arrangements (B, C, D), frame joints (E, F), and a bottom section (G, H).

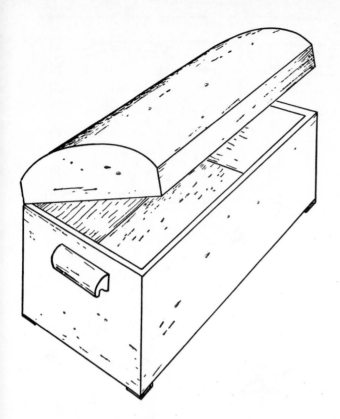

Fig. 5-12. *A box with a curved lid is often called a* cabin trunk.

glued and nailed on, but it could come inside the other parts.

The top is made of 5/8-inch-by-1-inch strips (Fig. 5-13E) with a slight bevel on each edge to make close joints. This can be planed by eye, or you can set a saw or jointer to about 3 degrees and try the fit of experimental pieces. Glue the strips to each other and use pins, sunk and stopped, as well as glue at the ends. Sand the outside to a smooth curve.

Separate the lid from the box and plane the edges. Use two brass 2-inch hinges. There could be a brass lock. Put small square feet under the corners (Fig. 5-13F). These could be leather if the box is to stand on a polished surface. You could add brass handles at each end or make some from wood (Fig. 5-13G).

**Materials List for Cabin Trunk**

| | |
|---|---|
| 2 sides | 5/8 × 9 1/2 × 23 |
| 2 ends | 5/8 × 11 × 13 |
| 12 tops | 5/8 × 1 × 23 |

## BEDROOM BOX

Not every chest has to be made to stand up to rough treatment. For more settled conditions, boxes were made in lighter form and with a good finish. The box in Fig. 5-14 could be used on the floor or put on a low stand or table for storage in a bedroom or elsewhere. There are two drawers and a lift-out tray (Fig. 5-14A). Any wood could be used, but a type that can be stained and polished will look best. Plywood could be used for some parts. The suggested size (Fig. 5-15A) is intended to stand on a low table. A larger box could have feet to stand on the floor.

The box and lid sides and ends are made as one, then cut apart. Corners may be dovetailed, although two-way nailing with a rabbet (Fig. 5-15B) is an alternative. Mark the positions of other parts on the ends (Fig. 5-15C) and cut out the front for the drawers (Fig. 5-15D). Make the drawer guide assemblies (Fig. 5-15E and F) with sizes matched to the drawer openings and drilled for

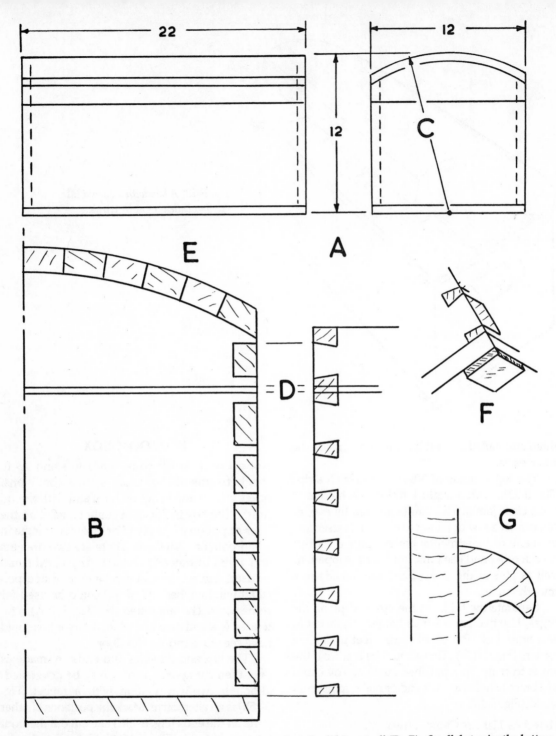

*Fig. 5-13. The cabin trunk (A, B, C) is made in one piece, then the lid is cut off (D, E). Small feet raise the bottom (F). Wooden handles are appropriate (G).*

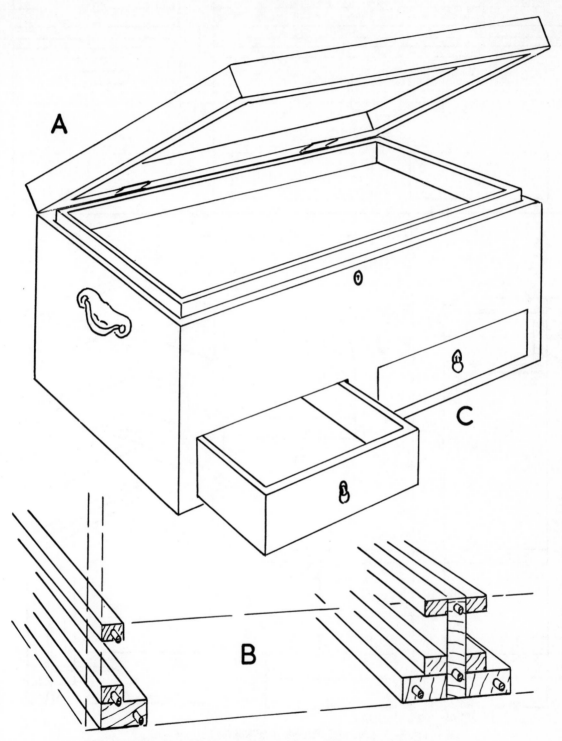

Fig. 5-14. This box of lighter construction has a lift-out tray and two drawers.

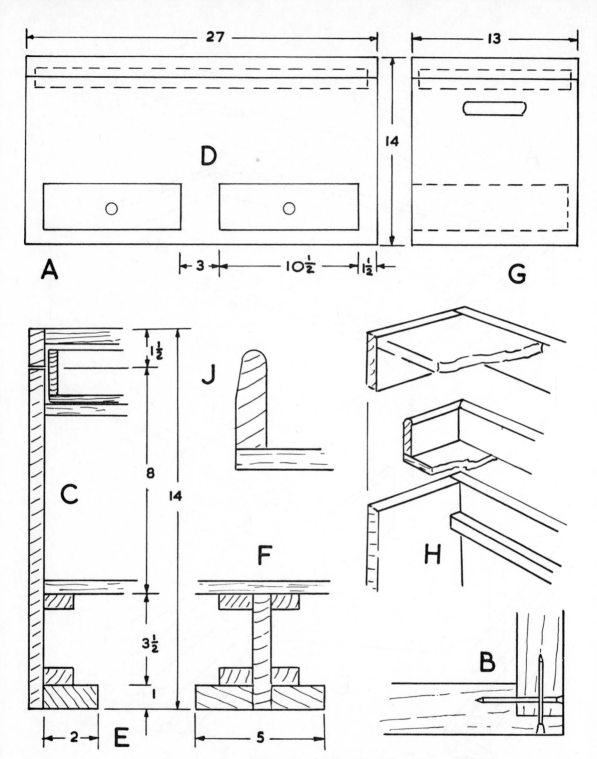

Fig. 5-15. Sizes and assembly details of the bedroom box.

dowels (Fig. 5-14B). Attach the outer guides to the ends. Assemble the sides and ends with the top inside them (Fig. 5-15G) and the drawer guides dowelled in. Separate the lid from the box and fit the bottom over the drawer guides. The tray projects into the lid. Fit supports for it (Fig. 5-15H). Make the tray with beveled edges (Fig. 5-15J) to clear the lid.

Make the drawers as previously described (see Fig. 4-8). Fit pulls or knobs. Hinge the lid and fit a lock and lifting handles, if you wish (Fig. 5-14C).

**Materials List for Bedroom Box**

| | |
|---|---|
| 2 ends | 5/8 × 14 × 14 |
| 2 sides | 5/8 × 14 × 28 |
| 1 lid | 5/8 × 12 × 28 |
| 1 bottom | 1/2 × 12 × 28 |
| 8 drawer guides | 5/8 × 1 × 13 |
| 4 drawer guides | 1 × 2 × 13 |
| 2 drawer guides | 1 × 4 1/2 × 13 |
| 2 tray supports | 1/2 × 1/2 × 27 |

| | |
|---|---|
| 2 tray sides | 3/8 × 1 1/2 × 27 |
| 2 tray ends | 3/8 × 1 1/2 × 13 |
| 1 tray bottom | 1/4 × 12 × 27 |
| 2 drawer fronts | 5/8 × 3 1/2 × 11 |
| 2 drawer backs | 1/2 × 3 × 11 |
| 2 drawer sides | 1/2 × 3 1/2 × 13 |
| 2 drawer bottoms | 1/4 × 11 × 13 |

## SLOPING LID BOX

Boxes with sloping hinged lids were made and used in many sizes from tall floor-standing boxes for bulk stores or table-standing boxes for household quantities, such as this example (Fig. 5-16A). It could be made of any available local wood, but resinous types should be avoided if the contents will be food.

The pair of ends (Fig. 5-16B) will settle sizes. Make the back, bottom, and front to match (Fig. 5-16C). The top and lid may overhang 1/2 inch all around (Fig. 5-16D). Assemble with glue and nails. Let in 1 1/2-inch brass hinges so the gap between the wood edges is narrow.

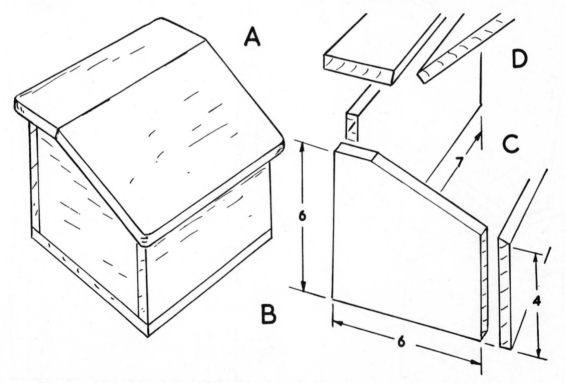

*Fig. 5-16. A box with a sloping lid is suitable for such things as foods that have to be scooped out.*

## Materials List for Sloping Lid Box

| | |
|---|---|
| 2 ends | 1/2 × 6 × 7 |
| 1 back | 1/2 × 6 × 8 |
| 1 front | 1/2 × 4 × 8 |
| 1 bottom | 1/2 × 7 × 8 |
| 1 top | 1/2 × 2 × 9 |
| 1 lid | 1/2 × 6 × 9 |

## DOWEL-HINGED BOX

When manufactured hinges were unobtainable, other means had to be used. Dowels made satisfactory and interesting pivots. This box (Fig. 5-17A) uses two pegs or dowels, so the lid goes back just past vertical (Fig. 5-17B). Construction is with nails.

Mark out the pair of ends (Fig. 5-17C) with the positions of other parts. Set back the front 1/2 inch, but set in the back 3/4 inch to give clearance for the lid.

Make the sides and ends. Make the lid. Round its long edges and the corners of the ends. Drill for 1/4-inch dowels in the ends but not the lid. Assemble the box and put the lid in position to drill through for the dowels. Put in two dowels and try the lid action. If satisfactory, glue the dowels in the lid.

## Materials List for Dowel-hinged Box

| | |
|---|---|
| 2 ends | 1/2 × 5 × 9 |
| 2 sides | 1/2 × 4 1/2 × 12 |
| 1 bottom | 1/2 × 5 3/4 × 12 |
| 1 lid | 1/2 × 8 × 12 |

## DADO-JOINTED BOX

This general-purpose small box (Fig. 5-18A) is made with lid and box sides separated after joining and with dado corner joints. The top and bot-

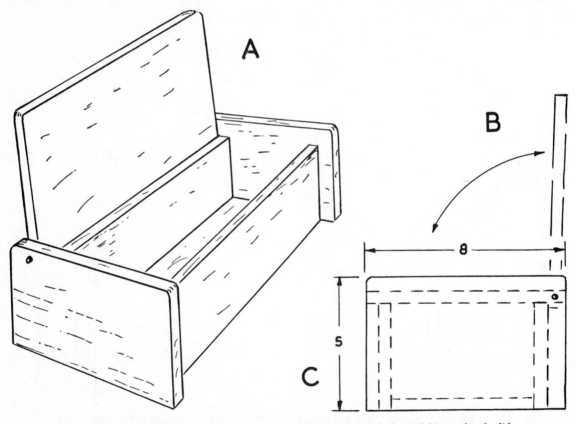

*Fig. 5-17. A box with raised ends can have dowel pivots instead of metal hinges for the lid.*

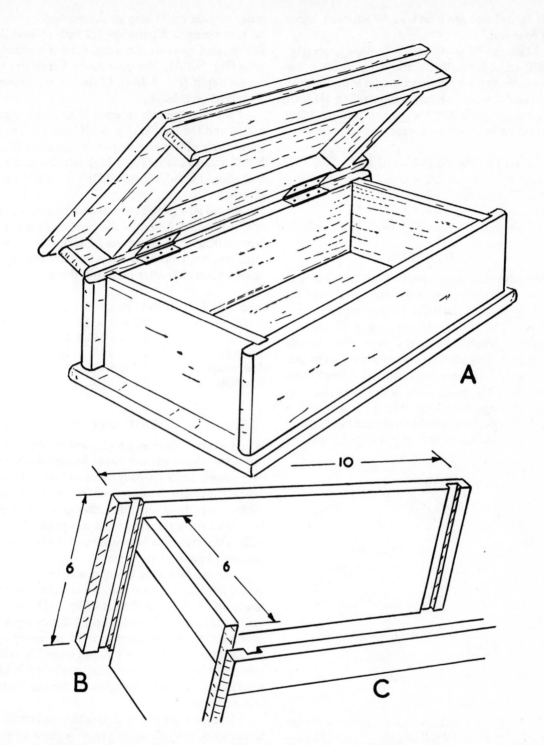

Fig. 5-18. Dado joints can be used in box corners if the sides overlap the ends. This box is made as one assembly, then the lid is sawn off the bottom part.

tom extend and are glued on All exposed edges are rounded.

Make the sides and ends with dado joints (Fig. 5-18B) and the cut lines marked (Fig. 5-18C). Assemble these parts, then cut the lid from the box.

Make the top and bottom extending 1/4 inch on all sides. Round the edges and corners. Glue on and let in a pair of hinges.

**Materials List for Dado-jointed Box**

| | |
|---|---|
| 2 ends | 1/2 × 6 × 7 |
| 2 sides | 1/2 × 6 × 11 |
| 1 top | 1/2 × 7 1/2 × 13 |
| 1 bottom | 1/2 × 7 1/2 × 13 |

## TOTE BOX

Boxes with central carrying handles were made in a great variety of sizes and designs and used for carrying small tools, nails, garden requirements, cutlery, and household cooking and cleaning materials. These tote boxes were often hastily made by nailing together offcuts of wood. The better ones, which have survived, have been more carefully made. Such a box is still worth having, and the suggested design (Fig. 5-19) is an example that could be adapted to suit your needs. Most joints are dadoes, which might depend only on

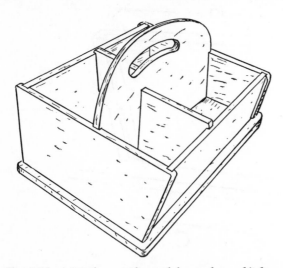

Fig. 5-19. A tote box can be used for garden or kitchen materials. In the shop it will hold tools or nails. This one has a central carrying handle.

glue, or pins could also be driven and covered with stopping. All parts are 1/2 inch or slightly thicker, and joints are about one-third of the thickness (Fig. 5-21A). The sides slope 1 inch in the 5-inch depth (Fig. 5-20A). Divisions are shown staggered (Fig. 5-20B).

Mark out the pair of ends (Figs. 5-20C and 5-21B) and the handle (Fig. 5-21C and D). From these parts obtain the shapes of the sides (Fig. 5-21E) and divisions (Fig. 5-21F), which stand 1/2 inch above the sides (Fig. 5-20D). Cut all the dado grooves.

Round all exposed corners and the edges that will be handled. Assemble the parts and mark the bottom from them to extend 1/2 inch all around. Glue and pin it on. If the box is for table use, glue cloth underneath after polishing the wood.

**Materials List for Tote Box**

| | |
|---|---|
| 2 ends | 1/2 × 5 × 14 |
| 2 sides | 1/2 × 5 1/4 × 14 |
| 1 handle | 1/2 × 8 1/2 × 14 |
| 2 divisions | 1/2 × 5 1/2 × 8 |
| 1 bottom | 1/2 × 12 × 14 |

## WOOD BOX

When wood is used as a fuel, particularly on an open fire, a large amount has to be kept ready for use, so early homes usually had a large box of logs near the fireplace. Boxes ranged from simple open containers to those with lids, although a semiopen box with a top for use as a shelf was popular (Fig. 5-22). This box would be equally useful where fires are used in a modern home.

Sizes can be altered to suit needs, but the suggested box is in the form of a 24-inch cube that extends up 18 inches at the back (Fig. 5-23) and is made with 3/4-inch boards and 1 1/2-inch square framing. The board widths could be anything available, but 6 inches or 8 inches would be convenient. All parts may be nailed, preferably with nails driven at alternate angles, in dovetail fashion, for strength.

Make the front (Fig. 5-23A) with boards nailed to uprights, then fill the edges with more strips. Make the back (Fig. 5-23B) in the same way. Board

edges could be tongued and grooved to keep the joints dustproof if the boards shrink.

The pair of ends overlap the back and front, with about 3/4 inch extending forward of the front. Reduce to about half width at the top (Fig. 5-23C). Put strips across, shortened to clear the uprights (Fig. 5-23D). Join the corners and make a bottom (Fig. 5-23E) to rest on the strips, either from tongue and groove boards or plywood.

Make the top (Fig. 5-23F) to extend at sides and front. Round all exposed edges and corners. There could be square blocks under the box bottom corners to act as feet.

## Materials List for Wood Box

| | |
|---|---|
| 2 uprights | 1 1/2 × 1 1/2 × 44 |
| 2 uprights | 1 1/2 × 1 1/2 × 26 |
| 8 rails | 1 1/2 × 1 1/2 × 24 |
| 2 rails | 1 1/2 × 1 1/2 × 14 |
| 15 boards | 3/4 × 6 × 26 |
| 6 boards | 3/4 × 8 × 44 |
| 1 board | 3/4 × 12 × 28 |

## CHEST OF DRAWERS

Chests were made with drawers as well as lids, and the obvious development was to make the entire piece of furniture into a block of drawers.

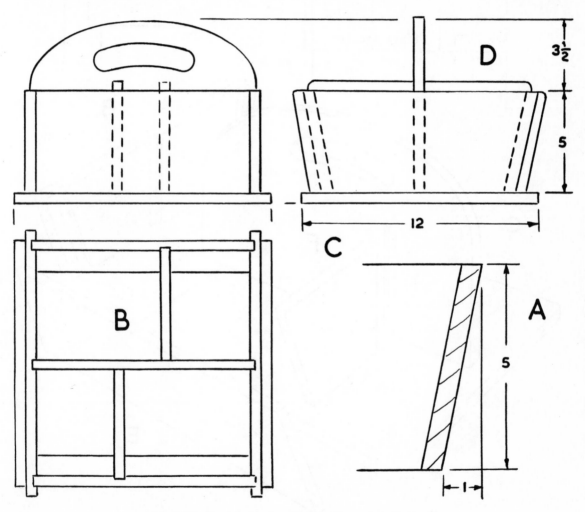

Fig. 5-20. The tote box has sloping sides and vertical ends.

These chests of drawers varied in size. Some Shaker chests were so high that a stool was needed to reach the upper drawers.

This chest of drawers (Fig. 5-24) is dated about 1800. The main parts of the original were made of oak with some internal and drawer parts made of softwood. The back and drawer bottoms were softwood pieces about 1/2 inch thick with tongued and grooved joints. Unless you are determined to make a true replica, these parts could be plywood.

The size (Fig. 5-24A) is suitable for bedroom use, with ample storage for clothing, sheets, and

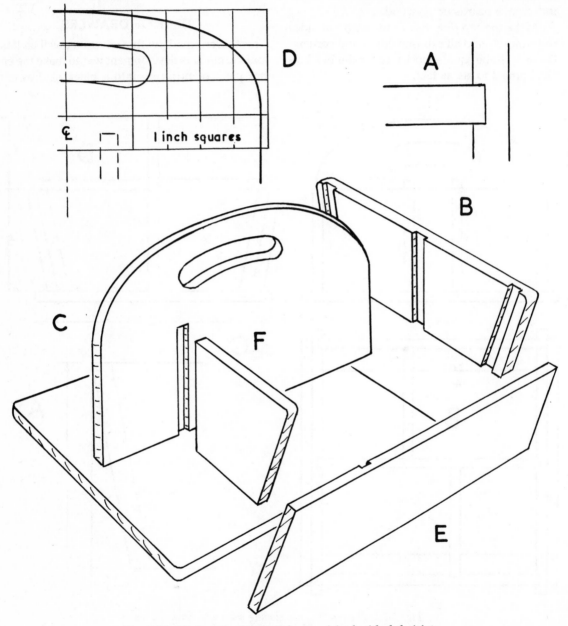

Fig. 5-21. *Most parts of the tote box are joined with dado joints.*

*Fig. 5-22. A box for firewood has to be large and strong. This one has a top that can be used as a shelf.*

The 2 1/2-inch top and middle rails may have single tenons. Assemble these parts with the panels fitted in the grooves.

Mark the drawer positions (Fig. 5-25E). At the bottom and middle these will come over rails. At the other two positions put packing strips against the panels (Fig. 5-25F and G) with their inner surfaces level with the uprights to act as drawer guides.

Make the five frames that fit between the ends (Fig. 5-25H). Put beads on the front edges (Fig. 5-25J) if you have beaded the ends. Tenon the corners (Fig. 5-25K) and tenon another piece across the center of each frame (Fig. 5-25L). It is needed to take the division on the top two frames, but it also provides stiffness on the others. The division between the top drawers (Fig. 5-25M) may be beaded on the front edge and should have similar corner joints to the horizontal frames.

Prepare for 1/2-inch dowels at 4-inch intervals where the frames, ends, and divisions meet. Place end dowels on an edge about 1 inch in.

Assemble the carcass, pulling all joints tight and checking squareness by comparing diagonals. Fit the back to hold the assembly square.

At the bottom, fit molding the same depth as the frame across the front and ends (Fig. 5-24B). If possible, use the pattern of molding as you will use on the edges of the top.

The feet are the same at the back as the front. Cut them to shape (Fig. 5-24C) and miter where they meet. Make up each pair with blocks inside the miter and at the straight edges for attaching to the bottom of the carcass (Fig. 5-24D). Fit the feet with glue and a few screws upwards through the blocks.

The drawers have 3/4-inch hardwood fronts to match the wood of the carcass, but the other parts could be softwood with traditional dovetail corner joints. In the original chest of drawers the sides and back are under 1/2 inch thick. This would be weakened by a groove for the bottom. Instead, the 3/8-inch bottom, with its grain across, goes under the sides. A 1-inch wide runner fit below (Fig. 5-26A). The bottom is grooved into the front, and the runners stop against the front (Fig. 5-26B).

blankets. The drawers are graduated in their depths, which gives a better appearance than making them all the same. There is some beading around the front edges and moldings on the top and bottom. Feet lift the chest above the floor. To maintain the traditional appearance, decorative brass bail handles should be used.

Construction is simpler than might be expected. The two ends are framed, and the top frame, bottom, and the three divisions are basically the same. The divisions may be dowelled to the ends, although in the original chest of drawers there would have been tenons on the ends of the long parts.

Start by making a pair of ends (Fig. 5-25A). Cut beads (Fig. 5-25B), if you wish, on the inner edges of the fronts. Rabbet the rear edges to suit the back panel (Fig. 5-25C). Groove to take the end panels. Cut pieces for the top, middle, and bottom with panel grooves. The 4-inch-wide bottom joins the uprights with double tenons (Fig. 5-25D).

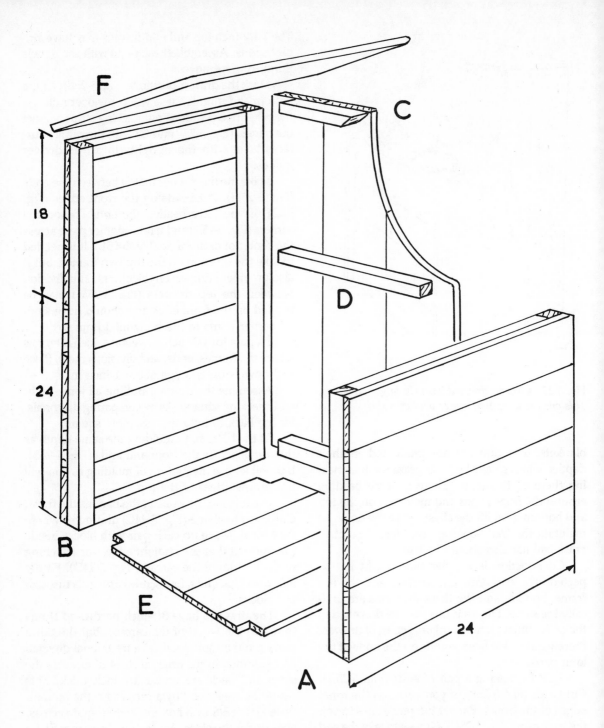

Fig. 5-23. *The wood box is assembled from boarded panels.*

An alternative way of fitting the bottom is with fillets inside (Fig. 5-26C). This also provides a wide bottom bearing surface and was common in much early construction. Another alternative is to thicken the sides and groove them (Fig. 5-26D). Except for these possible variations in fitting the bottom, the drawers are made as already described (see Figs. 4-8 and 4-21).

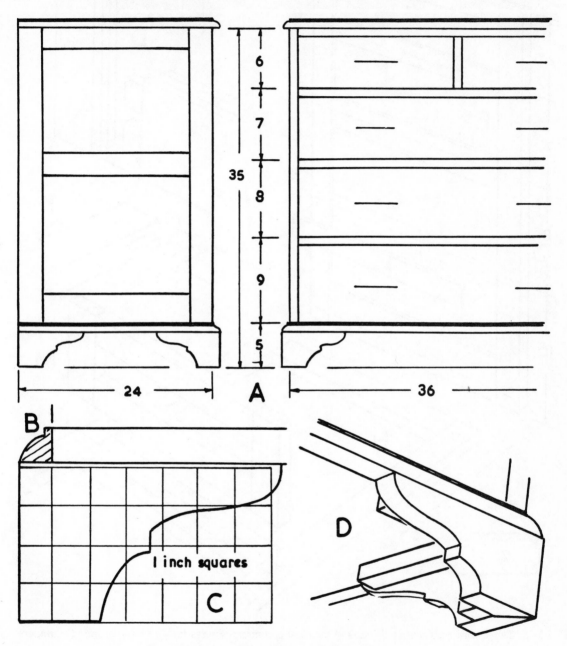

Fig. 5-24. Sizes and foot details of the chest of drawers.

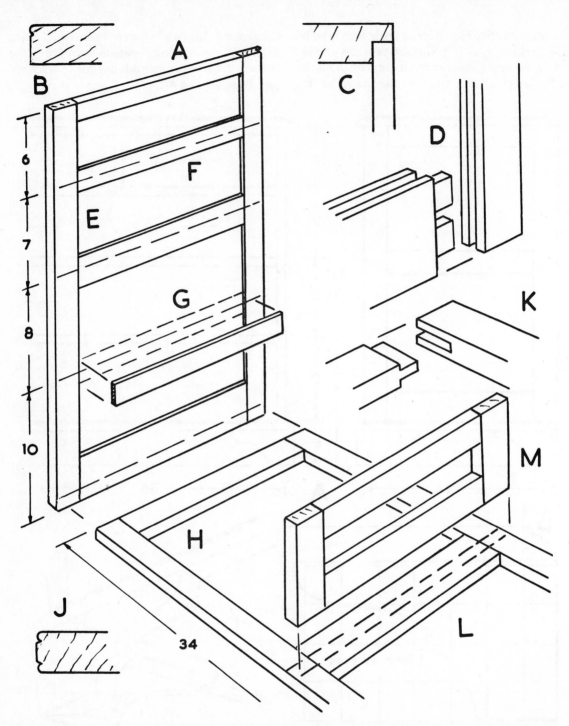

*Fig. 5-25. The paneled ends control the sizes of the chest of drawers. Frames fitted to them separate the drawers.*

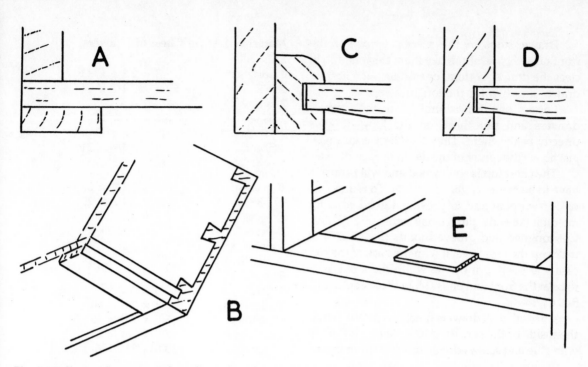

Fig. 5-26. Drawer bottoms can fit underneath with runners (A, B), fit into fillets (C), or into notched sides (D). A stop (E) goes on the rail under a drawer.

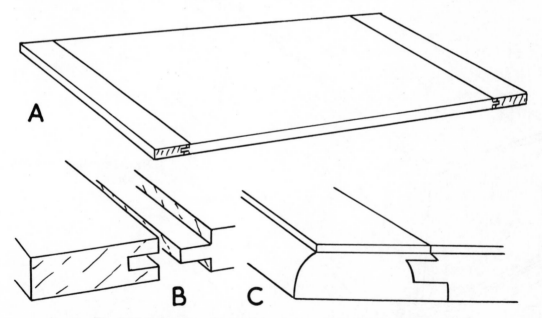

Fig. 5-27. Ledgers keep the top flat and are molded with the main part.

Drawer stops are thin pieces of wood on the front rails (Fig. 5-26E). Make them thin enough to clear the drawer bottom, one under each narrow drawer and two for the long drawers.

Locate handles centrally on the narrow drawers and put those on the long drawers directly below them. They look best if arranged just above the center of the depth of each drawer.

The chest top is solid wood and will probably have to be made by gluing boards. To reduce the risk of warping and to provide a good edge for molding the ends, put ledgers across (Fig. 5-27A). Cut tongued and grooved joints (Fig. 5-27B) to make up the top. Level it with the back of the carcass and overlap it by the width the molding is to be at the front and ends. Mold these edges (Fig. 5-27C).

Check that all drawers function correctly while the inside of the carcass is accessible. Fit the top with glue and screws driven upwards from inside.

**Materials List for Chest of Drawers**

*Ends*

| | |
|---|---|
| 4 uprights | 7/8 × 2 1/2 × 33 |
| 4 rails | 7/8 × 2 1/2 × 24 |
| 2 rails | 7/8 × 4 × 24 |
| 2 panels | 3/8 × 18 × 12 |
| 2 panels | 3/8 × 18 × 15 |
| 4 fillers | 1/4 × 2 1/2 × 21 |

*Dividers*

| | |
|---|---|
| 10 pieces | 7/8 × 2 1/2 × 36 |
| 10 pieces | 7/8 × 2 1/2 × 25 |
| 5 pieces | 7/8 × 4 × 25 |
| 2 pieces | 7/8 × 2 × 25 |
| 2 pieces | 7/8 × 2 × 7 |

*Base*

| | |
|---|---|
| 8 feet | 7/8 × 4 × 9 |
| blocks from | 7/8 × 7/8 × 60 |
| 1 molding | 7/8 × 7/8 × 40 |
| 2 moldings | 7/8 × 7/8 × 26 |
| 1 back | 3/8 × 31 × 36 |

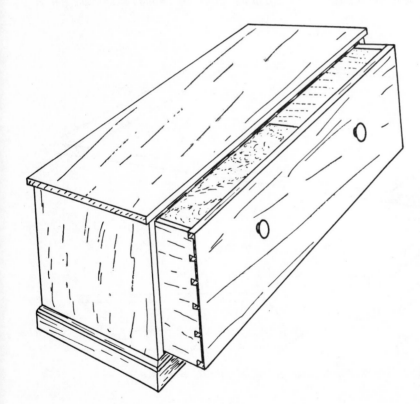

Fig. 5-28. A large chest with one large drawer.

*Top*
1 Board     7/8 × 25 × 36
2 clamps    7/8 × 4 × 26

*Top Drawers*
2 fronts    3/4 × 5 1/8 × 18
4 sides    1/2 × 5 × 24
2 backs    1/2 × 4 1/2 × 18
1 bottom    5/16 × 24 × 18
4 runners    5/16 × 1 × 24

*Second Drawer*
1 front    3/4 × 6 1/8 × 36
2 sides    1/2 × 6 × 24
1 back    1/2 × 5 1/2 × 36

1 bottom    5/16 × 24 × 36
2 runners    5/16 × 1 × 24

*Third Drawer*
1 front    3/4 × 7 1/8 × 36
2 sides    1/2 × 7 × 24
1 back    1/2 × 6 1/2 × 36
1 bottom    5/16 × 24 × 36
2 runners    5/16 × 1 × 24

*Fourth Drawer*
1 front    3/4 × 8 1/8 × 36
2 sides    1/2 × 8 × 24
1 back    1/2 × 7 1/2 × 36
1 bottom    5/16 × 24 × 36
2 runners    5/16 × 1 × 24

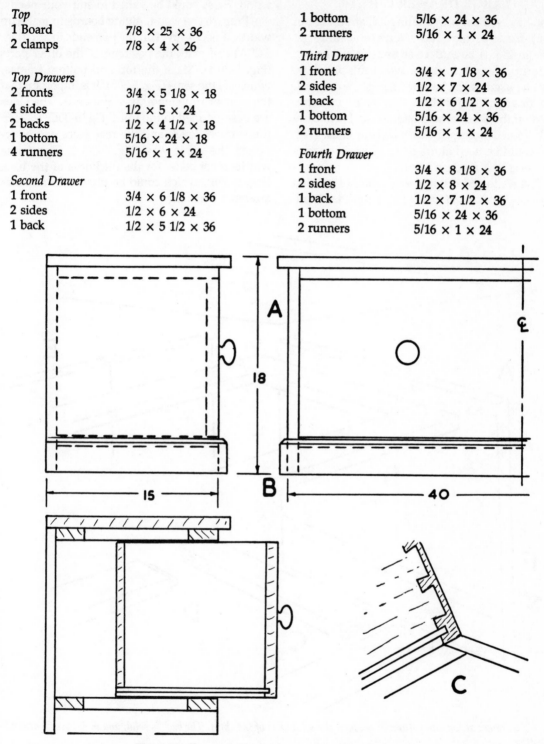

Fig. 5-29. Sizes and drawer details of the large drawer chest.

## LARGE DRAWER CHEST

If you have a chest with a lifting lid, anything put on top has to be removed when you want to get at the inside. A large drawer under a strong top will form a blanket chest that avoids this difficulty. It can be used as the base for a cupboard, wardrobe, or any other furniture that would be better raised off the floor, as was often desirable in early earth-floored homes. Such a drawer chest (Fig. 5-29) could be used alone or as a base for something else in a modern home.

The well-used original was made of painted softwood, but it could look good in polished hard-wood. Sizes could be varied to suit your needs.

Prepare the wood, gluing boards to make up widths if necessary. Cut the two ends to size (Fig. 5-29A) and mark the positions of the other parts (Fig. 5-30A). Make the top and bottom frames, which are the same (Fig. 5-30B). It is important that the drawer run smoothly at the ends. The sides are best tenoned to the front (Fig. 5-30C) to keep the surfaces level, and the rear piece can be tenoned the other way (Fig. 5-30D). The frame widths must allow for the thickness of the back (Fig. 5-30E), which could be plywood or boards arranged vertically.

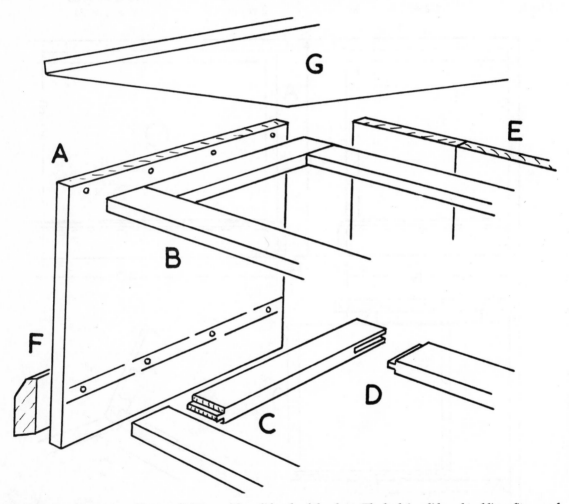

*Fig. 5-30. Frames at top and bottom fit between the solid ends of the chest. The back is solid, and moldings fit around the bottom.*

114

Join all these parts with glue and nails, screws, or dowels. For a clear polished finish, choose dowels as they will not show.

At the bottom make a plinth (Fig. 5-29B) to fit at the front and ends. It should reach to within 1/8 inch of the top of the bottom frame. Mold or bevel it and miter the corners (Fig. 5-30F). Make the top (Fig. 5-30G) level at the back, but overhang it about 1 inch at the sides and front. Delay fitting it with screws through the top frame until you have made and adjusted the drawer. Its edges could be molded to match the plinth.

The drawer should have dovetailed corners and be made in a similar way to that described earlier (see Figs. 4-8 and 4-21), except for the treatment of the bottom. The drawer and its contents will be heavy, so broad bearing surfaces are advisable. The bottom could be plywood or strips of solid wood. Groove the drawer front, but let the drawer sides come above the bottom. Nail or screw through and put a broad bearing strip under each side (Fig. 5-29C). Adjust the lengths of the drawer sides so the front stops level when they hit the back. Two widely spaced round knobs will probably be better than metal handles.

## Materials List for Large Drawer Chest

| | |
|---|---|
| 2 ends | 7/8 × 15 × 19 |
| 2 frames | 7/8 × 2 1/2 × 42 |
| 2 frames | 7/8 × 2 1/2 × 38 |
| 4 frames | 7/8 × 2 1/2 × 15 |
| 1 plinth | 5/8 × 3 × 42 |
| 2 plinths | 5/8 × 3 × 17 |
| 7 backs | 5/8 × 6 × 19 |
| 1 top | 7/8 × 16 × 44 |
| 1 drawer front | 7/8 × 13 × 40 |
| 2 drawer sides | 5/8 × 12 1/2 × 15 |
| 1 drawer back | 5/8 × 12 × 40 |
| 1 drawer bottom | 3/8 × 14 × 40 |
| 2 drawer strips | 3/8 × 2 × 15 |

# Six

# Racks and Stands

In any home, whether pioneer, colonial, or modern, there is a need for supports of various sorts. Some hold washed clothing to dry, some hold blankets, and others are used for display or for drying herbs. Other stands store bowls and other washing needs. Such dry sinks might not be needed today for their original purpose, but they can be converted to other interesting uses.

Many early racks were very simple, although functional. Elaboration might not increase usefulness, although it might improve appearance. Some racks give an opportunity to use up narrow offcuts from larger jobs. Several racks are either small in themselves or can be folded into a small space.

## QUILT RACK

A basic frame consists of two legs with feet of sufficient spread to give stability and usually three rails. Such a frame was originally used mainly for drying towels or wet clothing, but in a bedroom it could become a quilt rack (Fig. 6-1). The ends are two inches square and the rails are 1 inch × 2 inches. It could be hard or softwood. Joints are mortise and tenon. They could be wedged from outside, but traditionally they were pegged

across—in this case you could use 3/8-inch dowels (Fig. 6-2A).

Prepare the wood and mark all joints. Leave tenons a little too long for planing level later. Round the rail edges (Fig. 6-2B). Round the legs

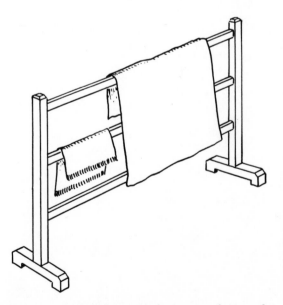

Fig. 6-1. A quilt rack is a simple structure that can also be used for drying towels and clothing.

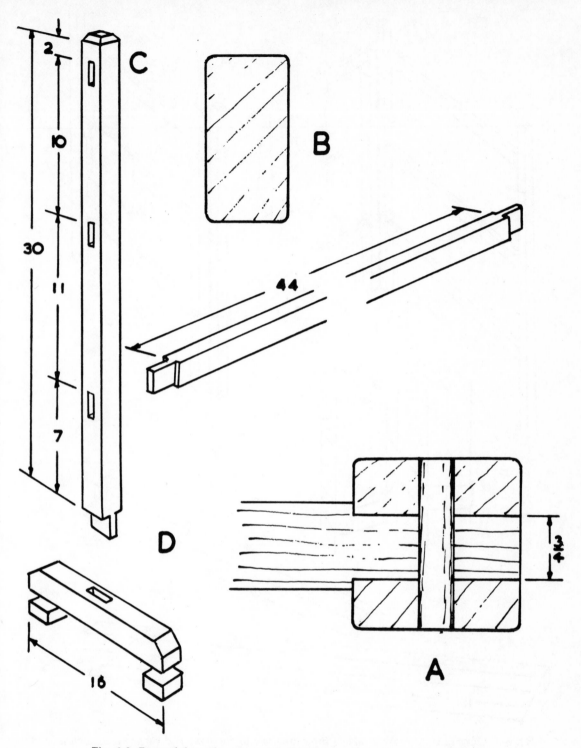

Fig. 6-2. Parts of the quilt rack are joined with pegged mortise and tenon joints.

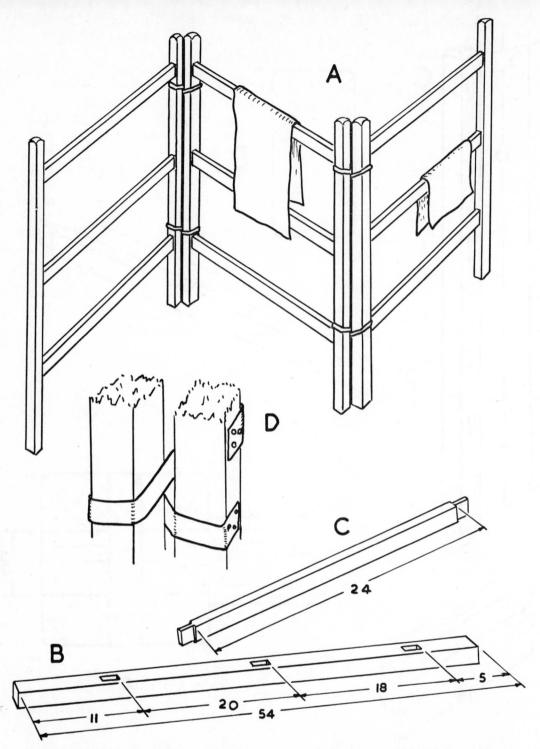

Fig. 6-3. Capacity is increased by adding three parts to a drying frame and hinging them with tape.

similarly and either round or chamfer the tops (Fig. 6-2C).

Make the feet (Fig. 6-2D) with square blocks glued under their ends. Glue and peg the legs into the feet first. See that they are square and make a pair, then add the rails, again checking for squareness and absence of twist.

**Materials List for Quilt Rack**

| | |
|---|---|
| 2 legs | 2 × 2 × 34 |
| 2 feet | 2 × 2 × 17 |
| 4 blocks | 1 × 2 × 2 |
| 3 rails | 1 × 2 × 50 |

### HINGED DRYING FRAME

The value of a simple rack can be increased by hinging two or three frames together to make a drying rack, or "clothes horse," that will fold flat and supports itself without feet (Fig. 6-3A). The frames can be of lighter construction, because of the mutual support, and 1 1/2-inch-square legs and 3/4-×-1 1/2-inch rails are suggested. There could be hinges between the sections, but an arrangement of stout tape or webbing allows folding both ways. General construction is similar to the quilt rack (see Fig. 6-2).

Make six legs (Fig. 6-3B) and nine rails (Fig. 6-3C), prepared for mortise and tenon joints. Round all edges and chamfer or round the tops of the legs. Assemble the frames. Check that they match. Wedge or pin the tenons.

Hinges are formed with tape or 1-inch-wide webbing and tacks taken in a figure-eight manner around the legs (shown loosely in Fig. 6-3D). Start on the rail side of one leg. Turn the cut end under the tack securely. Follow tightly around as shown and tack again. Also tack on the rail side of the other leg. Try the action.

**Materials List for Hinged Drying Frame**

| | |
|---|---|
| 6 legs | 1 1/2 × 1 1/2 × 56 |
| 9 rails | 3/4 × 1 1/2 × 29 |

### TURNED DRYING FRAME

There is an advantage in being able to hang as much as possible high on a frame, so some dry-

ing frames were made with two or three top rails as well as more lower ones. Turning was popular, as it allowed a better finish on poorly seasoned wood. You might not have the same reason for making a rack in this way, but its attractive appearance justifies the method (Fig. 6-4). Use a wood with a close grain for easy turning. A hardwood is advisable and could be 1 1/4 inches square. Softwood should be slightly larger.

Prepare the wood square and locate centers at the ends so it turns accurately. Mark out the positions on the posts (Fig. 6-5A), on the crossbar (Fig. 6-5B), and the base (Fig. 6-5C), allowing some waste wood at the ends for mounting in the lathe. Turn between the square parts, using your own ideas, if you wish. Cut the halving joints (Fig. 6-5D) and the mortise and tenon joints (Fig. 6-5E). Drill 5/8-inch holes for the rails and feet, going as deep as possible without the drill point breaking

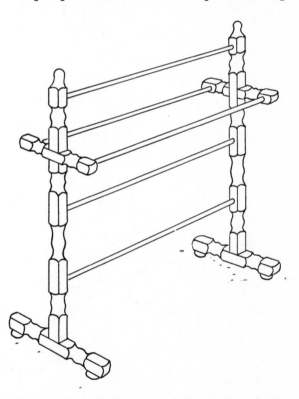

*Fig. 6-4. This drying frame has several rails. The end parts are turned between the square sections where the rails are attached.*

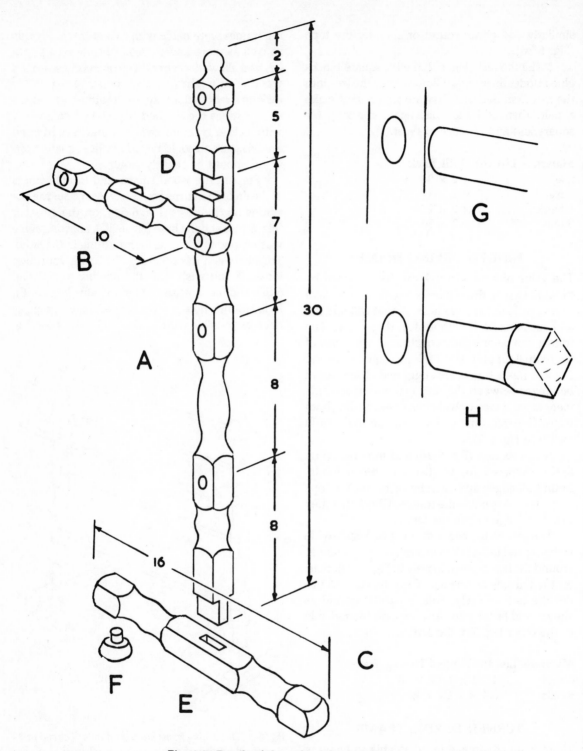

Fig. 6-5. Details of the ends of the drying frame.

through. Turn feet (Fig. 6-5F) with dowels to fit the holes.

The rails can be made to suit needs or available space. The frame looks best, however, if it is longer than it is high; 40 inches is suggested.

Rails could be 5/8-inch dowel rods (Fig. 6-5G). An early woodworker would not have had prepared dowel rods and was more likely to use square pieces. If you want to make a more authentic reproduction, use square rods reduced to round at the ends (Fig. 6-5H).

Assemble with glue only and be careful to get all parts fitting squarely. Take sharpness off angles but do not round edges excessively.

**Materials List for Turned Drying Frame**

| | |
|---|---|
| 2 posts | 1 1/4 × 1 1/4 × 33 |
| 2 crossbars | 1 1/4 × 1 1/4 × 13 |
| 2 bases | 1 1/4 × 1 1/4 × 19 |
| 4 feet | 1 1/4 × 1 1/4 × 4 |
| 5 rails | 3/4 × 3/4 × 42 |

## SHAKER TOWEL RACK

As with many other pieces of furniture, the

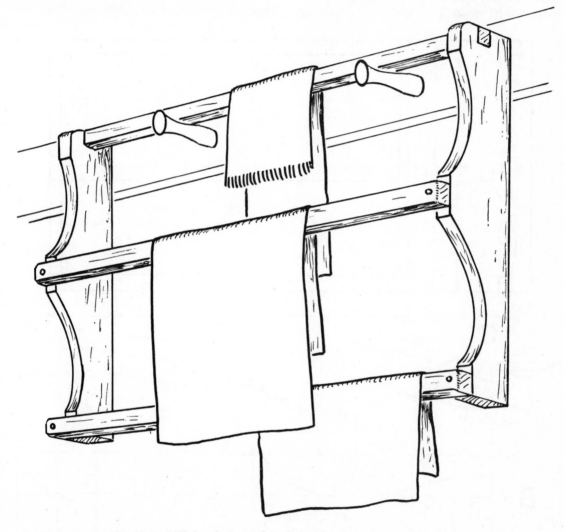

Fig. 6-6. A Shaker drying rack is designed to hang by a rail from pegs.

Shakers made their drying racks to hang on the pegs arranged high on the wall. This is such a rack (Fig. 6-6). It could be made of wood 7/8 inch thick and left untreated or finished with varnish. Sizes could be varied to suit needs, but if there are existing pegs, the length should be arranged to suit their spacing. As suggested, there is a hanging rail and two towel rails (Fig. 6-7A).

Mark out the two ends (Fig. 6-7B) and wood for the rails. To take the downward load, the top rail has single dovetails (Fig. 6-7C). The two lower rails fit on the surface and may be dowelled (Fig. 6-7D), which would be preferable to nails or

screws. Take sharpness off exposed edges and assemble the rack squarely.

**Materials List for Shaker Towel Rack**

| 2 ends | 7/8 × 4 × 25 |
| 1 top rail | 7/8 × 7/8 × 37 |
| 2 rails | 7/8 × 1 1/4 × 37 |

## WALL DRYING ARMS

Arms that pivot can fold flat against a wall, then be turned outwards when needed. There could be any number of arms, but three is a reasonable maximum number. If there are more, they would

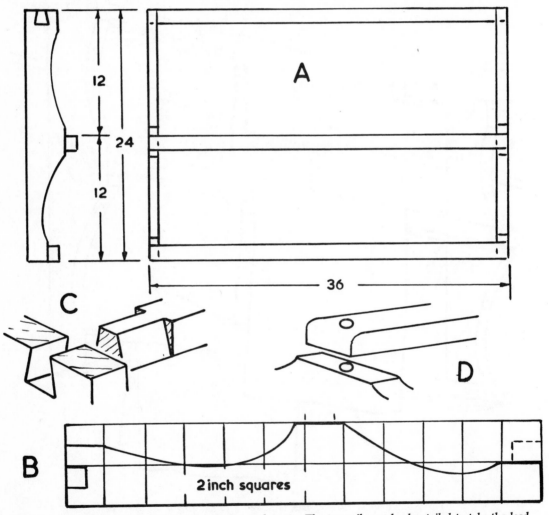

*Fig. 6-7. Sizes and shapes of the Shaker drying rack parts. The top rail may be dovetailed to take the load.*

have to be made shallower and might then sag after long use, as some early examples do. A single arm is shown (Fig. 6-8,) but the drawing of two arms (Fig. 6-9A) could be extended to three.

A close-grained hardwood is advisable. It should have a reasonably straight grain to reduce the risk of warping.

Make the arms (Fig. 6-9B and C) tapering from 3/4 inch deep 4 inches from the inner end to about 5/8 inch round at the tip. Leave the thick ends with square edges but well round the extending parts.

The support (Fig. 6-9D) has mortise and tenon joints. Drill for screwing to the wall and for a 1/4-inch hardwood dowel as pivot. Use a drill press or a drill guide to make the holes squarely through all parts. If the dowel rod is allowed to project slightly, it is easy to withdraw if you ever need to take the assembly apart.

### Materials List for Wall Drying Arms

| | |
|---|---|
| 2 arms | 3/4 × 1 1/2 × 18 |
| 1 back | 1/2 × 2 × 9 |
| 2 blocks | 1/2 × 2 × 4 |
| 1 pivot | 6 × 1/4 round |

## DROP-ARM DRYING RACK

The alternative to folding swinging arms is to arrange for them to drop down. This wall four-arm rack is based on one made as a full circle herb drying rack seen in a Cape Code home. It was on a central post with feet and had eight arms. This rack (Fig. 6-10) is only half of that shape and more suitable for any hanging or drying purpose in a modern home.

Because some of the cuts in the main part have to be across the grain, use a dense hardwood for strength. The top may be any wood. The arms may be straight-grained hardwood. If sizes are altered, be careful to arrange the shape so the pivot rods can be fitted in clear of the next projection.

Mark out the shape of the main part (Fig. 6-11A). The arms are at a 45-degree angle to each other, with the rear ones 22 1/2 degrees to the back. First draw their centerlines. Draw curves at the following radii: 2 1/4 inches (inner ends of slots), 4 inches (centers of pivot rods), 4 5/8 inches (outsides). With these lines as guides, complete the outline. Check that there will be clearance for the drill when you make the pivot holes (Fig.

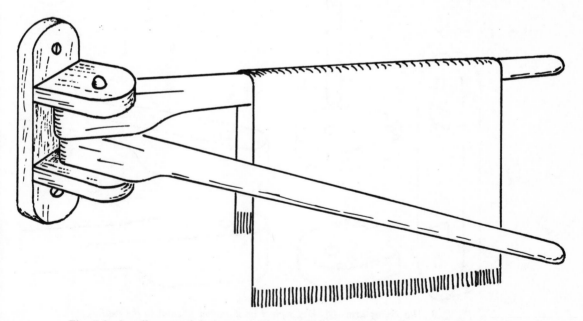

*Fig. 6-8. A wall-mounted drying arm. There could be one, two, or three swinging arms.*

6-11B). Cut the shape and lightly round edges (Fig. 6-11C). Drill for 1/4-inch pivots.

Make the top (Fig. 6-11D) to overlap the sockets by 3/4 inch (3-inch radius) (Fig. 6-11E). Glue it to the main part. Cut the back to shape and join to the main part with glue and screws (Fig. 6-11F). The assembly should be square or tilted up slightly, not down.

The four arms must fit in the grooves and can be 18 inches long. At each inner end cut a slot (Fig. 6-11G). When on a pivot rod, it should come clear of the top when pulled out and allowed to swing down. When pushed in, the slot must allow the arm to go under the top to the end of the groove.

**Materials List for Drop-Arm Drying Rack**

| | |
|---|---|
| 1 main part | 1 × 4 1/2 × 10 |
| 4 arms | 1 × 1 × 19 |
| 1 top | 1/2 × 3 1/2 × 8 |
| 1 back | 3/4 × 4 × 14 |

## CEILING DRYING RACK

Hot air rises, so the best drying area is at the top of a room. Because it is also the least cluttered

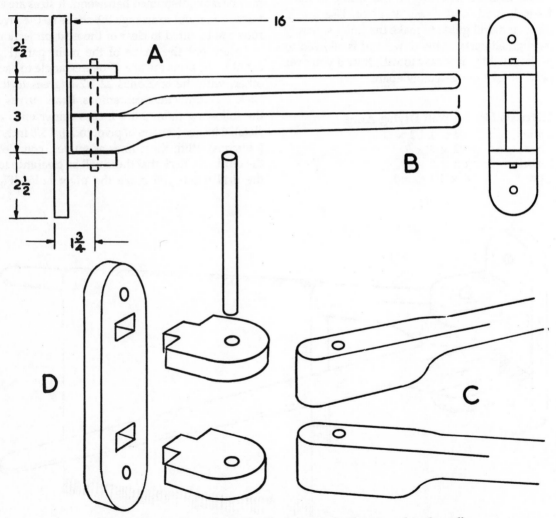

*Fig. 6-9. The drying arms (A, B, C) pivot on a bracket screwed to the wall.*

place, clothing and other things to be dried were hauled up to the ceiling. It is still a good place for drying.

This rack has four rails, 8 feet long, but they could be any length to suit your needs. They are hoisted up with a rope through pulleys screwed to the ceiling (Fig. 6-12). Any wood can be used, but the long rails are best made of straight-grained softwood.

Prepare the four rails and lightly round all edges and ends (Fig. 6-12A). The two ends may be 5/8 inch thick (Fig. 6-12B). Make notches to suit the rails. To strengthen where the load comes on cross grain, put a strip before drilling the hole (Fig. 6-12C) for the rope. Glue and screw or nail the parts together.

Arrange a single pulley above where each end will come and a double pulley in line with them close to the wall (Fig. 6-12D). Put a metal cleat below it on the wall (Fig. 6-12E). Knot the rope at the place that will hook on the cleat when the rack is fully raised (Fig. 6-12F). Have sufficient loop below it to hook on when the rack is at a level for loading.

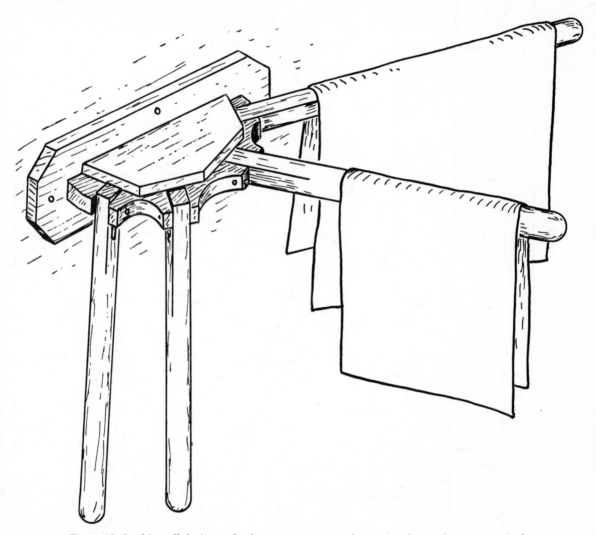

Fig. 6-10. In this wall drying rack, the arms are arranged to swing down when not required.

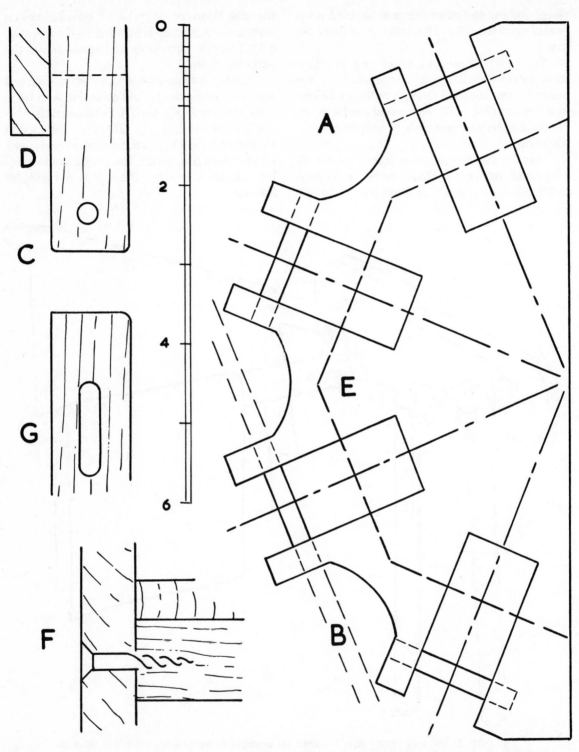

Fig. 6-11. *The layout of the top of the rack (A-E). The back is screwed on (F), and each arm is slotted (G).*

**Materials List for Ceiling Drying Rack**

| | |
|---|---|
| 4 rails | 3/4 × 1 1/2 × 96 |
| 2 ends | 5/8 × 5 × 20 |
| 2 end stiffeners | 3/8 × 2 × 6 |

## CURTAIN RODS AND BRACKETS

Wooden curtain rods and brackets will give a traditional look to a window. Some rods for large windows are fairly massive, but for the windows in a smaller home, a piece of 3/4-inch hardwood dowel rod will be stiff enough for a window width up to about 48 inches. The brackets should be 1-inch thick hardwood. The design shown in Fig. 6-13A uses knobs at the end to prevent the rod from sliding.

For a 3/4-inch dowel rod, the socket can be 7/8 inch with its center 1 inch from the wall (Fig. 6-13B). Mark the hole center and draw the other parts of the shape around it. Drill first and cut the outlines of two matching brackets. Smooth the cut parts and take sharpness off the edges. Drill for fixing screws (Fig. 6-13C).

Allow some clearance in the length of the rod and drill 3/8-inch holes 1/2 inch deep centrally in its ends. You might be able to buy standard drawer pull knobs, or you could turn them if you have the use of a lathe (Fig. 6-13D). Glue the knobs in place, unless you expect to move and shorten the rod.

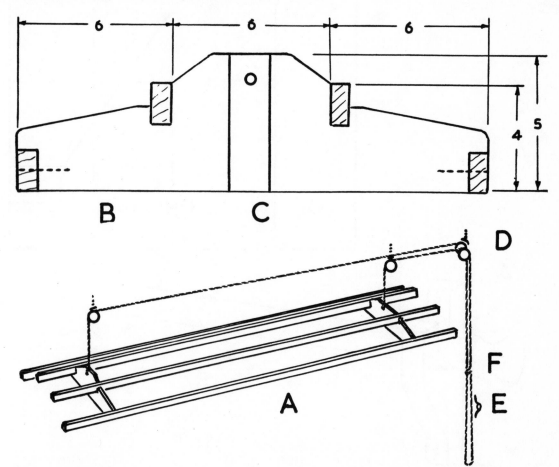

Fig. 6-12. A ceiling drying rack. The long rails (A) fit over stiffened ends (B, C) and are hoisted by ropes using pulleys and a cleat (D, E, F).

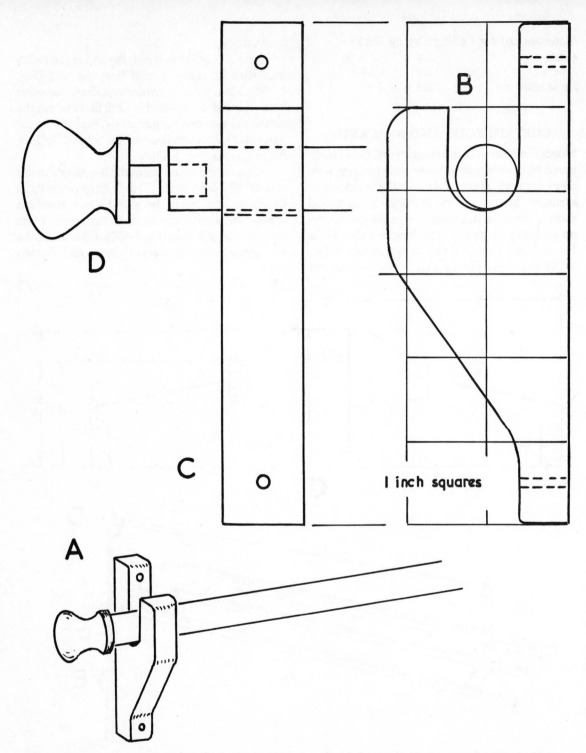

Fig. 6-13. A wood curtain rail (A) is supported by brackets (B, C), and knobs prevent endwise movement (D).

1 inch squares

| 1 rod | 48 × 3/4 round |
|-------|----------------|
| 2 brackets | 1 × 2 1/4 × 7 |
| 2 knobs | 1 1/2 × 1 1/2 × 4 |

## COAT RACK

Hooks for hanging clothing can be arranged on or against a wall or on a free-standing rack (Fig. 6-14A). A modern rack might have metal hooks, but early makers had to fashion wooden hooks.

Because weight is an advantage that provides steadiness, you could choose a heavy hardwood for all parts.

Mark out the post (Fig. 6-14B) with the positions of the other parts. Its bottom can be left square, but the top can be chamfered, rounded, or decorated with a turned knob.

Join the legs and hooks to the post with dowels (Fig. 6-15A) or mortise and tenon joints (Fig. 6-15B). Allow for the chosen joints when

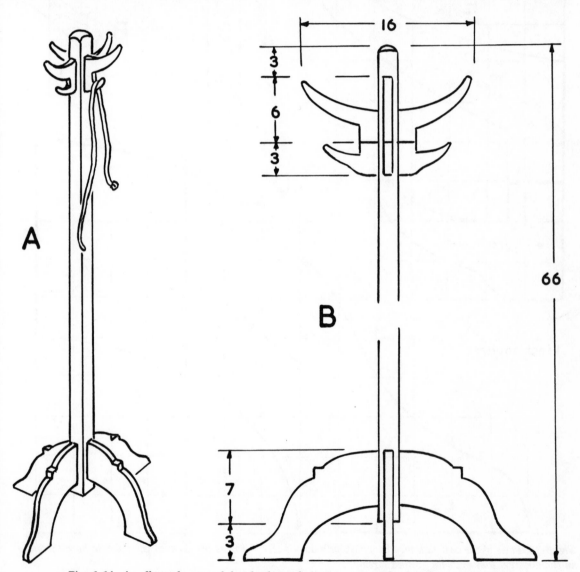

*Fig. 6-14. An all-wood coat rack has hooks made in two parts and a broad spread of feet.*

marking out the post and other parts.

The feet (Fig. 6-15C) have a small step in the outer profile (Fig. 6-15D). Besides providing decoration, this is used for clamping the joint during assembly. It might be advisable to leave it thicker until after assembly in case it becomes marked by the clamp. Round the outer edges of the feet.

To get the greatest strength from the grain

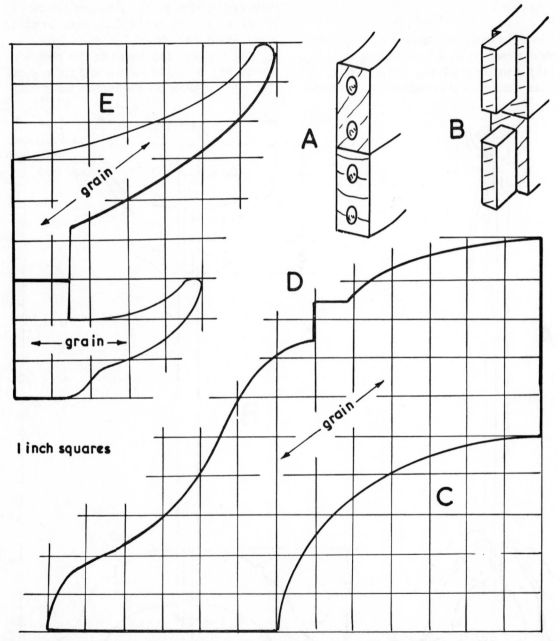

*Fig. 6-15. Parts of the coat rack may be joined with dowels (A) or tenons (B). Shaped parts should have the grain in the direction that provides greatest strength.*

directions, make the hooks in two parts (Fig. 6-15E). The flat surfaces will help in clamping. Taper and round the points of the hooks. Glue the parts together before joining to the post.

Check that the rack stands upright when viewed from any direction. Corrections can be made by planing the bottoms of feet.

### Materials List for Coat Rack

| | |
|---|---|
| 1 post | 2 × 2 × 68 |
| 4 feet | 1 × 6 × 18 |
| 4 hooks | 1 × 3 1/2 × 10 |
| 4 hooks | 1 × 3 × 7 |

## WASHSTAND

In homes without piped water, a washstand was an important piece of furniture. It took the form of a table, ledged around the top, and with a broad shelf. There might have been a drawer. The stand held a bowl and pitcher, both large enough for personal ablutions and other washing needs. In a modern home, the stand might just be decorative in itself or used for flowers or a lamp or as a bedside table. Early washstands were mostly softwood, but any wood could be used.

This project is a typical early washstand (Fig. 6-16) with drawer and towel rails. Sizes (Fig. 6-17A) should suit most needs. Construction is with traditional joints, but dowels may be used. Although the legs could be left square, they are better turned.

Make four matching legs (Fig. 6-18A). Mark the positions of rails and start the turned parts 1 1/2 inches from them. At the front, the 5-inch drawer is between 1-inch rails. The other top rails are to the same depth. The bottom rails are 1 inch by 2 inch all around.

Prepare the rails. For the top, deep rails use double tenons (Fig. 6-18B). Use a tenon at each end of the rail under the drawer (Fig. 6-18C), but dovetails are better at the top (Fig. 6-18D).

On the side rails put drawer runners at the bottom (Fig. 6-18E) and kickers (Fig. 6-18F) at the top. Thicken above the runners with guides (Fig. 6-18G) level with the insides of the legs.

Make plain tenons on the bottom rails (Fig. 6-18H) and have the shelf ready (Fig. 6-18J) to fit in as you assemble, so it keeps the framework square. Make up the ends first, then join them with the long parts and shelf.

The top comes level with the legs at the back but overhangs at the ends and front. Frame it (Fig. 6-17B) with dovetailed corners and screws upwards into the back and ends. Fix the top to the framework with screws up through the drawer kickers and the front rail.

If towel rails are to be fitted, use 5/8-inch dowel rods. Make blocks to glue and screw to the legs and fit under the top (Fig. 6-17C).

The drawer can be made in the standard way (see Figs. 4-8 and 4-21) with the front level with the legs or projecting about 1/8 inch. Fit one or two knobs or metal handles.

*Fig. 6-16. A traditional washstand might have other uses today. This one has towel rails, a shelf, and a drawer.*

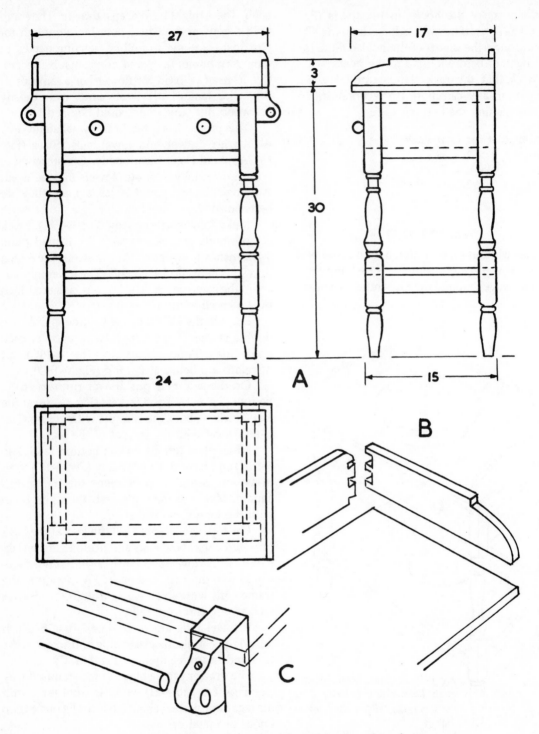

Fig. 6-17. Sizes and details of the towel rails and top frame.

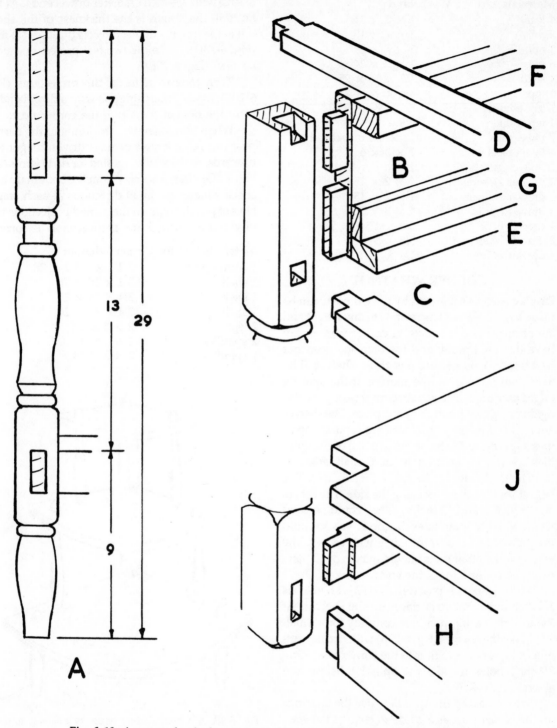

Fig. 6-18. A pattern for the legs and how the parts of the washstand are assembled.

133

## Materials List for Washstand

| | |
|---|---|
| 4 legs | 2 × 2 × 31 |
| 2 rails | 1 × 7 × 15 |
| 1 rail | 1 × 7 × 24 |
| 6 rails | 1 × 2 × 24 |
| 1 shelf | 1/2 × 15 × 25 |
| 1 top | 3/4 × 17 × 28 |
| 2 top frames | 5/8 × 3 × 19 |
| 1 top frame | 5/8 × 4 × 29 |
| 2 towel rails | 18 × 5/8 dowel rod |
| 4 towel blocks | 1 × 3 × 6 |
| 2 drawer guides | 1/4 × 1 × 15 |
| 2 drawer kickers | 1 × 2 × 15 |
| 2 drawer runners | 1 × 2 × 15 |
| 1 drawer front | 1 × 5 × 22 |
| 1 drawer back | 5/8 × 4 1/2 × 22 |
| 2 drawer sides | 5/8 × 5 × 16 |
| 1 drawer bottom | 1/4 × 15 × 24 |

## CORNER WHATNOT

Display shelves separated by turned posts can be made as four-legged long stands to any height and are often termed *whatnots*. A corner version can have three supports, and the rear one need not be turned. This project has three shelves (Fig. 6-19), but there could be more and the spacing might be varied. The square corner post provides rigidity by going through in one piece. The shelves are reduced in size, and there are separate spindles supporting the front corners. All of the spindles are within the capacity of a small lathe.

The total height is 36 inches (Fig. 6-20A). The largest shelf is 18 inches along the side. The others are 15 inches and 12 inches. They could be solid wood with the grain lines diagonal, or you could use plywood and cover the edges with veneer. The wood for the other parts should match, or all parts could be stained the same color.

Make the corner post (Fig. 6-21A) with notches 1/4 inch deep on two surfaces for the shelves. At the top, drill a 1/2-inch hole centrally for a finial.

Make the shelves (Fig. 6-20B) with circular outlines and notched to fit into the corner post. Drill 3/4-inch holes to take the spindles below and above (Fig. 6-21B).

When making the spindles, use the spacings on the corner post as a guide to lengths between shoulders. Turn the spindles between shelves (Fig.

6-20C) with 3/4-inch diameter dowel ends. At the bottom, the length is the thickness of the shelf, but at the top, the dowel projects through 1/2-inch (Fig. 6-20D). Make the two feet project in a similar way (Fig. 6-20E).

Turn tops to glue on the projections (Fig. 6-20F). Make a matching one with a dowel end to fit in the hole at the top of the corner post.

When you assemble, the joints to the corner post can have screws or nails driven diagonally upwards, in the way suggested for dado joints (see Fig. 2-1G). Start assembly from the bottom up and check squareness in all directions at each stage. Do not put the tops on the turned projections until you are satisfied that the assembly is correct.

## Materials List for Corner Whatnot

| | |
|---|---|
| 1 corner post | 1 1/2 × 1 1/2 × 38 |
| 1 shelf | 3/4 × 18 × 26 |
| 1 shelf | 3/4 × 15 × 23 |
| 1 shelf | 3/4 × 12 × 20 |
| 2 legs | 2 × 2 × 10 |
| 2 spindles | 2 × 2 × 17 |
| 2 spindles | 2 × 2 × 18 |

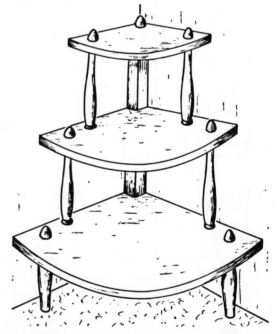

Fig. 6-19. A corner whatnot serves as a display unit in a part of the room that might not otherwise be used.

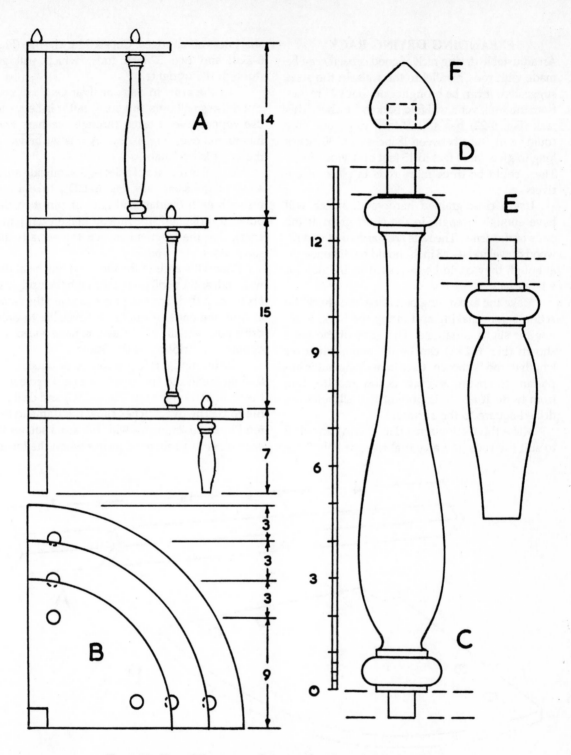

Fig. 6-20. Sizes of the corner whatnot and patterns for the turnings.

## EXPANDING DRYING RACK

An adjustable drying rack of good capacity can be made with rods parallel to the wall. In the sizes suggested, it can be brought out about 25 inches from the wall, yet it will fold back to 5 inches. This rack (Fig. 6-22) has six, 24-inch rods, but they could be anything between 18 inches and 30 inches long to give you 9 feet to 15 feet of drying space. There could be three more rods in place of the rivets.

Use a close-grained hardwood, which will have enough strength in the short grain at the ends of the arms. The rails are hardwood or softwood dowel rods—3/8 inch should be stiff enough, although they could be increased to 1/2 inch for a large rack.

Make the expanding parts first and check the action before making and fitting the back, to allow for slight variations. The sizes of the ends shown (Fig. 6-25A) can be the same whatever length of rod is chosen. Care in marking out is important to ensure accurate action and freedom from twist. It is also important that all holes are drilled square to the surface.

Make the twelve arms (Fig. 6-23A) and drill to suit the rods and a central rivet or bolt. Take sharpness off all edges. Cut six 24-inch rods (Fig. 6-22B) and two 27-inch rods, which will go through the uprights.

Join the arms in pairs at their centers. You could use small nuts and bolts, but it is better to use copper rivets, taken through washers and hammered over (Fig. 6-22C). A washer between the arms is optional.

Assemble the pair of sides so that outside arms all slope the same way (Fig. 6-22D). Take a rod through each overlap and glue or pin it to the outer arm (Fig. 6-23B). As you make each joint, check that the lengths between the arms is the same along each rod.

Round the ends of the rods that will be at the wall end, as they will project through the uprights. Fix them in their arms so projections are the same at opposite ends. It might be advisable to only drive pins partially until after you have tested the opening and closing of the frame.

The two uprights (Fig. 6-23E) come outside the folding frame and are joined by a bar to screw to the wall. Mark them out (Fig. 6-23C) and drill for the rods. The two notches allow the frame to extend to about 25 inches with the arms square to each other or to about 15 inches when the lower

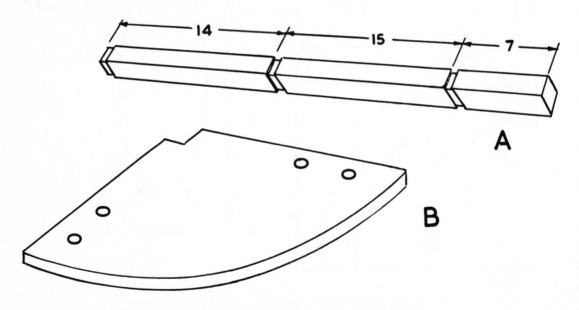

*Fig. 6-21. Details of the corner post (A) and shelf (B).*

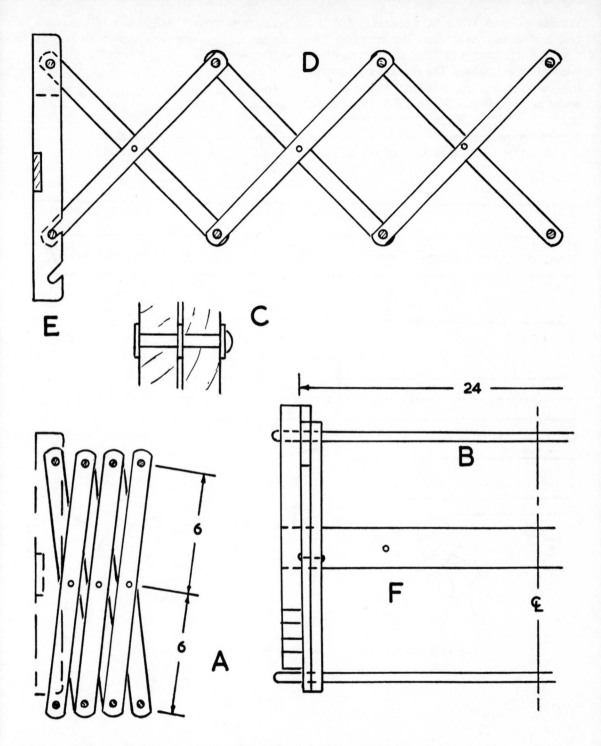

Fig. 6-22. *The expanding drying rack uses a rod in notches to hold the parts in either of two open position, or it drops to allow folding.*

notches are used. When the frame is folded, the rear bottom rod goes below the uprights. You could arrange notches in different positions if you want other extensions. The notches cut into the holes at 45-degree angles but make them slightly wider at their mouths (Fig. 6-23D). At the tops, put strips inside (Fig. 6-23E) to allow for the thickness of the outer arms.

Let the back into its notches (Fig. 6-23F) and screw from the rear. Adjust its length to give a little clearance over the outer arms of the frame. Drill for screws to the wall (Fig. 6-23F).

**Materials List for Expanding Drying Rack**

| | |
|---|---|
| 12 arms | 1/2 × 3/4 × 15 |
| 2 uprights | 1 × 1 1/2 × 14 |
| 1 bar | 1/2 × 2 × 28 |
| 6 rods | 25 × 3/8 round |
| 2 rods | 28 × 3/8 round |

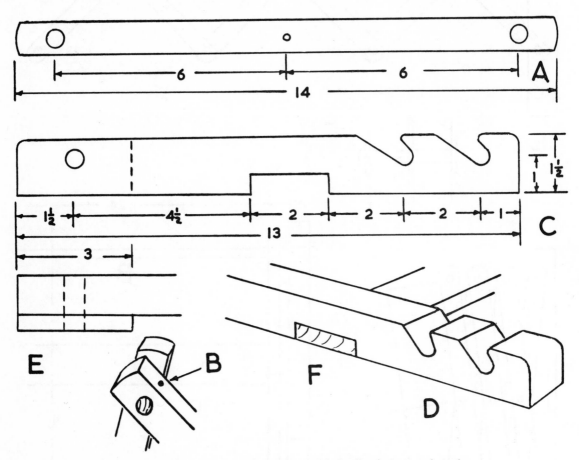

Fig. 6-23. Sizes of arms and uprights, with details of pivots and notches.

# Seven

# Hanging Cupboards and Cabinets

The next step after making a block of shelves is to fit one or more doors. Besides protecting the contents from dust and from falling out, the doors give a tidy appearance to what might be a varied collection of articles. If the contents are to be displayed while being protected, the doors could have glass panels.

Most doors are hinged to open sideways, but a door can be hinged at the bottom so it becomes a flap with a working surface. It could hinge upwards to give good access to the interior. Sliding doors were little known in early furniture, so if you want to make a reproduction, avoid these.

Metal hinges were either nonexistent or rather clumsy blacksmith-made ones. These looked good on large doors but were inappropriate to the usual size of wall cupboard. Consequently, methods of wood-to-wood hinging were used and are interesting to reproduce.

Many early cupboards were made of plain wide boards. If you want your work to accompany chests and tables made in this way, use similar methods of making cupboards. Once the means of converting wood to regular sizes became common, doors were more often paneled, as was commonly done in Europe. These were not very different from modern paneled doors.

## DOWEL-HINGED CABINET

This is an example of a wall cabinet made from plain boards and with a door that swings without metal hinges (Fig. 7-1). The suggested sizes would suit a medicine cabinet (Fig. 7-2A). They could also be modified to suit any size, although if much bigger it would be advisable to brace the door to prevent warping.

Make the pair of sides and mark the positions of other parts (Fig. 7-2B). The back (Fig. 7-2C) goes between the sides and need not project below the bottom shelf.

Top and bottom are cut around the sides (Fig. 7-2D) far enough to overlap the door and give enough strength in the end grain to take the load of the pivots. If a shelf is to be fitted, nail cleats to the sides (Fig. 7-2E) so the shelf will rest on them.

Parts are nailed, as they would have been in an original cabinet. In better work there would be dado joints. Glue and nail the parts together. From this assembly measure the size of the door. Drill for 1/4-inch dowels (Fig. 7-2F). Round the inner edge of the door to clear the sides as it swings.

The handle could be a block of wood or a turned knob. Any fastener might be fitted, but a

very early cabinet would have had a hook (twisted wire) over a nail in the door.

## Materials List for Dowel-hinged Cabinet

| | |
|---|---|
| 2 sides | 5/8 × 7 × 21 |
| 1 back | 5/8 × 9 3/4 × 19 |
| 1 top | 5/8 × 8 1/2 × 13 |
| 1 bottom | 5/8 × 8 1/2 × 13 |
| 1 door | 3/4 × 11 × 15 |
| 1 shelf | 1/2 × 6 × 11 |
| 2 cleats | 1/2 × 3/4 × 6 |

## PANELED-DOOR CABINET

This cabinet (Fig. 7-3) has a family likeness to the previous project. It might have been made up to a century later, however, by a cabinetmaker who had seasoned wood of good quality and facilities

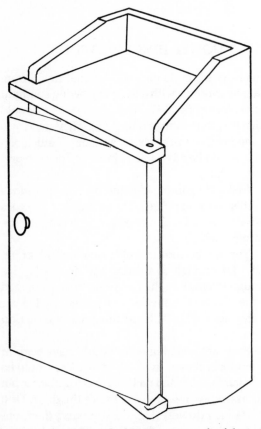

*Fig. 7-1. A dowel-hinged cabinet is an example of the type of door arrangement that can be made without metal hinges.*

for doing accurate handwork.

The cabinet could be made of any wood, but it would look good in an attractive hardwood, stained and polished. The sizes suggested (Fig. 7-4A) would make a roomy medicine chest. The back could be plywood or hardboard, but for an authentic reproduction, it would have to be solid wood.

Prepare the wood for most parts as accurate joints can only be made by reference to pieces that have to fit. Start with the pair of sides (Fig. 7-4B). Rabbet the rear edge for the back parts. Square the fronts of the top and bottom grooves but leave the inside shelf grooves rounded as they come from the router. The best joint for the bottom is a dovetail (Figs. 7-4C and 7-5A). Do the edge shaping.

Make the top and bottom with stopped dado joints (Fig. 7-5B) and the inside shelves to fit their grooves (Fig. 7-5C). Cut the bottom dovetails. Assemble these parts, then fit the back (Fig. 7-5D) as high as the top of the cabinet top piece, then fit a shaped thicker piece above that (Fig. 7-5E).

At the front, glue strips each side of the doorway (Figs. 7-4D and 7-5F). Make the door with only a little clearance all around, then plane it to size after assembly. Make sufficient grooved pieces (Fig. 7-4E). Leave the door sides overlong until after the joints are cut and assembled. Make corner joints with tenons cut back (Fig. 7-5G). Prepare the panel (Figs. 7-4F and 7-5H) to fit the grooves without touching their bottoms. Do not use glue on the panel edges. Square the door as you glue the corner joints. Fit hinges to one side and a knob or handle to the other side. If the catch you use does not also act as a stop, a small block on the bottom will prevent the door going in too far.

## Materials List for Paneled-Door Cabinet

| | |
|---|---|
| 2 sides | 5/8 × 7 × 22 |
| 1 top | 5/8 × 6 3/4 × 13 |
| 2 bottoms | 5/8 × 6 3/4 × 13 |
| 2 shelves | 1/2 × 4 × 13 |
| 1 back | 1/4 × 11 1/2 × 20 |
| 2 door parts | 3/4 × 1 1/4 × 15 |
| 2 door parts | 3/4 × 1 1/4 × 11 |
| 1 door panel | 1/2 × 8 × 12 |
| 2 doorway sides | 3/4 × 1 × 14 |

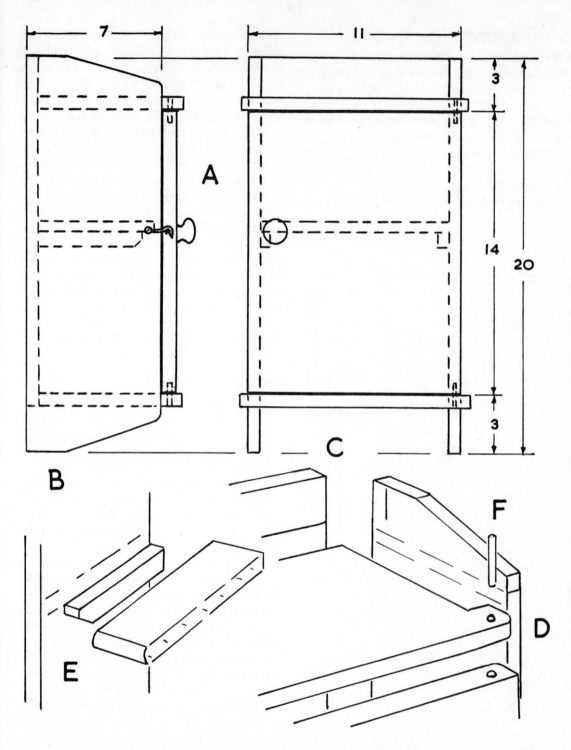

Fig. 7-2. Sizes and assembly details of the dowel-hinge cabinet.

## DROP-FRONT CABINET

It is convenient for a cabinet that holds first-aid or similar equipment to have a front that drops to give a working surface. This small cabinet is based on an early design and includes a rail for a folded towel (Fig. 7-6), which might be needed in an emergency. The cabinet could be made without metal parts if dowels are used as pivots, but it would be stronger to use screws and cover their heads with dowel plugs (Fig. 7-7A).

The key parts are the sides. Mark them from the squared drawing (Fig. 7-7B). Cut stopped dado joints for the top (Fig. 7-7C) but make full-length grooves in the bottom (Fig. 7-7D). If you wish to have a shelf, cut grooves for it. The pivot holes must be located so the front flap does not drop lower than horizontal (Fig. 7-7E). To allow for wear it is better to first arrange it to tilt upwards slightly. The towel rail can be a 5/8-inch dowel rod with holes taken halfway through (Fig. 7-7F). Make and fit the top, the bottom rail, and then the back, which is glued between the other parts.

Make the door to fit easily and mark through the side screw holes. Any handle could be used, but a piece of round rod with a flat on it (Fig. 7-7G) might have been used originally. If a catch is needed, use an inconspicuous ball type. If the catch does not act as a stop, put a small block of wood centrally under the top.

### Materials List for Drop-Front Cabinet

| | |
|---|---|
| 2 sides | 5/8 × 6 1/2 × 16 |
| 1 top | 1/2 × 6 × 8 |
| 1 bottom | 1/2 × 5 × 8 |
| 1 door | 1/2 × 6 × 10 |
| 1 back | 1/2 × 6 × 8 |
| 1 rail | 8 × 5/8 round |

### MIRROR-FRONT CABINET

If a mirror or plain glass is to be fitted into a door, it is unwise to put it in grooves, as would be done with a wood panel, because it could not be replaced, if ever necessary, without breaking the frame. It is more usual to fit the glass into rabbets and hold it there with strip wood fillets (Fig. 7-8A), fixed with pins, so they can be sprung out to replace the glass. If a mirror is used, its back can be protected by a piece of card held under the fillets.

Simple miters are difficult to strengthen sufficiently to take the loads of a door, and it is better to use mortise and tenon joints. The tenons need not go through, and there have to be long and short shoulders to allow for the rabbet (Fig. 7-8B). It is always wiser to start with the mortised piece too long (Fig. 7-8C), to prevent the grain breaking out, then trim it level after assembly.

This bathroom cabinet (Fig. 7-9) has a top and bottom that overhangs the door, which could have

*Fig. 7-3. A wall cabinet with a raised panel door and a shelf below.*

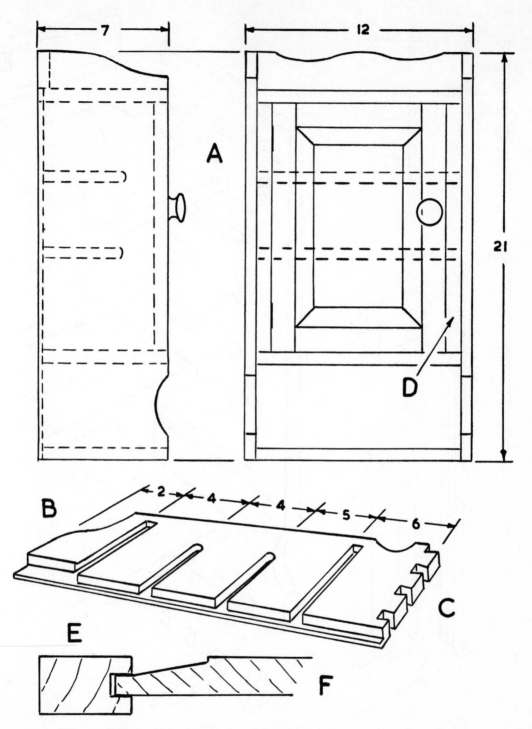

Fig. 7-4. Sizes of the paneled-door cabinet. Details of a side, which controls other sizes, and a section through the edge of a door panel.

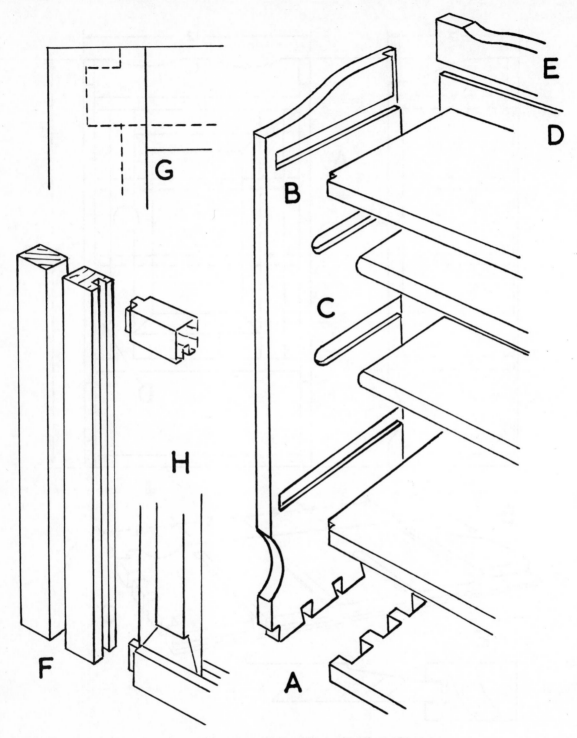

Fig. 7-5. Assembly details of the paneled-door cabinet.

144

hinges at one side or pivot pins at top and bottom. The door is shown with a wider bottom rail, which is common practice, but it could be the same width as the other rails.

The best cabinet corner joints are dovetails (Fig. 7-8D). Details are similar to earlier cabinets. Make the cabinet before the door, then measure the space to get the sizes of the wood for the door frame.

Make the door frame with shouldered mortise and tenon joints and trim the outside to size. Allow a little clearance at the edges of the mirror. Make fillet widths to match the frame section both ways and fit them with pins, at about 3-inch spacing. Let in 2-inch hinges and add a knob and a catch.

## Materials List for Mirror-Front Cabinet

| | |
|---|---|
| 2 sides | 5/8 × 5 × 14 |
| 2 top/bottom | 5/8 × 6 × 12 |
| 1 back | 3/8 × 9 × 11 |
| 2 door sides | 3/4 × 1 1/2 × 13 |
| 1 door top | 3/4 × 1 1/2 × 11 |
| 1 door bottom | 3/4 × 2 1/2 × 11 |
| 4 fillets | 3/8 × 3/8 × 10 |

## CLEATED CORNER CUPBOARD

A corner cupboard to use space that might otherwise be empty was, and still is, a good idea. Such a cupboard is a block of shelves fitted with a door. The expert method of construction uses dadoes for the shelves, but cutting long grooves might have been too difficult for some early woodworkers. Al-

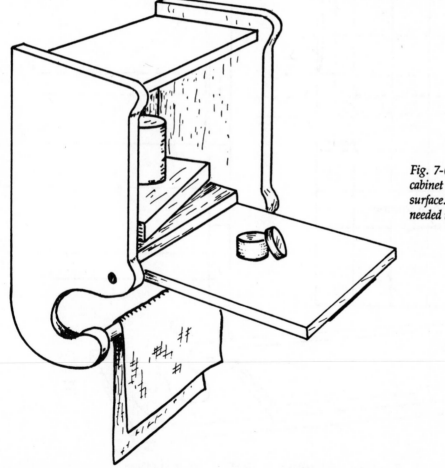

Fig. 7-6. The door of a drop-front cabinet opens to provide a working surface. A towel below might be needed if this is a first-aid cabinet.

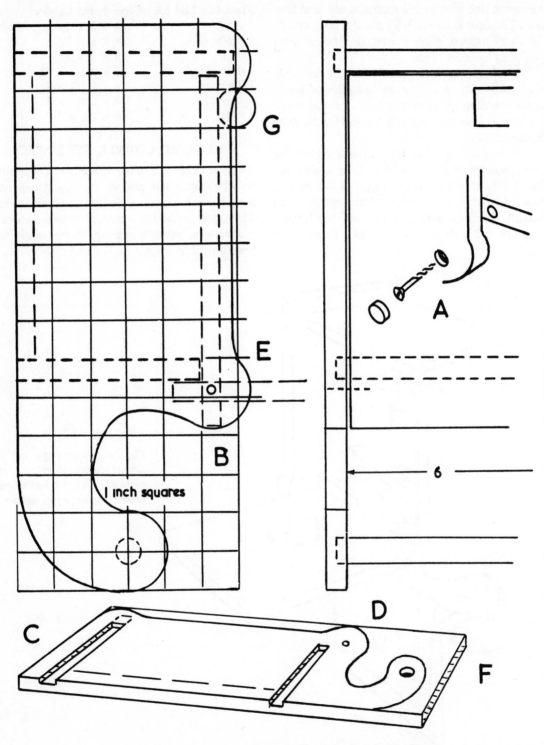

1 inch squares

Fig. 7-7. Shapes and constructional details of the drop-front cabinet.

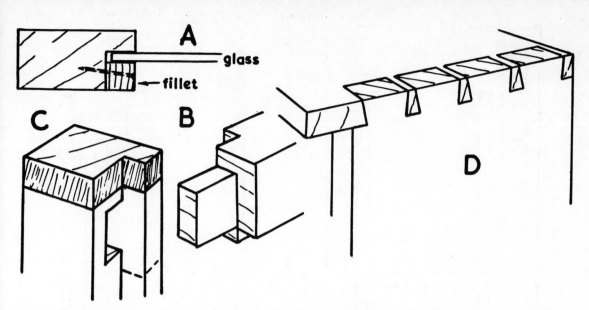

Fig. 7-8. If a door is to have a mirror or glass panel, it is better to use fillets in a rabbet (A) than to put it in a groove. Corner joints are arranged to suit (B, C). Dovetails are best for the cabinet.

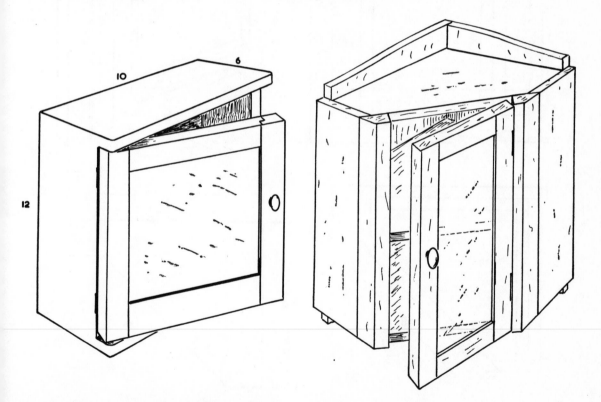

Fig. 7-9. A bathroom cabinet door could turn on dowel or screw pivots, or ordinary hinges could be fitted at one edge.

Fig. 7-10. A corner cabinet can be made from solid wood and fitted with a glass door.

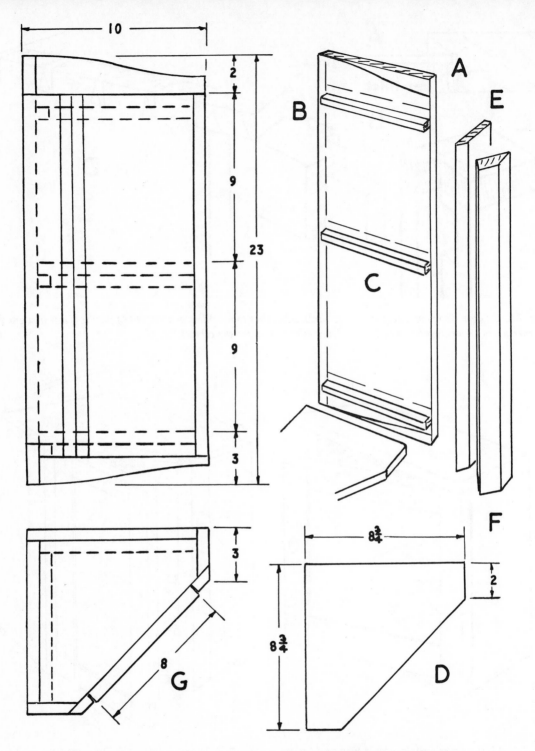

Fig. 7-11. Sizes and constructional details of the cleated corner cupboard.

though long grooves are easily cut with a router or other tools, this corner cupboard (Fig. 7-10) avoids grooves by using cleats to support the shelves. Most of the parts are glued and nailed, with the front nails set below the surface and covered with stopping. The door may have a wood or glass panel. A local hardwood would be appropriate for an authentic reproduction.

The two backs (Fig. 7-11A) are the same, except one overlaps the other (Fig. 7-11B). Mark the positions of the shelves and fit cleats (Fig. 7-11C). Shape the top and bottom.

Check the angle of the corner of the room. If it is not square, set an adjustable bevel to the angle and use that instead of a square when making the three shelves, which are all the same (Fig. 7-11D). They are best made with the grain parallel with the front edge.

Glue and nail the backs together. Fit the shelves to the cleats with nails through the backs.

Make the two sides (Fig. 7-12E) long enough to cover the edges of the top shelf and the bottom cleat. The bevel of the front edge should match the angle of the shelves. Fit the sides and make the two fronts (Fig. 7-11F) the same length as the sides. They should fit over them and leave a gap about 8 inches wide (Fig. 7-11G).

The door fits between the fronts and overlaps the shelves. It will be thicker than the front strips, so round its projecting edges. The simplest door is a single solid piece of wood, but a framed door will look better. There could be a plain or raised wood panel (Figs. 7-4 and 7-5) or a glass panel could be let in (Fig. 7-8). Fit hinges and a handle. The middle shelf will act as a door stop.

### Materials List for Cleated Corner Cupboard

| | |
|---|---|
| 1 back | 5/8 × 9 3/8 × 24 |
| 1 back | 5/8 × 8 3/4 × 24 |
| 3 shelves | 5/8 × 8 × 14 |
| 6 cleats | 5/8 × 5/8 × 10 |
| 2 sides | 5/8 × 3 × 24 |
| 2 fronts | 5/8 × 2 × 24 |
| 2 door sides | 3/4 × 1 1/2 × 24 |
| 2 door ends | 3/4 × 1 1/2 × 10 |

## CORNER CUPBOARD WITH OPEN SHELF

Many federal and colonial period corner cup-

boards included an open shelf, usually below the part with a door. The back might have continued above the cupboard, although if that was intended to be positioned fairly high on the walls, as in this example (Fig. 7-12), the top was finished flat. The glass door includes some top shaping, and the part below the cupboard includes some curves. Main

Fig. 7-12. This corner cupboard is of more advance construction and has a shelf at the bottom.

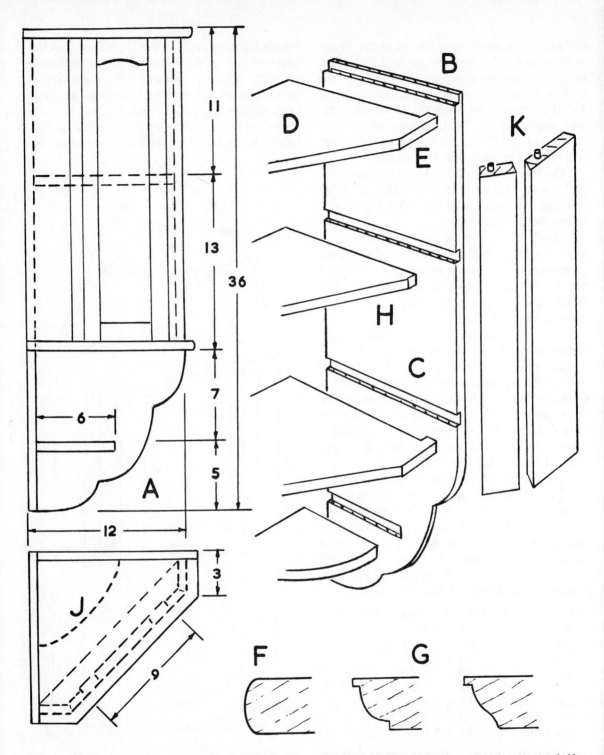

Fig. 7-13. Sizes and the method of joining the parts and possible edge moldings for the corner cupboard with open shelf.

parts have dado joints. A good hardwood with a polished finish will look attractive.

The backs could fit into each other with a rabbet, but you could use a nailed or screwed overlap, as in the last project. Mark out the two backs to the sizes in Fig. 7-13A. Cut a rabbet at the top (Fig. 7-13B) but at the other joints prepare dadoes (Fig. 7-13C). Curve the lower edges around the shelf. The top (Fig. 7-13D) and bottom are similar. Check the wall corner and make the top and bottom corners to suit. These parts extend 1 1/4 inches past the rabbet and dado ends (Fig. 7-13E) and are cut to hide them. The projecting edges may be rounded (Fig. 7-13F) or molded (Fig. 7-13G).

Cut the inside shelf straight across (Fig. 7-13H). The small lower shelf is similar, although it looks best with a curved front edge (Fig. 7-13J), and it could be molded.

Each front and side could be overlapped, as in the last project, but the joint looks better with a glued miter, then there can be dowels at top and bottom (Fig. 7-13K). Assemble the parts. There may be screws through the backs, but elsewhere glue should be sufficient. See that the door opening is square.

Move the door with 1 1/2-inch sides and 2-inch top and bottom. Cut rabbets 3/8 inch deep and 1/2 inch wide in the sides and bottom. For the top, mark a curve about 3/8 inch deep and cut the rabbet 1/4 inch further (Fig. 7-14A), so the glass can be used with a square edge. Make the tenons as wide as the wood will allow (Fig. 7-14B). Tenons can be wider on the straight bottom piece. When fitting the glass, shape the top fillet to match the frame. Fit hinges and a handle. A piece of wood under the top will act as a door stop.

## Materials List for
## Corner Cupboard with Open Shelf

| | |
|---|---|
| 1 back | 5/8 × 12 × 38 |
| 1 back | 5/8 × 11 3/8 × 38 |
| 1 top | 3/4 × 12 × 20 |
| 1 bottom | 3/4 × 12 × 20 |
| 1 shelf | 5/8 × 8 × 18 |
| 1 shelf | 5/8 × 6 × 11 |
| 2 sides | 5/8 × 3 × 24 |
| 2 fronts | 5/8 × 3 × 24 |
| 2 door sides | 3/4 × 1 1/2 × 24 |
| 2 door ends | 3/4 × 2 × 9 |
| 2 fillets | 3/8 × 3/8 × 24 |
| 1 fillet | 3/8 × 3/8 × 9 |
| 1 fillet | 3/8 × 3/4 × 9 |

## WIDE CORNER CUPBOARD

One of the problems with making a cupboard fully fitted into a corner is that the wider you want the front, the deeper the distance has to be from the door to the point at the back. If what you are making is primarily for storage, all that extra space will be valuable, but if you want to display pottery, trophies or other fairly small things, it would be

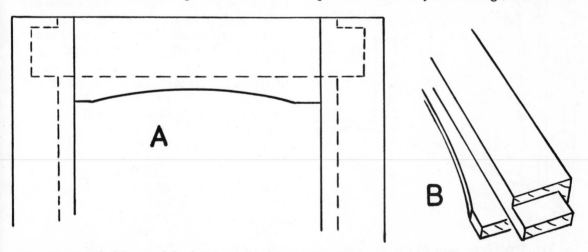

Fig. 7-14. Detail of the top of the door frame showing how the glass is cut square behind a shaped frame edge.

better if there was a back not too far in and parallel with the door. This can be arranged by cutting off the point of the triangle in the vertical view. The effect is to leave a gap in the corner of the room, but that can be disguised by making the top a full triangle.

This wide corner cupboard (Fig. 7-15) has three display shelves and a door with a shaped surround, but the glass is cut square. The amount of the triangular point to be cut away can be varied. As shown (Fig. 7-16A), the parts are cut to leave a back-to-front internal width of about 9 inches.

Copy this drawing full size—using the square corner of a piece of plywood or hardboard is one way. This will show you the widths and angles

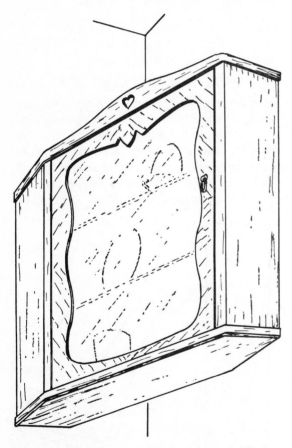

*Fig. 7-15. A wide corner cupboard need not go fully into the angle of a corner.*

of the various parts that have to be cut. The height suggested (Fig. 7-16B) will make a cupboard of reasonable proportions.

Top and bottom are the same and can be marked from your drawing (Fig. 7-17A). Make the two sides overlap these pieces. Add 1-inch square strips at the front and cleats for the shelves (Fig. 7-17B). Make the back by gluing several pieces together (Fig. 7-17C) or with tongue and groove joints. If exact authenticity is not required, use plywood. The pair of fronts (Fig. 7-17D) overlap the sides and top and bottom, and are beveled to glue against upright strips (Fig. 7-17E) set square to the front edge to form door posts.

Make the shelves (Fig. 7-17F) with their fronts rounded and level with the inner edges of the door posts. Notch to fit around the corner posts. Assemble all parts, with the back last.

The door is made in two thicknesses (Fig. 7-18A) with a mitered 1 1/2-inch frame inside the front, which is made of four pieces joined at the centers of the edges (Fig. 7-18B, C, and D). If the front pieces are made with the grain diagonal, they will be stronger and the grain lines will form a pattern. Round the front edges of the shaped parts. Glue the door parts and fit the assembly to the case with hinges, knob, and catch.

Put strips at the bottom (Fig. 7-17G), mitered where they meet. Put similar strips at the tops of the side parts, but a wider piece with a heart motif is suggested for the center (Fig. 7-18E).

Fit the glass panel with a little clearance and with nailed fillets (Fig. 7-18F) all round.

**Materials List for Wide Corner Cupboard**

| | |
|---|---|
| 1 top | 3/4 × 9 1/2 × 30 |
| 1 bottom | 3/4 × 9 1/2 × 30 |
| 2 shelves | 5/8 × 8 × 30 |
| 2 sides | 5/8 × 9 × 28 |
| 2 fronts | 5/8 × 5 × 28 |
| 4 posts | 1 × 1 × 28 |
| 1 back | 1/2 × 18 × 28 |
| 1 trim | 1/2 × 1 × 24 |
| 4 trims | 1/2 × 1 × 7 |
| 1 trim | 1/2 × 4 × 24 |
| 4 door parts | 5/8 × 1 1/2 × 27 |
| 4 door parts | 3/8 × 11 × 18 |

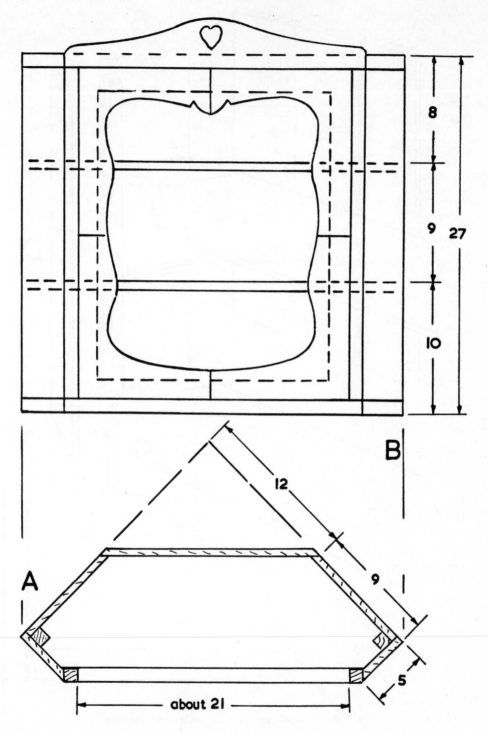

Fig. 7-16. Suggested sizes of a wide corner cupboard.

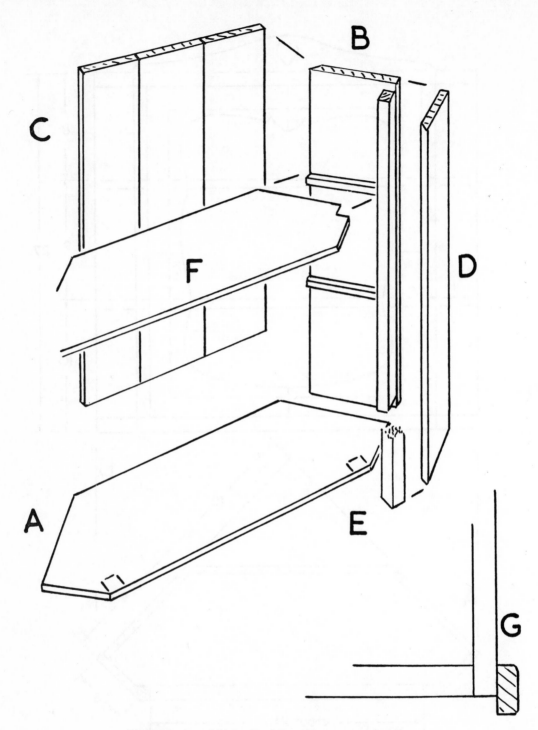

Fig. 7-17. Assembly details of the wide corner cupboard.

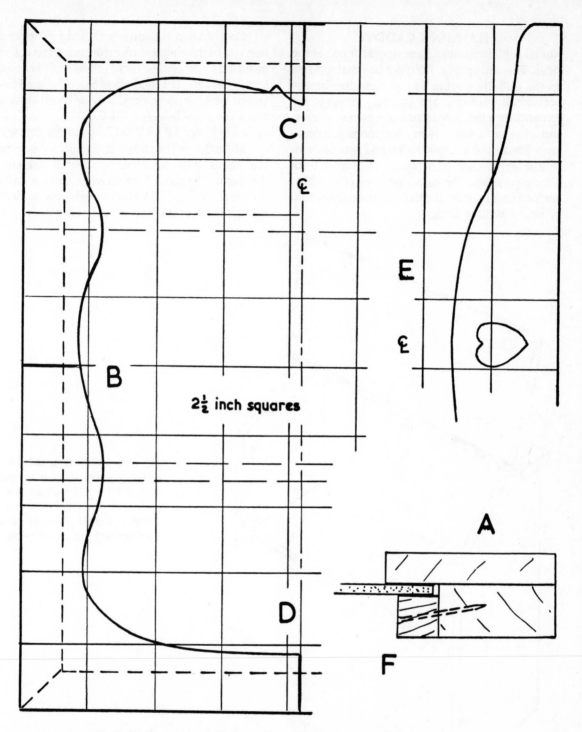

C

₵

E

₵

B

2½ inch squares

A

D

F

*Fig. 7-18. Pattern for the door and the shaped top of the wide corner cupboard.*

## HANGING CADDY

Not all cupboards need have doors hinged at the sides. This caddy (Fig. 7-19) is a box that mounts on the wall. Its sloping lid and front flap hinges horizontally and opens to give easy access to the contents. In a hall you could store gloves, scarves, and other small items. Near a telephone you could keep directories, address books, and note pads inside or on the shelf. The flap then lowers to form a writing surface. The sizes suggested (Fig. 7-20A) are for a small caddy. If enlarged, the caddy could become a writing desk.

Construction is shown with dado joints and dowels. In the simplest construction, parts could be nailed together. The back is shown as plywood let into rabbets, but solid wood could be fitted between the ends. Any wood may be used. Do not make the parts less than 1/2 inch thick, and the ends are better 5/8 inch to allow for the dadoes.

Make the pair of ends (Fig. 7-20B). Rabbet the rear edges. If the lid slopes at about 30 degrees, the flap will be about 7 inches wide. Cut the dado for the shelf (Fig. 7-20C) far enough back to clear the thickness of the flap. At the other dado, the

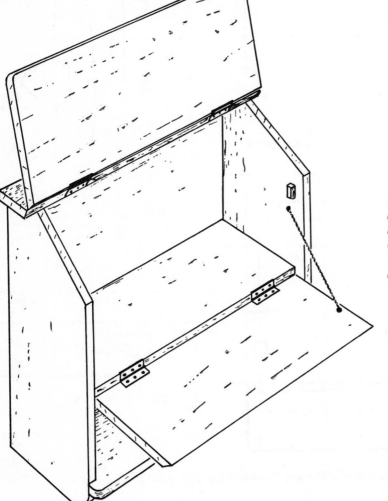

Fig. 7-19. This hanging caddy has an opening front as well as top and a shelf below. The whole thing could store gloves and other small things, or it could offer storage and a writing surface near a telephone.

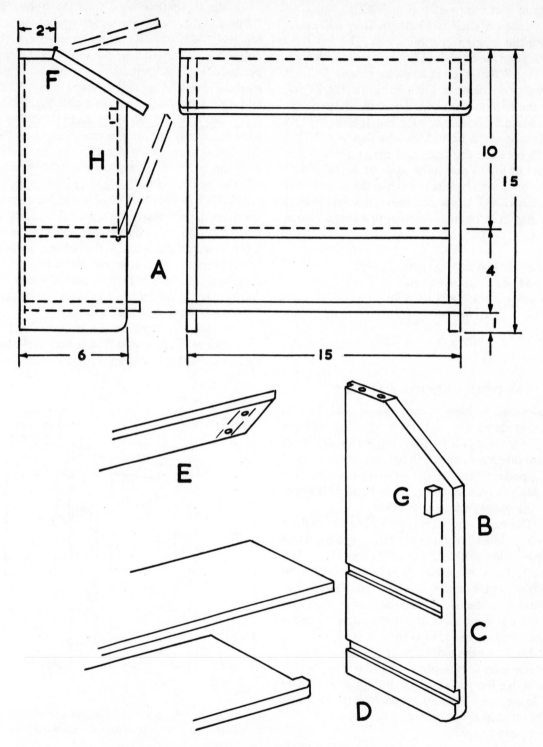

Fig. 7-20. Sizes and assembly details of the hanging caddy.

bottom is cut to overlap (Fig. 7-20D).

Make the shelf and bottom. They will determine the lengths of other parts. The top (Fig. 7-20E) and the lid should be cut to meet with a miter (Fig. 7-20F), then notched for hinges. Drill for dowels into the ends. Put stop blocks (Fig. 7-20G) for the flap on the ends. Assemble these parts.

Make the lid to match the length of the top and overhang at the front. Make the flap (Fig. 7-20H) to fit between the ends and hinge to the shelf. Bevel its top to match the slope of the lid. There is no need for a handle or catch as the lid will hold the flap closed. Use a cord with screw eyes to hold the flap in its open position or fit a hinged metal strut.

## Materials List for Hanging Caddy

| | |
|---|---|
| 2 ends | 5/8 × 6 × 16 |
| 1 shelf | 1/2 × 5 1/4 × 16 |
| 1 top | 1/2 × 2 × 17 |
| 1 lid | 1/2 × 6 × 17 |
| 1 flap | 1/2 × 7 1/2 × 16 |
| 1 back | 1/4 × 15 × 15 |

## DOUBLE-DOOR CABINET

Dust was a problem in early homes, and one reason for doors was to keep it out. The problem might not be as acute today, but reasonably dustproof doors are still worth having. In this cabinet or cupboard (Fig. 7-21), the top overlaps the pair of doors, which overhang the bottom. At the center the doors fit into each other.

The suggested sizes (Fig. 7-22A) will make a useful cabinet for many purposes, but the same construction could be used for other sizes. Any wood could be used. A softwood might be painted, but a clear finish on a good hardwood would be attractive. The back is shown as plywood, but if you want to be more authentic in the reproduction, use thin vertical boards.

Mark out the sides first (Fig. 7-23A). Rabbet the rear edge for the plywood and widen the rabbet above the top shelf for the upper back. The dado grooves for the top goes across, the two shelf grooves stop at 6 inches, and the bottom fits into a stopped grove.

Make the bottom level with the front (Fig. 7-23B) and the shelves the same length. Make the top (Fig. 7-23C) wide enough to overhang the doors slightly and cut it around the sides. The upper back (Fig. 7-22B) fits above the top, to which it can be screwed from below. Shape it (Fig. 7-23D) and cut the ends of the sides to match (Fig. 7-23E).

When you assemble there could be screws or nails diagonally up through some joints (see Fig. 2-1G) to supplement the glue. Have the back ready so it can be fitted to keep the assembly square.

The framed doors could have plywood panels (Fig. 7-22C), or you could make raised panels from solid wood, particularly if you are using an attractive hardwood. Make the doors to come under the top with a little clearance. At the bottom, it would be better for the doors to extend about 1/8 inch below the cabinet bottom than for part of it to show. At the sides, allow for the doors fitting over (Fig. 7-22D) and let in two 3-inch hinges.

On the front surfaces, the sides and top of each door is 2 inches wide. The bottom looks better 3 inches wide. At the center the door stiles have

Fig. 7-21. A wide cabinet needs double doors. These are arranged to give the contents good protection against dust.

overlapping rabbets. To keep the 2-inch front width, one stile has to be wider by the amount of overlap (Fig. 7-22E).

Groove the wood for the panels and cut the rabbets so the front surfaces will close level. Use mortises and tenons at the corners. The doors will

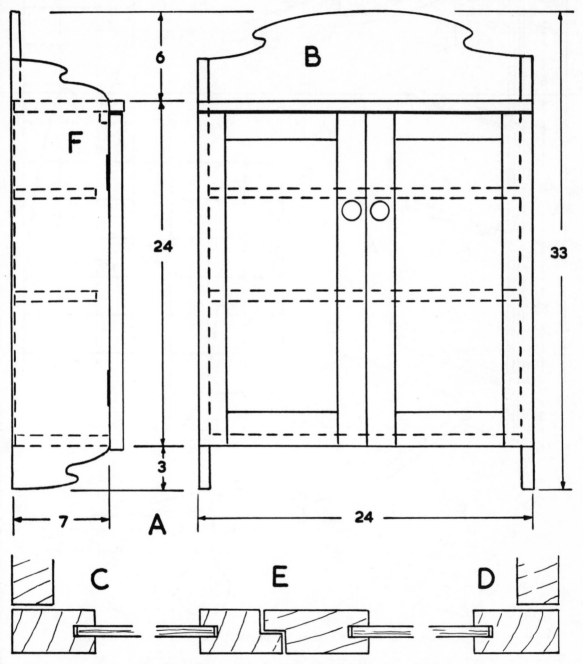

Fig. 7-22. Sizes and door sections for the double-door cabinet.

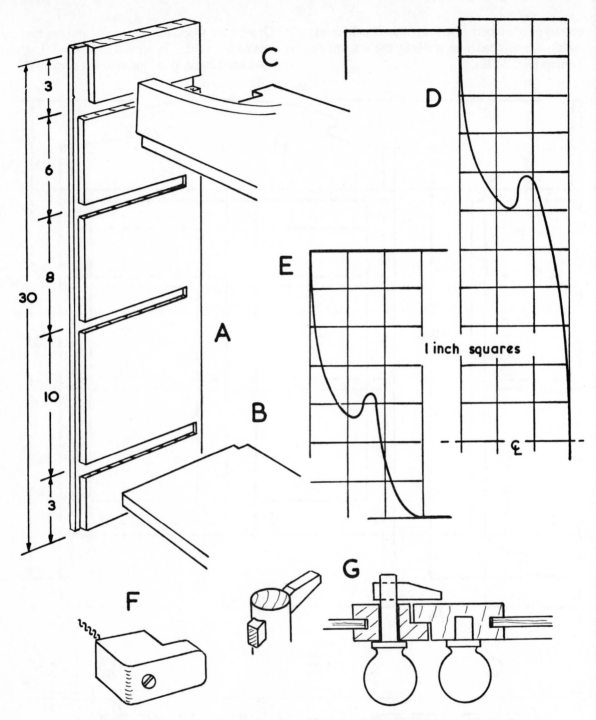

Fig. 7-23. Assembly details (A, B, C), shapes to cut (D, E), and wooden fasteners (F, G).

shut against the cabinet bottom. Put a strip across at the top (Fig. 7-22F) to act as a dust stop.

To fasten the doors, you can use a metal bolt inside the door with the wider stile, downwards into a hole, then the other door can have a knob with a catch to turn and hold it. You can make wooden catches, similar to those often used on early doors. Instead of the bottom bolt make a turn button on a screw at the top (Fig. 7-23F) to close behind the dust strip. For the other door turn a knob with a dowel long enough to go through and have a catch slotted in (Fig. 7-23G). Make a matching knob without the extension for the other door.

## Materials List for Double-Door Cabinet

| | |
|---|---|
| 2 sides | 5/8 × 7 × 32 |
| 1 bottom | 5/8 × 6 3/4 × 26 |
| 2 shelves | 5/8 × 6 × 26 |
| 1 top | 5/8 × 8 × 26 |
| 1 upper back | 5/8 × 6 × 26 |
| 1 back | 1/4 × 24 × 24 |
| 1 dust strip | 5/8 × 5/8 × 24 |
| 3 door stiles | 1 × 2 × 26 |
| 1 door stile | 1 × 2 3/8 × 26 |
| 2 door rails | 1 × 2 × 12 |
| 2 door rails | 1 × 3 × 12 |
| 2 door panels | 1/4 × 11 1/2 × 27 |

# Eight

# Standing Cupboards

In earlier homes there were floor-standing storage units that were called a variety of names beside cupboards. There were dry sinks, where water was brought to a bowl in a pitcher from an outside source, but the low part also provided storage. There were vegetable bins and pie or food safes with ventilating panels in doors and side. Cupboards, often more like modern storage units, were called jelly cupboards. Although you might not want any of these items—or reproductions of them—for their original purposes, they will fit in with other country furniture to give the desired overall effect while serving as side tables or storage places for the many things needing cupboard space in a modern home.

Some early units stood higher and had shelves or other cupboard space above the working top, forming the unit into a hutch or dresser. Even if not wanted for its original purpose, such a unit would display plates, cups, and trophies, or act as a bookcase. Many storage units from over a century ago were not so very different from modern furniture. A Shaker wall-to-ceiling unit is almost the same as some modern built-in furniture.

Many early storage units, like much other furniture, was of fairly heavy construction due to the difficulty of preparing thin boards. In some of the better work, if the widths needed in larger cupboards were difficult to make up from boards, they were framed and paneled. Backs and other hidden parts would have been made with several boards, probably with tongue and groove joints in better construction. Today you may use plywood if extreme accuracy in reproduction is not of first importance. Of various pieces of country furniture, cupboards have the greatest number of wider areas to cover.

Any wood can be appropriate. Some cupboards were made of several woods and finished with paint. For a modern reproduction to look the part, the paint should be drab and certainly not a modern high gloss.

## SOLID-BOARD JELLY CUPBOARD

Early furniture had to be planned to suit available wood, and logs were often converted to boards of one size. This jelly cupboard (Fig. 8-1A) is designed around boards 12 inches wide and 3/4 inch to 1 inch thick. Shelves, ends, and back use full-width boards. The fronts were made from a board cut down the middle. The door could be a single board or may be framed with pieces made by cutting a board into four. The top has pieces glued to width.

The sizes suit 12-inch boards (Fig. 8-2A) and can be adapted if your boards are a different width. Mark out the boards for the ends (Fig. 8-1B) as they control sizes of other parts. Put cleats across at top and shelf positions. The feet shapes (Fig. 8-2B) are the same on all parts. The two boards that make the back (Fig. 8-1C) have a cleat at the top, but lower down they are nailed to the shelves.

Make and fit the shelves (Fig. 8-1D) and the back. Make the front strips and join them with a cleat and a strip between (Fig.8-1E). Nail them to the sides and shelves. For a single-board door (Fig. 8-1F), fit it to match the space and put three

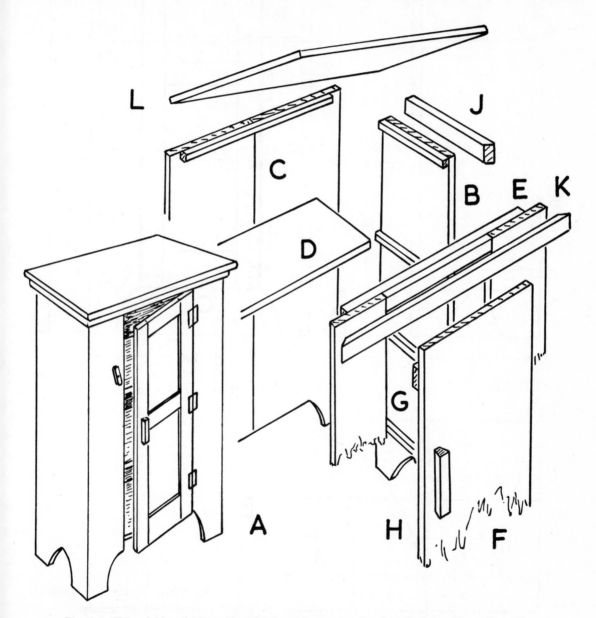

Fig. 8-1. This solid-board jelly cupboard follows the constructional methods used by early settlers.

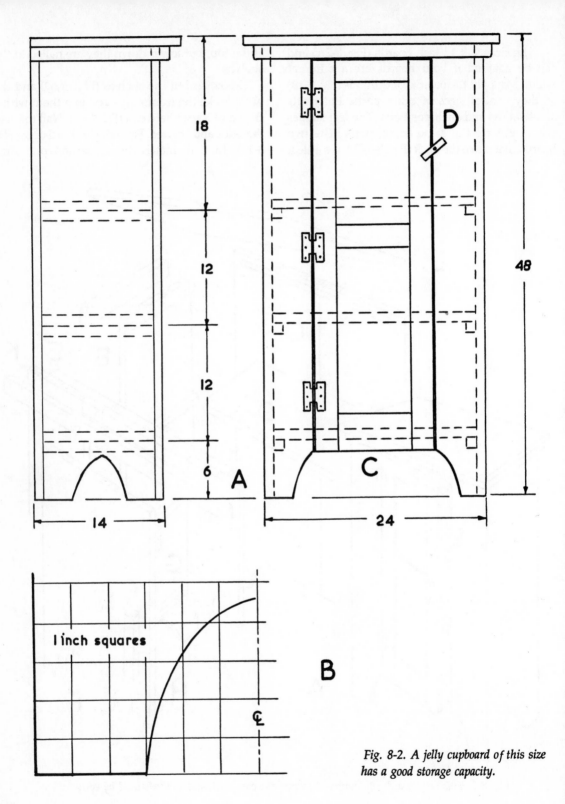

18

12

12

6

A

14

D

48

C

24

1 inch squares

B

C̵L

Fig. 8-2. A jelly cupboard of this size has a good storage capacity.

ledgers across (Fig. 8-1G) to prevent warping. For a framed door (Fig. 8-2C), fit the panels into grooves, but simple bevelling at the front would be more appropriate to this design than modern raised panels. Hinges should be on the surface, and the H-type would be suitable. A simple tapered block (Fig. 8-1H) would be an appropriate handle. A wood turnbutton (Fig. 8-2D) can hold the door closed.

At the top, make border strips at the sides (Fig. 8-1J) and the front (Fig. 8-1K), with either molded or rounded edges, and a top to overhang them (Fig. 8-1L) with rounded edges. A painted finish would be appropriate.

## Materials List for Solid-Board Jelly Cupboard

| | |
|---|---|
| 2 sides | 1 × 12 × 48 |
| 2 backs | 1 × 12 × 48 |
| 1 front | 1 × 5 3/4 × 48 |
| 3 shelves | 1 × 12 × 24 |
| 8 cleats | 1 × 1 × 13 |
| 2 cleats | 1 × 1 × 24 |
| 1 top | 1 × 14 × 30 |
| 3 tops | 1 × 2 × 14 |
| 1 top | 1 × 2 × 28 |
| 1 door | 1 × 12 × 44 or panel material |

## TRADITIONAL JELLY CUPBOARD

Once wood production and its seasoning had improved, those with some cabinetry skills were able to make jelly cupboards more suitable to take their place along side other good quality furniture. This jelly cupboard is typical of many made in the eastern states (Fig. 8-3A). In the sizes shown (Fig. 8-4A) it could be used as a side table with storage, a stand for a lamp or television set, or a stand beside a bed.

If made of softwood, it might have a painted finish. A good hardwood could have a clear finish, preferably without a high gloss. The inside could be painted and the outside polished.

Make the pair of ends (Fig. 8-3B). Drill the cleat for screws upwards into the top. The shelf has a stopped dado, but the groove for the bottom goes through. The fronts (Fig. 8-3C) fit onto the sides and into the notched bottom (Fig. 8-3D). The back is made of vertical boards and overlaps the sides (Fig. 8-3E). The shelf is a plain board (Fig. 8-3F). Assemble these parts and add a cleat along the top edge of the back, drilled for screws into the top. You could use glue with nails set below the surface and covered with stopping, or you could put dowels in the long joints at the front. Fit a notched strip across (Fig. 8-3G) behind the fronts and drilled for screws.

At the bottom a base goes around the ends and front (Fig. 8-3H). Mold its top edge and arrange it 1/4 inch below the top surface of the bottom (Fig. 8-4B). Cut away underneath to leave corner feet (Fig. 8-4C). Miter the corners. Glue and screw on from inside. The corners may be strengthened with blocks glued in. Another block could go behind the front for screwing up into the bottom.

The top is a plain board. Its edges can be molded.

Make the door in the usual way. The grooves for the panel could be towards the front (Fig. 8-4D). Tenon the corners. Hinges could be let in between the edges, but H-hinges on the surface will look traditional. A turned knob and a wood turnbutton are appropriate.

## Materials List for Traditional Jelly Cupboard

| | |
|---|---|
| 2 ends | 1 × 10 × 28 |
| 1 back | 1 × 21 × 28 |
| 2 fronts | 1 × 3 × 28 |
| 1 shelf | 1 × 9 × 22 |
| 2 cleats | 1 × 1 × 12 |
| 1 cleat | 1 × 1 × 22 |
| 1 cleat | 1 × 2 × 22 |
| 1 base | 1 × 5 × 26 |
| 2 bases | 1 × 5 × 15 |
| 2 door sides | 1 × 3 × 25 |
| 2 door ends | 1 × 3 × 17 |
| 1 door panel | 1/2 × 10 × 18 |

## SIMPLE DRY SINK

It is unlikely that you will want to use a dry sink for its original purpose, but it can make an attractive piece of furniture for storage and for displaying plants and foliage. This dry sink (Fig. 8-5A)

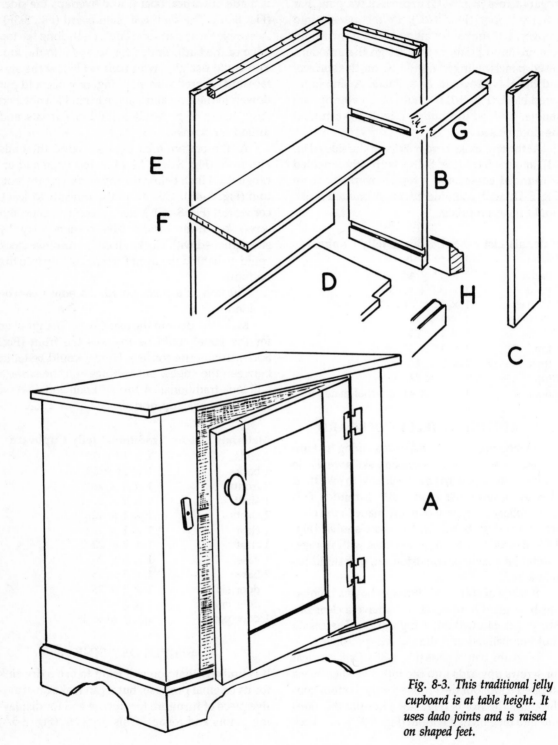

E

F

B

G

D

H

C

A

Fig. 8-3. *This traditional jelly cupboard is at table height. It uses dado joints and is raised on shaped feet.*

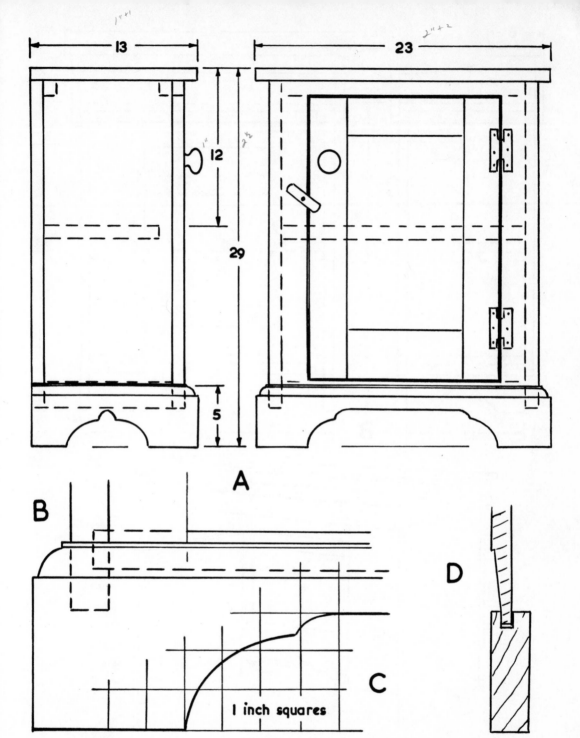

Fig. 8-4. Suggested sizes for the traditional jelly cupboard with details of feet and the door panel.

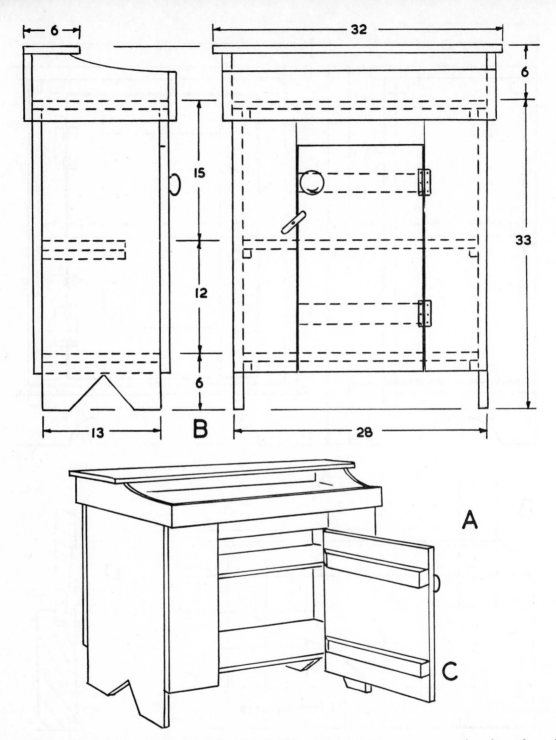

*Fig. 8-5. A dry sink might not be needed for its original purpose today, but it can serve as a work surface or be used for display.*

is of simple construction and typical of early design, although shorter than many originals (Fig. 8-5B). It would suit a room with a primitive theme or might find a place on patio or yard. Any wood could be used, and woods could be mixed if you use the common painted finish. Wide solid boards are needed, although pieces could be glued to make up the width. Thicknesses should not be less than 3/4 inch. Nailed construction is appropriate.

Make the pair of ends with cleats across and feet cut at the bottom (Fig. 8-6A). Cut boards for the bottom and shelf (Fig. 8-6B and C). Have boards ready for the back (Fig. 8-6D), then nail the bottom and shelf in place and add the back with a cleat across its top edge. Let the back reach far enough to cover the cleats under the bottom.

The front has the same overall size as the back but is made of two boards (Fig. 8-6E) with a 4-inch strip (Fig. 8-6F) across and a short piece to make up the thickness at the front (Fig. 8-6G). Nail on this assembly. Put a small projecting block at one side of the opening to act as a door stop. The door is made from boards glued to make the width and with ledgers across to prevent warping (Fig. 8-5C). Use surface hinges and fit a knob or handle and a turnbutton.

Nail on the top (Fig. 8-6H) and trim its edges level so the splash boards will fit upright as they overlap about 2 inches. Shape the splash board ends (Fig. 8-6J) and nail them to the main ends, then add the front, back, and shelf. Well round all exposed edges of the splash boards.

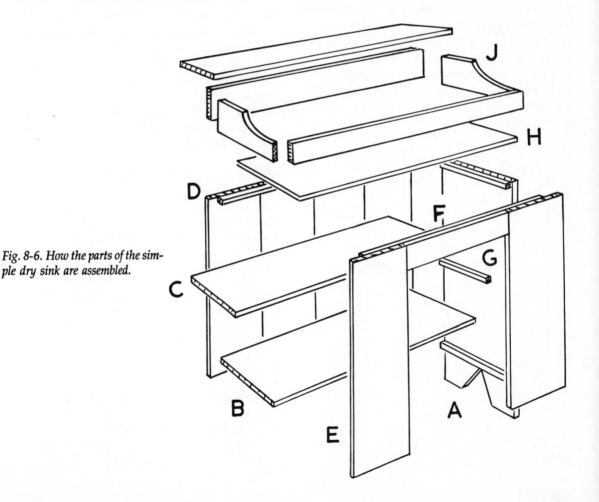

Fig. 8-6. How the parts of the simple dry sink are assembled.

## Materials List for Simple Dry Sink

| | |
|---|---|
| 2 ends | 3/4 × 13 × 34 |
| 1 bottom | 3/4 × 13 × 28 |
| 1 shelf | 3/4 × 9 × 28 |
| 6 cleats | 3/4 × 3/4 × 14 |
| 1 top | 3/4 × 15 × 30 |
| 4 backs | 3/4 × 7 × 31 |
| 2 fronts | 3/4 × 7 × 31 |
| 1 cleat | 3/4 × 3/4 × 28 |
| 1 cleat | 3/4 × 4 × 28 |
| 1 filler | 3/4 × 4 × 16 |
| 1 door | 3/4 × 14 × 28 |
| 2 ledgers | 3/4 × 2 × 14 |
| 2 splash boards | 3/4 × 7 × 15 |
| 1 splash board | 3/4 × 5 × 32 |
| 1 splash board | 3/4 × 7 × 32 |
| 1 shelf | 3/4 × 6 × 34 |

## SHAKER DRY SINK

The Shakers put their design skill to bear on dry sinks and produced functional and attractive examples. This project can be completed in two forms. There may be an open version (Figs. 8-7 and 8-8A), with corner shelves and pegs, or one with enclosed shelves for the pitcher, soap dishes, and other items (Fig. 8-8B). The lower part of the sink is the same.

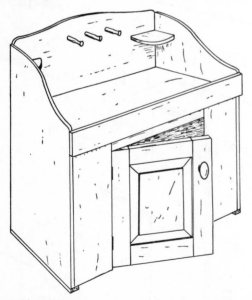

*Fig. 8-7. A Shaker dry sink is simple and uses their typical turned pegs.*

The ends are the pieces that control the sizes of many other parts. For the enclosed top (Fig. 8-9A), join boards and rabbet the edge for the back. Attach cleats. The sink top rests on the ends and goes underneath the shelf assembly (Fig. 8-9B), which will be the same length as the inner shelf and bottom. Assemble these parts and add the back, which could be plywood or vertical solid boards. Fit the division (Fig. 8-9C) and its shelf with the vertical pieces (Fig. 8-9D) at the ends. Make the top with a small overhang.

At the front, the piece across above the door (Fig. 8-8C) may be dowelled into the upright pieces, then the assembly fitted against the bottom and under the top. Make the door with mortise and tenon joints and a flat or raised panel (Fig. 5-12). Fit it with hinges let in or on the surface. Fit splash boards at the sides and front, setting the rounded top edges level with the shelf (Fig. 8-8D).

For the open top, the sink top is full width and the shaped sides are not as high. Even if the lower back is plywood, it will be better to make the piece that is visible 3/4-inch solid wood. The corner shelves can have dado joints, and the pegs can be the usual Shaker pattern (see Fig. 2-4). In either case, put strips across under the ends as feet to lift them off the floor.

## Materials List for Shaker Dry Sink (with enclosed shelves)

| | |
|---|---|
| 2 ends | 3/4 × 18 × 45 |
| Cleats from | 3/4 × 3/4 × 240 |
| 1 sink top | 3/4 × 12 × 34 |
| 1 bottom | 3/4 × 18 × 34 |
| 1 inner shelf | 3/4 × 10 × 34 |
| 1 shelf assembly | 3/4 × 8 × 34 |
| 1 shelf assembly | 3/4 × 2 1/4 × 34 |
| 1 open shelf | 3/4 × 6 × 22 |
| 1 division | 3/4 × 6 × 12 |
| 2 uprights | 3/4 × 1 1/2 × 12 |
| 1 shelf top | 3/4 × 9 × 36 |
| 2 fronts | 3/4 × 6 × 36 |
| 1 front | 3/4 × 4 × 22 |
| 2 door sides | 3/4 × 4 × 26 |
| 2 door sides | 3/4 × 4 × 17 |
| 1 splash board | 3/4 × 5 × 36 |
| 2 splash boards | 3/4 × 5 × 20 |
| 2 feet | 1 × 2 × 20 |

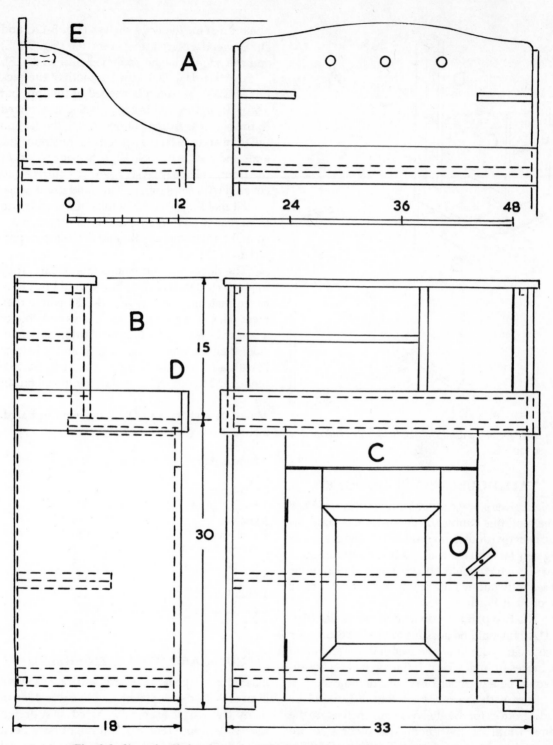

Fig. 8-8. Sizes of a Shaker dry sink, with alternative open (A) or closed (B) tops.

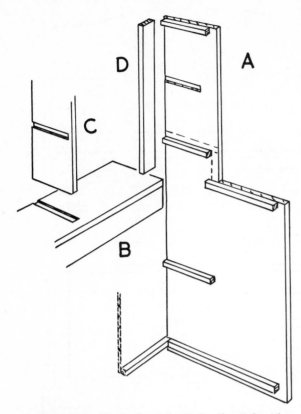

*Fig. 8-9. Assembly details of the Shaker dry sink with a closed top.*

## TALL DOUBLE-DOOR CUPBOARD

Height gives storage space without using up floor area, and this cupboard (Fig. 8-10) has good capacity in two double-door sections without extending very far from the wall. All of the parts are solid boards, which could be any wood, but pine or other softwood would be appropriate for a clear or painted finish.

The two parts are divided at the center (Fig. 8-11A). It would be possible to use the design for a cupboard with only one pair of doors and a top 36 inches from the floor. If the top half is chosen, it could be a cupboard to stand on a table.

Start with the two ends (Fig. 8-12A). Make dado grooves for the shelves. Four shelves are the same width as the ends. The other two are notched to project between the two sides (Fig. 8-12B). Make the fronts to go over the ends and

notch them for the wide shelves (Fig. 8-12C and D). Dowel the piece across at the top (Fig. 8-12E) and the one below the bottom shelf (Fig. 8-12F).

Use boards to make up the width of the back (Fig. 8-12G). A batten is needed at the top, but lower down the boards can be nailed or screwed to the shelves. At the bottom, shape the feet on the front and use these as patterns for marking the ends and back. Assemble all parts made so far. At the front, nails may be set below the surface and covered with stopping, or you could use dowels.

Fit molding around the tops of the ends and front (Fig. 8-12H). A simple cove is shown, but it could be any section. Make and fit the top to project over the molding.

The doors are four boards (Fig. 8-12J). They might have square edges, but it would be better to cut matching rabbets (Fig. 8-12K) where they meet. This keeps out dust and allows one door of a pair to be fastened with a turnbutton or bolt inside, then the other closes over it and is held to it with a turnbutton outside or a catch. Surface hinges and knobs will provide a traditional finish.

### Materials List for Tall Double-Door Cupboard

| | |
|---|---|
| 2 ends | $1 \times 12 \times 72$ |
| 4 backs | $1 \times 9 \times 72$ |
| 1 back batten | $1 \times 2 \times 36$ |
| 2 fronts | $1 \times 4 \times 72$ |
| 1 top front | $1 \times 5 \times 30$ |
| 1 bottom front | $1 \times 3 \times 30$ |
| 3 shelves | $1 \times 12 \times 36$ |
| 2 shelves | $1 \times 14 \times 36$ |
| 2 doors | $1 \times 15 \times 31$ |
| 2 doors | $1 \times 15 \times 25$ |
| 8 ledgers | $1 \times 3 \times 13$ |
| 1 molding | $2 \times 2 \times 42$ |
| 2 moldings | $2 \times 2 \times 17$ |
| 1 top | $1 \times 17 \times 44$ |

## CUPBOARD WITH OPEN SHELVES

Extending a cupboard upwards with open shelves is an obvious development, and this was done in many ways. This example is based on a design seen in Vermont (Fig. 8-13). It might have been called a pewter cupboard. It could have been used for display or for a more practical purpose in a

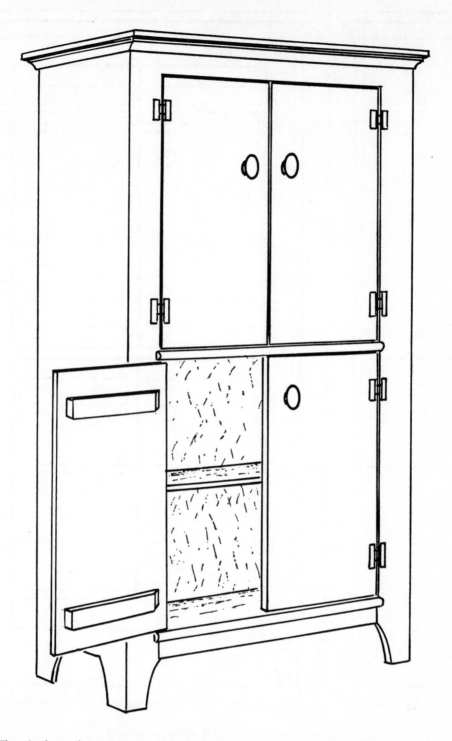

Fig. 8-10. There is plenty of capacity in a cupboard of double height. This one is of solid-board construction and made in the way used by early settlers.

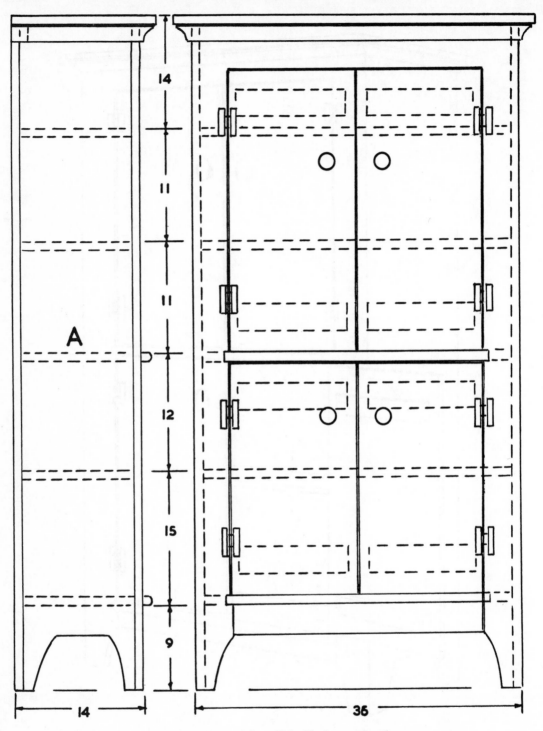

Fig. 8-11. Sizes of the tall double-door cupboard.

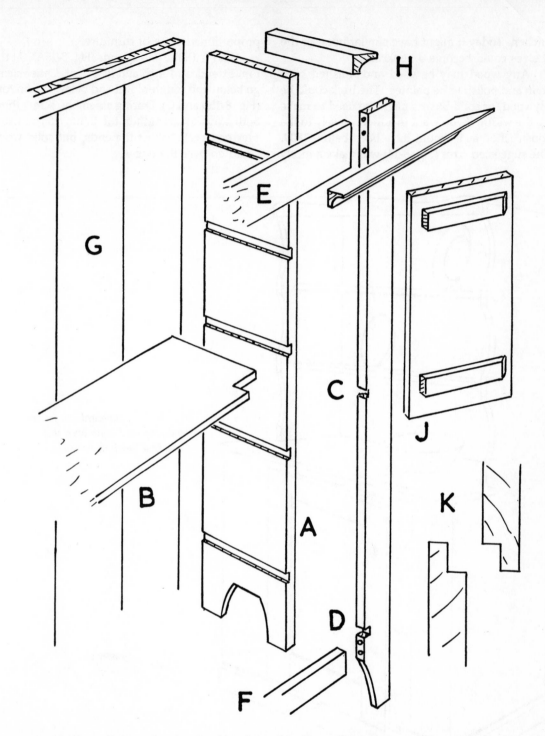

Fig. 8-12. *How the parts of the tall cupboard are brought together. The end (A) is the key part that settles many other sizes.*

kitchen. Today it might have similar uses, or the shelves could become a bookcase.

Any wood may be used and finished with stain and polish or be painted. The back could be plywood, or solid boards might be used to make up the width, if you want to adhere closely to the construction as it would have been before 1800. The suggested sizes (Fig. 8-14) will make a nicely proportioned piece of furniture.

Start with the pair of ends (Fig. 8-15A). At the top, extend up 1 inch and fit a cleat. Other cleats go below the counter level and below the bottom (Fig. 8-15B and C). During assembly, screw them both ways to strengthen the joints. If you use a plywood back, rabbet the ends, but solid wood could go over the edges.

*Fig. 8-13. A cupboard can be extended upwards with open shelves to make a hutch or bookcase.*

Make the bottom to notch around the fronts (Fig. 8-15D) and provide a 2-inch piece notched similarly (Fig. 8-15E) to fit against the cleats and around the fronts (Fig. 8-15F). Make the two fronts (Fig. 8-15G). The shelves are the same length as the bottom. The countertop fits in like a shelf, but it projects 1 inch at the sides and front, with rounded edges (Fig. 8-15H and J). Assemble these

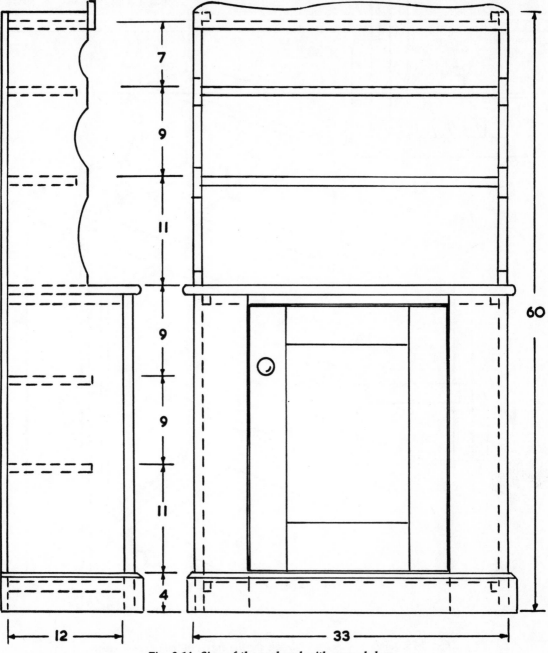

*Fig. 8-14. Sizes of the cupboard with open shelves.*

177

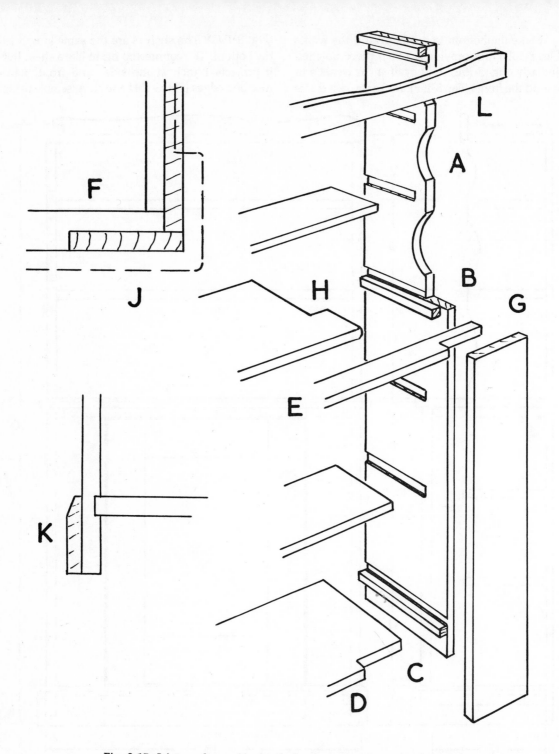

Fig. 8-15. Joints and assembly details for the cupboard with open shelves.

parts squarely. Nail the back securely to everything it crosses.

Fit a plinth (Fig. 8-15K) to the ends and front with its top slightly below the surface of the bottom and with corners mitered. The upper edges can be beveled or molded.

A strip across the front (Fig. 8-15L) prevents anything put on top from falling off. It could be straight, but it could match the cutaway sides if given some simple curves.

A single door is shown with a plain panel, but the panel could be raised, or you could make a pair of doors. Door construction should be with grooves and mortise and tenon joints (see Fig. 5-12). A round knob or a strip wood handle would be suitable, and hinges could be let in or on the surface.

**Materials List for Cupboard with Open Shelves**

| | |
|---|---|
| 2 sides | 1 × 12 × 62 |
| 6 cleats | 1 × 1 × 13 |
| 2 fronts | 1 × 6 × 35 |
| 1 counter support | 1 × 2 × 34 |
| 1 bottom | 1 × 13 × 34 |
| 1 top | 1 × 9 × 34 |
| 2 shelves | 1 × 9 × 34 |
| 2 shelves | 1 × 8 × 34 |
| 1 counter | 1 × 14 × 37 |
| 1 plinth | 3/4 × 4 × 36 |
| 2 plinths | 3/4 × 4 × 15 |
| 1 top front | 3/4 × 3 × 37 |
| 2 door sides | 1 × 4 × 30 |
| 1 door top | 1 × 4 × 18 |
| 1 door bottom | 1 × 5 × 18 |
| 4 backs | 3/4 × 9 × 62 |

## PIE SAFE

In the days before refrigeration, a pie safe or cupboard was used to store food with maximum ventilation but secure against insects and rodents. Some pie safes were quite large and were prominent pieces of furniture in an early kitchen. More likely, it was on a porch or other place where there was a good circulation of air. The original need for a pie safe has passed, but it is an interesting piece of furniture and can still provide storage.

A large pie safe might not be acceptable in many modern homes, but a smaller version is worth making. This project (Fig. 8-16), seen in Georgia, is a sideboard or serving table as well as a pie safe.

Protection from insects while allowing ventilation was arranged in several ways. The Shakers and others used cloth netting. Wire mesh screening was used, but pierced tin was popular and is the type suggested for this project. Holes are punched in tinplate panels. For good ventilation there have to be plenty of holes, and there is scope for arranging many patterns. Some early designs were geometrical, but some were pictorial. If you plan your own design, arrange for plenty of holes and not very much unpunched metal. It might be possible to buy punch designs or ready-punched tin panels. You could, of course, complete the project with plain or raised wood panels instead of pierced tin. The finished article then becomes a normal sideboard or serving table with enclosed storage below.

Any wood could be used. Many pie safes were painted softwood, but if this is to take its place in a dining room, it would be better made of hardwood with a polished finish.

All of the framework is made of nominal 2-inch-by-2-inch wood, which finishes about 1 3/4 inches square. The panels are held by 5/8-inch square strips glued and pinned to the frame parts. Traditionally, this type of assembly was made with tenons and pegs driven through them. It would be less satisfactory to use dowels.

Mark out the legs (Fig. 8-17A) with the positions of the joints (Fig. 8-18A). Leave some extra wood at the top (Fig. 8-7B) until after the mortises have been cut or until after framework assembly. Allow for tenons being mitered inside the legs (Fig. 8-17C). At the lower rails, the tenons may be full depth but, at the top, cut them back (Fig. 8-17D) to avoid having open mortises. Taper the lower parts of the legs.

Assemble the end rails to the legs (Fig. 8-18B). Prepare the lengthwise rails (Fig. 8-18C) and the uprights (Fig. 8-18D). The back of the safe can be made the same as the front, with a fixed panel in place of the door. Make up the complete frame-

work. Compare diagonals to check squareness.

The door (Fig. 8-17E) is made in the same way as the framework, with the rails tenoned into the stiles. Let in two, 3-inch hinges and make a knob handle. The original fastener was a wood turnbutton, but you could use a ball or spring catch.

With modern glues the joints will be strong enough without pegging. To give the traditional appearance, however, put two, 1/4-inch dowels into each tenon (Fig. 8-17F) and plane their ends level outside.

The bottom fits inside on cleats (Fig. 8-18E) and is level with the undersides of the bottom rails (Fig. 8-17G). The bottom could be plywood or several thin boards glued together.

Cut the pieces of tinplate to fit the spaces. Your intended pattern of holes could be drawn directly on the surface, but if you use a paper pattern, it will serve for several panels when lightly stuck on or held temporarily with masking tape. Your punch should have a fairly slender point. You could grind the end of a center punch. Early panels were punched with nails. Lead makes the best surface to support the tin, but a piece of close-grained hardwood is suitable.

Try to use the same weight of hammer blow each time. Experiment on scrap metal first. Aim to get clear holes, though obviously not so big as to pass insects. You will soon get into a regular rhythm. If the tin buckles, hammer a board over

Fig. 8-16. This pie safe, which also forms a table, has pierced tin panels.

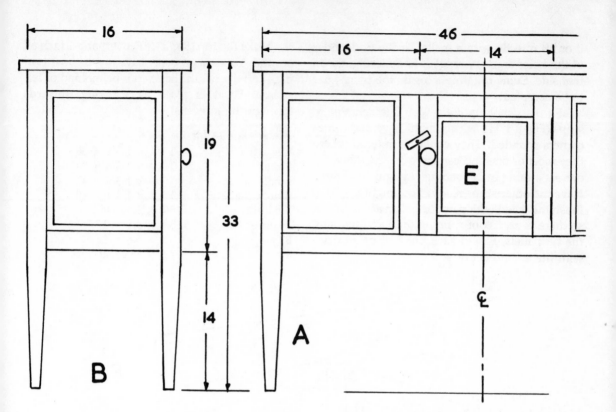

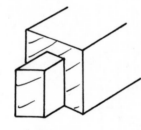

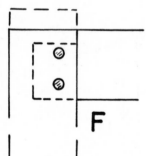

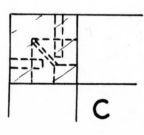

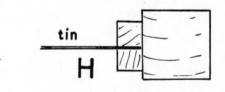

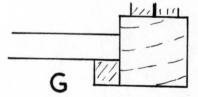

Fig. 8-17. Sizes and joint details of the pie safe.

it or hit directly with a mallet. If the undersides of the holes are very ragged, hammer lightly on that side. Some roughness inside the panels has to be accepted.

Fit the panels in place with 5/8-inch square strips (Fig. 8-17H), which might have their outer corners rounded. They could be mitered where they meet or one end can lap over the other. Fit one set around each opening with glue and pins. Have the other strips ready. You might prefer to finish the wood with paint or polish at this stage, so there is no risk of running onto and marking the tin panels. Fasten each piece of tin in place with the second set of strips.

Make the top (Fig. 8-18F) overhang 1 inch all around. You will probably have to glue boards to make up the width. Edges can be molded or left square. Fit it in place by screwing upwards through the top rails.

**Materials List for Pie Safe**

| | |
|---|---|
| 4 legs | 1 3/4 × 1 3/4 × 36 |
| 8 rails | 1 3/4 × 1 3/4 × 20 |
| 4 rails | 1 3/4 × 1 3/4 × 47 |
| 4 door frame | 1 3/4 × 1 3/4 × 18 |
| 1 bottom | 5/8 × 13 × 46 |
| 24 strips | 5/8 × 5/8 × 17 |
| 32 strips | 5/8 × 5/8 × 14 |
| 1 top | 7/8 × 18 × 50 |

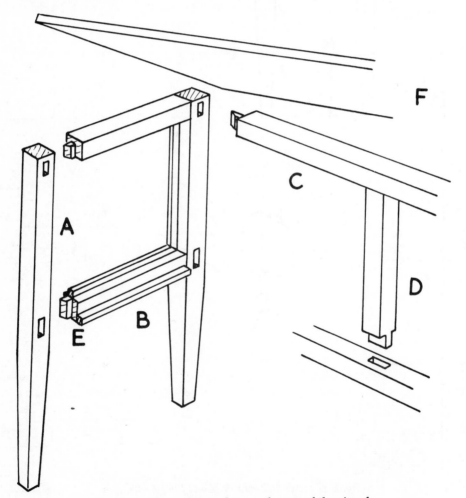

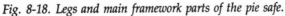

*Fig. 8-18. Legs and main framework parts of the pie safe.*

# Nine

# Chairs

More comfort than that provided by a stool or bench is welcomed, even when sitting at a table. If you want to relax, there has to be a back and probably arms. A satisfactory chair is much more than a bench with a back. A simple pattern with just a vertical back on a stool might be practical and suitable for brief use, but a chair needs to go some way towards matching the human body if it is to remain comfortable for longer use. If the body is to be accommodated, even an apparently simple chair will have curves and angles not immediately obvious. This means there have to be complications in construction that make some chairmaking more difficult than the production of most other furniture.

In particular the seat surface is important. A flat board might have a loose cushion. The Windsor chair has the wood shaped towards the body form. Cutting this satisfactory is difficult, and even then most users require a cushion.

It is more usual to only provide a seat frame with a flexible seat or upholstery. The flexible seat can be woven from a variety of materials, which can be decorative as well as functional. There were complications about the materials of early upholstery, but plastic or rubber foam makes seat padding simple (see Fig. 3-12E and F).

Woven seats can be made with cane, wood splints, fiber rush, seagrass, or cords made of natural or synthetic fibers. Natural rushes can be twisted into a rope form as they are used, but they have to be worked wet. It is better today to use prepared materials to make what is called a *rush pattern*, which is not as difficult to make as the finished seat appears to indicate.

To work a rush pattern, using seagrass, rush, cord or rope, prepare a few shuttles (Fig. 9-1A) for winding the cord on and a pointed rod (Fig. 9-1B) to help with the final tucks. Start by tacking inside a rail, then take the cord over the opposite rail, around the leg, and back over the first rail (Fig. 9-1C). That is the entire action. Go to the next leg and do the same (Fig. 9-1D). When you get to the first leg, put the turns inside the first. Keep a good tension all the time. As you continue, you will see that the pattern builds up from the corners, and the cords going from leg to let will be hidden. When you join in new line, make the knot on one of these parts.

If the top is square, both directions will fill at the same time. If it is oblong, fill the long way with figure-eight turns (Fig. 9-1E). If the shape is wider at the front, go twice around the front legs occasionally until the remaining spaces at front and

back are the same. At all stages keep the turns pressed along the rails towards the corners to get in as many turns as possible. Finally tack under a rail and push the end inside.

Some chairmakers, particularly the Shakers, preferred using a checker pattern of fabric tape in one or two colors. The tape is wrapped one way, then in the other direction it is woven over and under to make the pattern, preferably underneath as well as on top. To get the final tension right, you must judge the degree of slackness to be allowed in the first direction. This depends on the type of tape and experience with it.

For the usual chair shape, which is wider at the front, tack under the rail near a back leg and wrap squarely and closely over the frame (Fig. 9-2A), leaving a gap near each front leg, then finally tack underneath. That can be done with one long length. Using such a long piece the other way could be tedious, and you might prefer using shorter pieces tacked under where they join.

Work from the back, over and under, keeping the pieces tight and close (Fig. 9-2B). As you near the front, pry open the turns with a blunt knife or chisel.

For a tapered chair, tack one or more pieces of tape underneath as necessary to fill the front gap at each side (Fig. 9-2C) and work under turns

as far as possible towards the back. Either tack under when you have gone as far as you can or glue the new end under another tape.

With both methods of seating, padding may be included between the layers. In the original rush pattern, scrap rush was pushed in, or in both cases, cloth was used. Today, it would be better to use plastic foam—small pieces added as the rush pattern progresses or one big piece put in before weaving across the checker pattern.

## BASIC CHAIR

A substantial chair that could stand rough usage would have been valued in pioneer homes. Today, such a chair might not provide much comfort, but it could find a useful place in a rumpus room or on a patio. You might be glad of it in your shop as a support for wood being worked on as well as a resting place when you want to sit down.

Any wood could be used. Painted softwood might not look as good as polished hardwood, but it should stand up to rough treatment.

This chair (Fig. 9-3A) has vertical legs and a flat seat, which could be stood on. Its method of construction, although not its shape, is similar to many other chairs, so it provides an introduction to chairmaking.

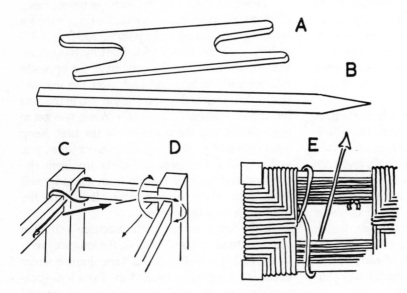

*Fig. 9-1. To work a rush pattern seat, you need some shuttles and a pointed stick (A, B). The line goes over and around the legs (C, D), then in a figure-eight fashion (E) to finish if the seat is not square.*

Mark out the two back legs (Fig. 9-3B) with a notch to half the thickness of the back (Fig. 9-3C). Mark out the front legs (Fig. 9-3D) to match the back legs.

The rails have plain tenons into the legs (Fig. 9-3E) except at the top of the front legs, where they should be cut down (Fig. 9-3F). The center bottom rail has square tenons (Fig. 9-3G).

Assemble the sides first, then join them with the other rails and back, which can be screwed or dowelled. Check that the assembly is square and the legs stand level.

Notch the seat around the back legs. Let it overhang about 1 inch at the sides and front. Round the edges and corners.

## Materials List for Basic Chair

| 2 legs | 2 × 2 × 29 |
|---|---|
| 2 legs | 2 × 2 × 17 |
| 7 rails | 1 × 2 × 16 |
| 1 back | 1 × 4 × 18 |
| 1 seat | 1/2 × 18 × 18 |

## CHAIR WITH RUSH PATTERN SEAT

This chair may be regarded as the next development after the basic chair. The seat is worked with rush, cord, or seagrass, and the back rails have some shaping, although it is still upright (Fig. 9-4A). The seat is level but is wider at the front. As a first step, draw the shape full size and symmetrical about a centerline (Fig. 9-5A). The legs are square to the back and front, and only the side rails have beveled ends.

Mark out the legs with rail positions (Fig. 9-5B). When covering with a rush pattern, it is usual to have the rails deeper at their middles (Fig. 9-4B). Reduce the 1 3/4-inch depth to 1 1/4 inches

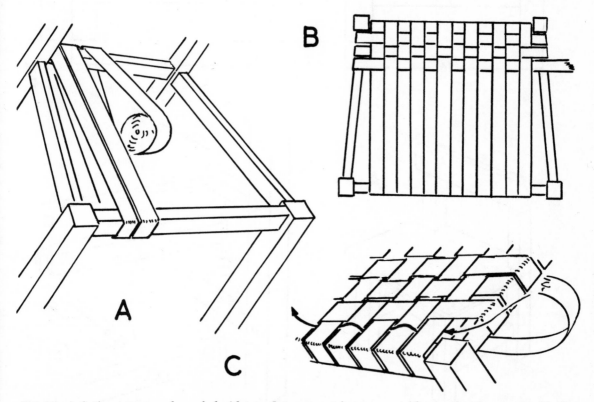

Fig. 9-2. A checker pattern can be worked with tape. Interweave strips one way with some the other way (A, B), then weave in fillers for the sides (C) if the chair frame tapers.

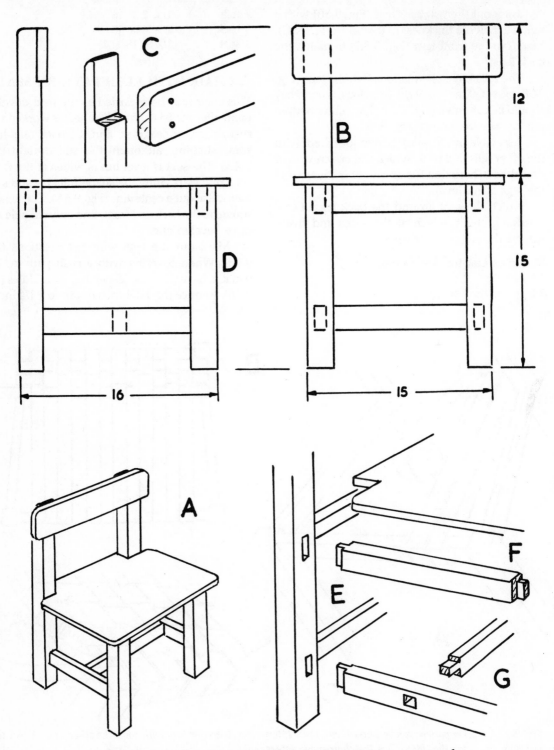

Fig. 9-3. A basic chair has upright legs and a flat seat. Joints are tenoned.

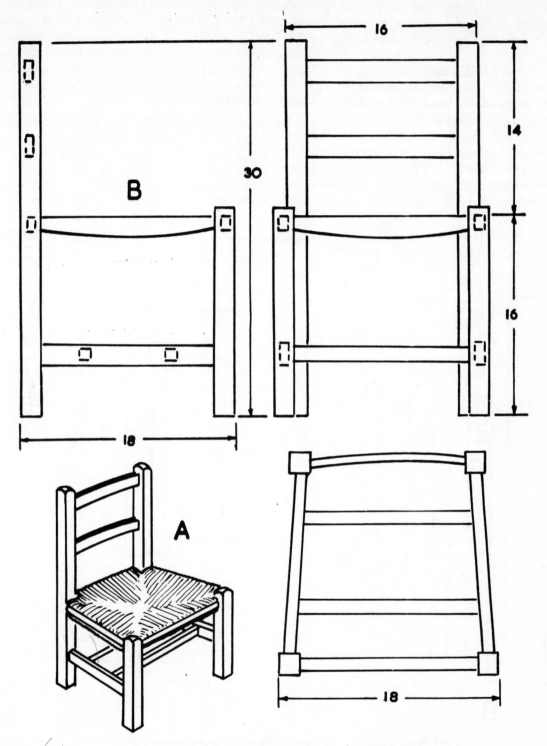

Fig. 9-4. This chair has a rush pattern seat and curved back slats.

at the ends. The other rails are parallel, and the joints are made in the same way as in the last project. Round (Fig. 9-5C) or chamfer the tops of the legs.

The two back slats are cut from wood 1 1/4 inches thick. The ends that tenon to the legs are reduced to half thickness, then the part between cuts to a curve 5/8 inch thick (Fig. 9-5D).

Assemble the back first and see that it finishes square and without twist. Join the bottom rails together, then assemble all parts to the back. Measure diagonals on the seat to see that it is symmetrical.

Apply finish to the wood before or after seating, but it is advisable to leave a final coat until the seat is finished. Work the rush pattern seat, as described earlier in the chapter. Traditional rush seats were protected around the edges with thin strips of wood nailed on (Fig. 9-5E). Add these if you wish.

### Materials List for Chair with Rush Pattern Seat

| 2 legs | 1 3/4 × 1 3/4 × 32 |
|---|---|
| 2 legs | 1 3/4 × 1 3/4 × 19 |
| 7 rails | 1 × 1 3/4 × 19 |
| 2 rails | 1 × 1 × 19 |
| 2 back slats | 1 1/4 × 1 3/4 × 17 |

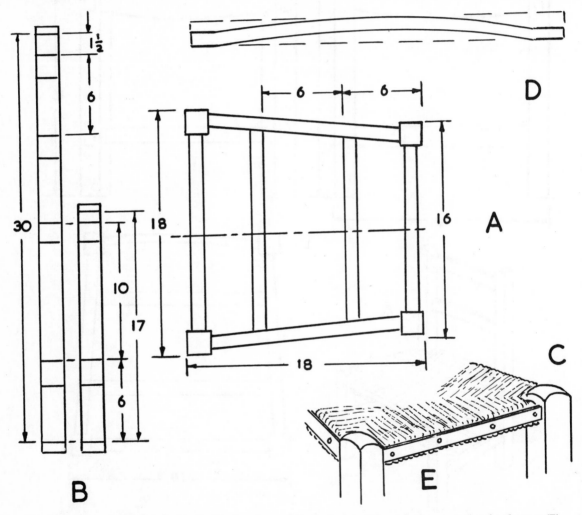

Fig. 9-5. Leg and seat details (A, B, C), the shape of the back slats (D), and edge protection for the seat (E).

## SHAKER LOW-BACK CHAIR

The Shakers used chairs with seats suitable for sitting on at a table but with backs low enough for the chair to be pushed under the table when out of use. It could also be hung on the wall pegs. This chair (Fig. 9-6A) is made of round rods, except for the back slats, and is intended to have a woven tape seat. A hard, close-grained hardwood, such as maple, is advisable to take the rocking strains that might come on joints when a sitter tilts the chair. All angles are square (Fig. 9-6B). Prepared dowel rods may be used, or you may turn the legs.

Make the legs with moderately rounded tops. Seat rails have to be on the same level, but side and crosswise rails are at different levels for greater strength. Make sure the lines of holes are marked at 90-degree angles to each other and use drills to make the holes a tight fit on the rods. For the lower rails, drill a little further than halfway through each leg (Fig. 9-6C). For the seat rails, drill to the middle and miter the meeting rod ends (Fig. 9-6D).

The 3-inch back slats reduce to 2 inches at their ends, with curved tops (Fig. 9-6E). Round the edges. Use 1/4-inch dowels into the legs (Fig. 9-6F).

Assemble the back and front and check that they match. Add the rods next the other way, checking squareness in all directions.

Weave a checker pattern seat. It would be possible to use a rush pattern with cords, if you wish. As corners are square, there are no complications with either method.

**Materials List for Low-Back Chair**

| | |
|---|---|
| 2 back legs | 29 × 1 1/2 round |
| 2 front legs | 20 × 1 1/2 round |
| 2 seat rails | 21 × 7/8 round |
| 2 seat rails | 17 × 7/8 round |
| 4 lower rails | 21 × 3/4 × round |
| 4 lower rails | 17 × 3/4 round |
| 2 slats | 1/2 × 3 × 21 |

## SHAKER WEAVER'S CHAIR

A weaver had to sit high, and the chair he used would make a very good modern bar stool. Construction is almost the same as the last project, with a higher seat, a single slat, and turned finials on the back legs (Fig. 9-7A).

Follow the instructions for the last project, except for the above differences. The finials are turned separately with dowels to fit holes in the tops of the legs (Fig. 9-7B). The seat could be woven tape or rush pattern.

**Materials List for Shaker Weaver's Chair**

| | |
|---|---|
| 2 back legs | 36 × 1 1/2 round |
| 2 front legs | 28 × 1 1/2 round |
| 4 seat rails | 18 × 7/8 round |
| 8 lower rails | 18 × 3/4 round |
| 1 slat | 1/2 × 3 × 18 |
| 2 finials | 1 1/2 × 1 1/2 × 5 |

## SHAKER HIGH-BACK CHAIR

For use at a table, when the chair does not have to push underneath, a high back is more comfortable. The low-back chair in Fig 9-6 might be extended upwards, but this project (Fig. 9-8) includes several improvements that could be included. The seat is tapered and the front rail is lowered. The back is given a slope and the three slats are curved. Otherwise, construction is the same as the last two projects.

Draw the plan view (Fig. 9-8A) and the slope of the back legs (Fig. 9-8B). These give you the angles to drill holes and the length of side rails.

Drill the tops of the front legs so the side rails come above the front rail (Fig. 9-8C) for increased strength. The woven seat top will then dip to the front for slightly more comfort. Back seat rails could be treated in the same way or mitered (see Fig. 9-6D).

The back slats could be flat, but they are better curved (Fig. 9-8D). Leave the ends near straight so there is enough wood around the dowel holes. Clean the surfaces in this direction before cutting the top curves.

Assemble the back and front squarely first, then join with the side rails. See that the chair stands level without twist.

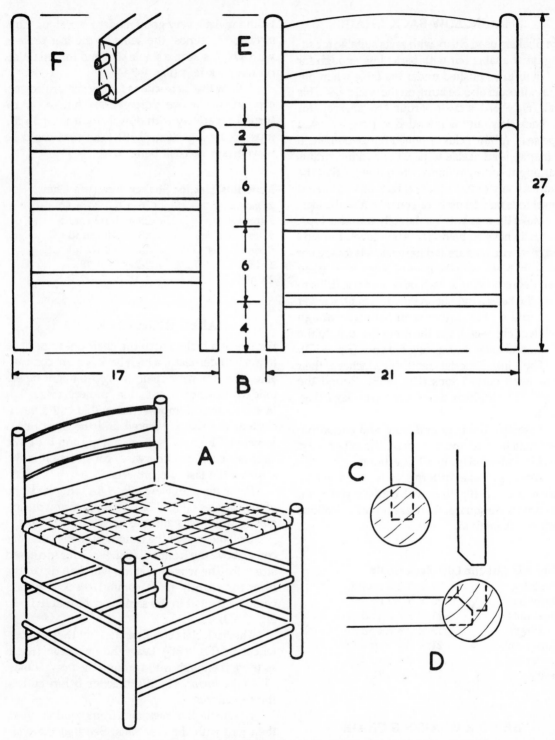

*Fig. 9-6. This Shaker chair has a back below table height. Legs and rails are round.*

**Materials List for Shaker High-Back Chair**

| | |
|---|---|
| 2 back legs | 39 × 1 1/2 round |
| 2 front legs | 20 × 1 1/2 round |
| 4 seat rails | 20 × 7/8 round |
| 8 lower rails | 20 × 3/4 round |
| 3 slats | 1 1/2 × 3 × 20 |
| 2 finials | 1 1/2 × 1 1/2 × 5 |

## UPHOLSTERED CHAIR

As settlement progressed and homes became more comfortable, the influence of British and other cabinetmakers was felt. Furniture developed a more advanced design and construction. This chair (Fig. 9-9) shows a Shearton influence. Mahogany is an appropriate wood. The shape aims at comfort, with a sloping padded seat wider at the front and rear legs that provide stability and back support in a good position.

The rear legs (Fig. 9-10A) are cut from a 4-inch width. The seat is 1 inch higher at the front than the back, but the front legs are square to the side rails (Fig. 9-10B). Mark the rear legs to match the angle of the side (Fig. 9-10C). Cut the two rear legs to shape and turn the front legs, leaving a little extra on the square tops (Fig. 9-10D).

Draw all or half the seat full size (Fig. 9-10E). Prepare the wood for the side rails with 1/2-inch rabbets to take the seat (Fig. 9-11A). The back and front rails are without rabbets. Use dowels or tenons for the joints. The front rails (Fig. 9-13B) are level with the front surfaces of the legs. The side rails are centered against the legs (Fig. 9-11C). Make up the front rail to the thickness of the leg with a strip (Fig. 9-11D). When you assemble, glue and screw a triangular block in each corner (Fig. 9-11E).

At the back, keep the rear legs parallel as you make the joints for the back rail (Fig. 9-11F). The

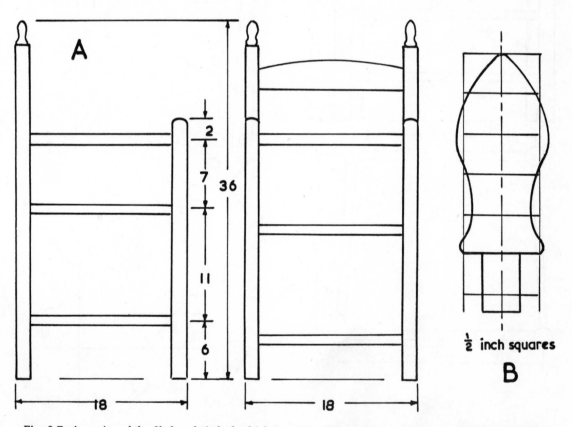

*Fig. 9-7. A version of the Shaker chair had a high seat (A). The rear legs were decorated with finials (B).*

191

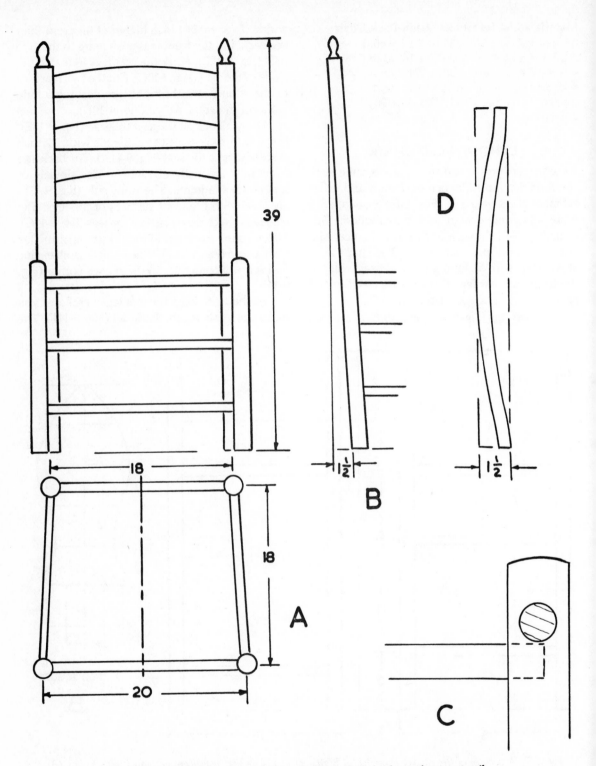

Fig. 9-8. Comfort is improved with a sloping back and a lower front seat rail.

leg and side rail are the same thickness (Fig.9-22G). Fit a strip to support the seat (Fig. 9-11H). As you assemble, see that the seat is symmetrical, the front legs square to the rails both ways, and the four legs stand level.

Cut the back curving across in a similar way to the slats in the last project, cut according to the profile in Fig. 9-10F. Fit it into the tops of the legs with glue and screws hidden with plugs.

Cut a seat with enough clearance for the cloth around its edges. Drill a few holes in it. Cover it with cloth over plastic or rubber foam (see Fig. 3-12).

## Materials List for Upholstered Chair

| | |
|---|---|
| 2 rear legs | 1 1/4 × 4 × 32 |
| 2 front legs | 2 × 2 × 19 |
| 2 side rails | 1 1/4 × 4 × 18 |
| 1 front rail | 1 1/4 × 4 × 21 |
| 1 back rail | 1 1/4 × 4 × 17 |
| 1 back | 1 1/2 × 5 × 22 |
| 1 seat | 1/2 × 17 × 18 |

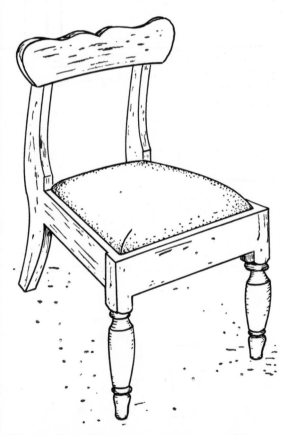

*Fig. 9-9. A side chair has more shaping, an upholstered seat for comfort, and turned front legs.*

## PEASANT CHAIR

In many parts of Europe there is a type of chair made from thick slabs. As much early wood available to immigrants was cut thick, some woodworkers from Germany would have turned to this design, which is a form of stool with a decorated back (Fig. 9-12). The main parts are hardwood about 1 1/2 inches thick, although edges may be thinned to give a lighter appearance. Legs are traditionally turned, although they could be octagonal if you do not have the use of a lathe.

It is advisable to mark out the back and seat, then drill holes and cut joints before shaping the outlines. The seat tapers from 16 inches to 14 inches. The leg holes are 2 inches from the edges and could be a 1 1/4-inch diameter. The drilling angles may be set by eye, as they are not crucial as long as opposite ones are a pair, but if you are able to set the angles on a drill press, the front legs may slope 12 degrees to front and side. The rear legs have the same slope to the side, but are 22 degrees to the rear (Fig. 9-13A).

The back has six tenons through the seat (Fig. 9-13B). Do not use dowels. They would not be strong enough. When you assemble, let the tenons project at first and tighten alternate ones with wedges (Fig. 9-13C).

Bevel under the seat (Fig 9-13D), if you wish. In original chairs many different outlines were used on the back, some of them quite elaborate, but a fairly simple outline is shown (Fig. 9-13E). The heart cutout should be large enough to put your hand through to lift the chair. Round all edges.

The legs (Fig. 9-13F) and method of fitting them are similar to the milking stools (Chapter 3). Take them through the seat and wedge them. To get their bottoms level, invert the chair over the edge of a bench and measure from the bench top to the same level on each leg, then cut and round

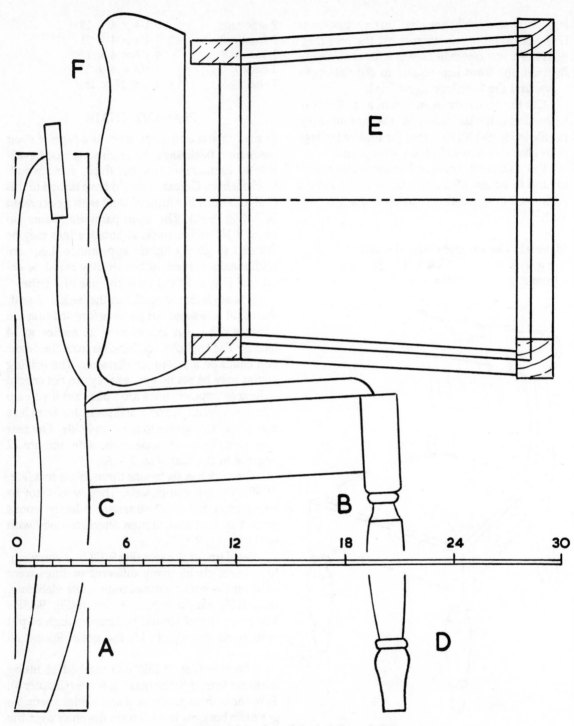

Fig. 9-10. Main sizes of the upholstered chair.

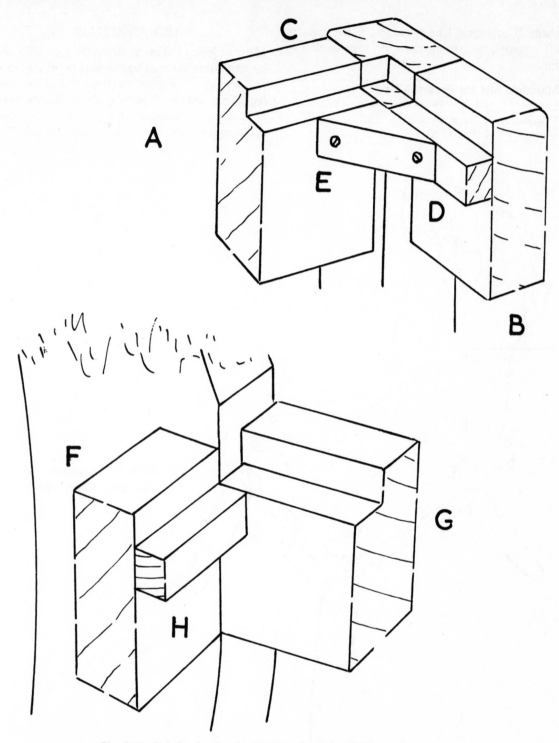

Fig. 9-11. Details of rail to leg joints at the front (A-D) and rear (F, G, H).

them. If octagonal legs are made, plane corners off square stock, then taper the tops to fit the holes.

**Materials List for Peasant Chair**

| | |
|---|---|
| 1 seat | 1 1/2 × 16 × 20 |
| 1 back | 1 1/2 × 16 × 25 |
| 4 legs | 2 × 2 × 20 |

## YARD ARMCHAIR

Many ordinary chairs can be made into armchairs by continuing the front legs up to support the arms and screwing the arms into the sides of the rear legs. This example (Fig. 9-14) shows the method of making an armchair. Chairs for indoor use could be made in a very similar way, but this one

Fig. 9-12. This peasant chair shows a European country influence.

is described for completion as an outside chair in the yard or on a patio or deck. For indoor use, there may be a solid or upholstered seat.

Wood of fairly stout section is specified. This should be a type naturally resistant to rot, or it should be treated with a preservative. Make joints with waterproof glue and, for additional strength, use dowels across tenons.

The sizes (Fig. 9-15A) will make a roomy chair. Start with the pair of rear legs (Figs. 9-15B and

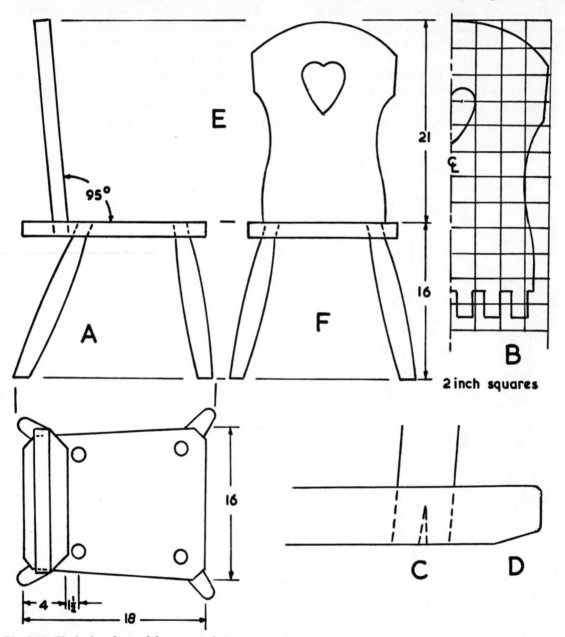

Fig. 9-13. The back and seat of the peasant chair are tenoned together. Legs are splayed and wedged through the seat.

197

9-16A). Mark out the positions of other parts and taper the ends. Make the front legs with matching positions (Fig. 9-16B) and enough left for the tenons at the top (Fig. 9-16C). The seat is two inches wider at the front than the back (Fig. 9-16C). Both front and rear seat rails (Fig. 9-16D and E) should have barefaced tenons to allow adequate width of wood beside the mortises. The lower rails (Fig. 9-16F and G) may have central tenons.

The side seat rails (Fig. 9-16H) have central tenons. The lower side rails must allow for the tapered leg (Fig. 9-16D).

Prepare the tops of the front legs for the joints to the arms, which can exert a considerable load when the chair is lifted or moved. Tenons could go through, but that would expose end grain to rain. It would be better to use stub tenons taken three-forths of the way through. Strengthen these with fox wedging (Fig. 9-15E). Use short wedges that will hit the bottom of the mortise as the joint is tightened and spread the tenon.

Put together the front and rear assemblies. Add the side rails and see that the framework stands true and symmetrical. Nail or screw on the seat boards (Fig. 9-15F). Notch around the legs (Fig. 9-16J), allowing the front edge to project (Fig. 9-15G). Round all exposed edges.

Fig. 9-14. This armchair is of simple construction and suitable for use outdoors.

Make the pair of arms (Fig. 9-16K). Their inner edges are parallel to each other, and they taper to the back. At the rear, glue and screw them to the legs. There could also be shallow grooves in the legs.

Round and screw on the two back boards (Figs. 9-15H and 9-16L). Screws in counterbored holes and covered with plugs are preferred.

**Materials List for Yard Armchair**

| | |
|---|---|
| 2 legs | 2 × 3 × 35 |
| 2 legs | 2 × 2 × 25 |
| 4 seat rails | 1 × 3 × 22 |
| 4 lower rails | 1 × 2 × 22 |
| 3 seat boards | 3/4 × 6 × 24 |
| 2 backs | 3/4 × 4 × 24 |
| 2 arms | 1 × 4 × 25 |

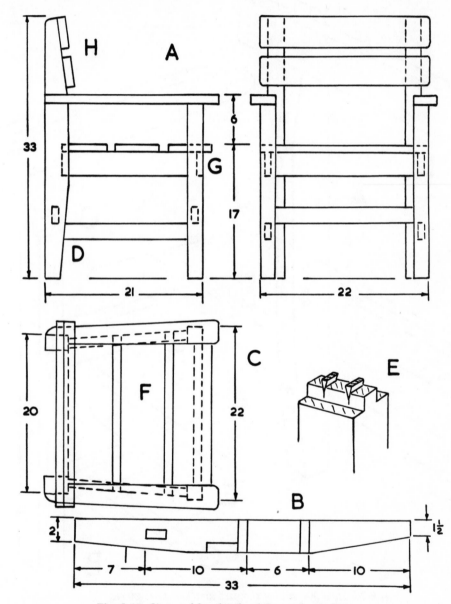

Fig. 9-15. Sizes and leg details of the yard armchair.

## VIRGINIA ROCKING CHAIR

Rockers have always been popular, and this project (Fig. 9-17) is modified from a chair seen in Virginia. Many chairs can be made into rockers, even if the rear legs are closer together than the front ones. This chair has a parallel arrangement. Its seat can be worked with a checker pattern interlaced tapes or be made into a rush pattern. The seat and lower rails are all round. The front legs are shown turned, but they could be square. They complement the shaped arms, however, which give character to the chair.

Make a full-size drawing of the main lines in the side view (Fig. 9-18A) to get the positions and

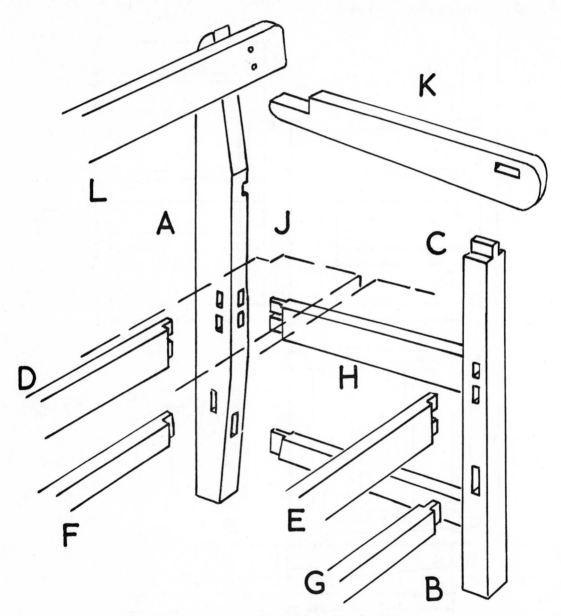

Fig. 9-16. How the parts of the yard armchair fit together.

angles of the parts. The back slopes at about 95 degrees.

The rockers extend at least 10 inches behind the rear legs. If they are cut to shape first, they can be put over your drawing to get the leg lengths. To draw the curves, make an improvised compass with an awl. Use a 72-inch radius for the outer curve and a notch 2-inches back to pencil the inner curve (Fig. 9-18).

Mark the rear legs (Fig. 9-19A). There is a tenon into the rocker, holes to suit rails, and mortises for the arms. The back slats are at 3-inch intervals and may be doweled. Drill the tops of the legs for the dowels on small knobs. Sizes are approximate—get exact sizes from your drawing.

The front legs (Fig. 9-19B) have matching rail hole spacings. The ends are reduced to fit 1-inch holes.

Dry assemble one or both sides while you make and fit the arms (Fig. 9-18C). Check actual sizes on your full-size drawing. Cut tenons and drill for the front legs. Well round all edges of the arms, particularly towards the front where the shaping is prominent.

When you are satisfied with the arms and other parts for the sides, assemble them. See that they match and are without twist.

The three slats (Fig. 9-18D) are cut to curves from thicker wood and taper to 3 inches at the ends. They could be tenoned, but dowels are suggested. Assemble these and the crosswise rails to the sides. Work the tapes or cords for the seat.

Fig. 9-17. This rocking chair has shaped arms, a rush pattern seat, and turned front legs.

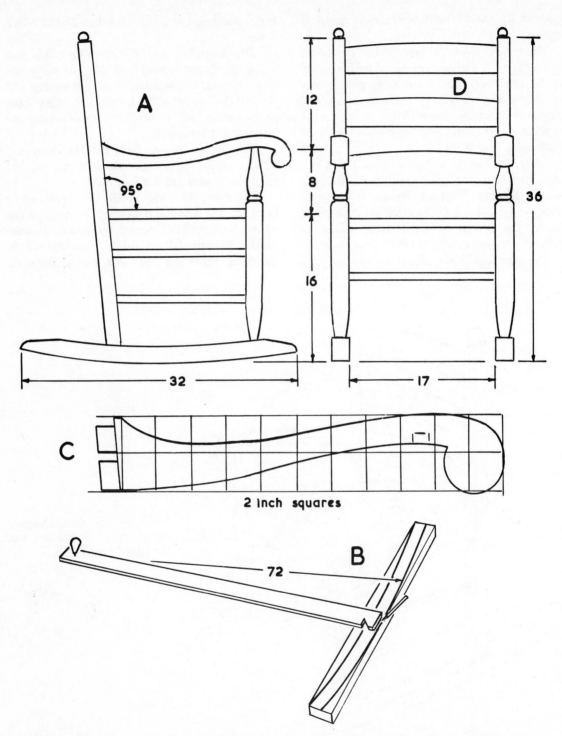

Fig. 9-18. Sizes of the rocking arm chair, the shape of its arms, and how to draw the curve of the rockers.

**Materials List for Virginia Rocking Chair**

| | | | |
|---|---|---|---|
| 2 rockers | 2 × 3 × 34 | 2 arms | 2 × 4 × 26 |
| 2 rear legs | 1 1/2 × 1 1/2 × 36 | 3 slats | 1 1/2 × 3 1/2 × 19 |
| 2 front legs | 2 × 2 × 18 | 4 seat rails | 21 × 1 round |
| | | 6 lower rails | 21 × 7/8 round |

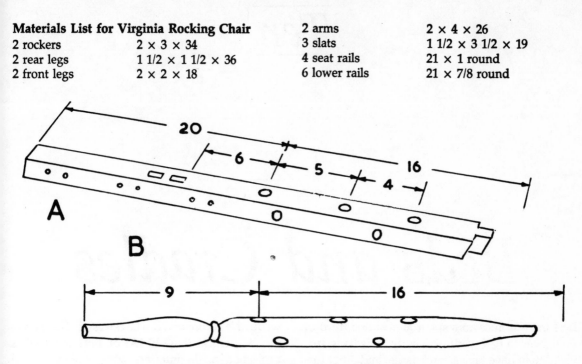

Fig. 9-19. Details of the legs for the rocking chair.

# Ten

# Beds and Cradles

Like us, our ancestors spent almost one-third of their lives in bed, yet fewer early beds have survived than have tables, cupboards, and other furniture. The design of the actual supports for the bedding has changed considerably and that might have affected survival, but the bed ends could still be used. In early beds a network of ropes formed the mattress support, or solid boards were used for the unyielding support for straw or feather padding.

Today, you might not want sagging ropes, but a solid wood base might be acceptable for modern, deep, resilient mattresses. In any reproduction, the head and foot can repeat an early example, but the part you sleep on can be of modern type.

One problem is obtaining rigidity between the bed sides and the two ends. If the joints could be permanent, there would be little difficulty, but it is usually necessary to disassemble a bed to get it through doorways. There are modern metal fittings for making these joints, but if you want to build your bed in the way used about two hundred years ago, you will have to manage without them.

Several variations on the mortise and tenon joint were used. A tusk tenon taken through and wedged is secure and can be released. The wedge can be vertical (Fig. 10-1A) or horizontal. This projection might interfere with pushing a bed against a wall and might be knocked by your legs. A pegged tenon need not project (Fig. 10-1B). Drill the hole in the tenon so driving the tapered peg pulls the joint tight (Fig. 10-1C). Drive the peg out with a punch to disassemble the bed.

Fitting a block permanently to the leg allows a tusk tenon to be used without anything projecting past the bed end (Fig. 10-1D). A semipermanent joint that was used had one or two metal angle brackets screwed to the wood (Fig. 10-2A).

Long bolts will make take-down joints. The bed side should have a shallow tenon for location, then the bolts go far enough in for the end grain to take the load (Fig. 10-2B). Put washers under the nuts in the pockets.

You might choose to use dowels in making the bed ends. Traditionally, however the joints between parts were nearly all mortises and tenons.

## FENCE-END BED

It might be that the need to erect fences in the fields inspired this design, but it is a popular country pattern (Fig. 10-3). It could be any width and

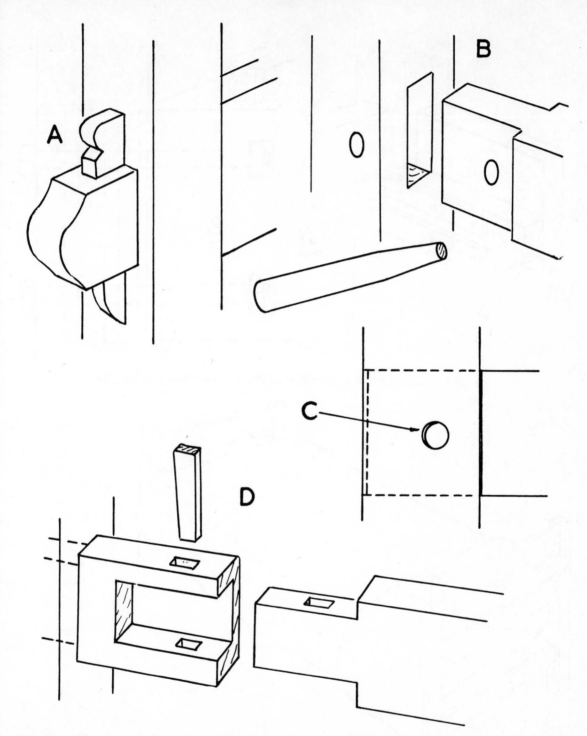

Fig. 10-1. Bed parts can be joined in several ways if metal parts are to be avoided. There can be tusk tenons wedged outside (A), pegged tenons (B, C), or tenons wedged through a fitted block (D).

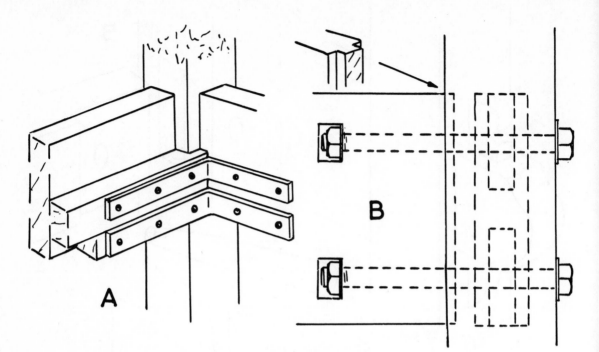

Fig. 10-2. Bed joints can be made with metal angle brackets (A) or long bolts (B).

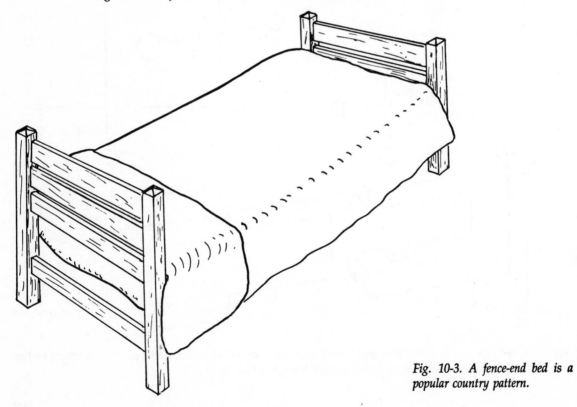

Fig. 10-3. A fence-end bed is a popular country pattern.

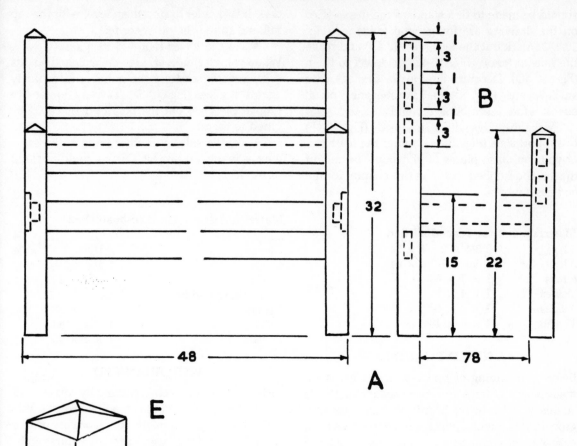

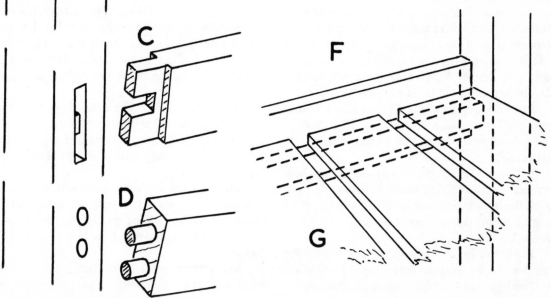

Fig. 10-4. *General assembly of the fence-end bed. Joints may be tenons or dowels. The mattress is supported on slats.*

should be made to fit a standard mattress—sizes on the drawing are for general guidance (Fig. 10-4A). Mark out the legs (Fig. 10-4B) and make the rails to tenon (Fig. 10-4C) or dowel to them (Fig. 10-4D). Decorate the tops of the legs with shallow cones (Fig. 10-4E). Take sharpness off all edges before assembling the ends.

Make the sides with strips inside (Fig. 10-4F) to support slats (Fig. 10-4G) under the mattress, or you could use pieces of plywood. Use any of the joints described earlier in this chapter for the bed assembly.

### Materials List for Fence-End Bed

| | |
|---|---|
| 2 legs | 2 3/4 × 2 3/4 × 34 |
| 2 legs | 2 3/4 × 2 3/4 × 24 |
| 6 rails | 1 × 3 × 48 |
| 2 sides | 1 × 4 × 80 |
| 2 sides | 1 × 2 × 80 |
| 15 slats | 1 × 4 × 48 |

## MATCHED-BOARD BED

Before the coming of plywood and other man-made boards of large area, one way of filling wide spaces was by using boards with tongue-and-groove edge joints. This ensured a freedom from spaces even when boards contracted. Prepared boards are available, or you can cut your own joints. In the simplest form, the two edges meet squarely (Fig. 10-5A). The gap is less obvious if it widens when a bead is worked on the tongued piece (Fig. 10-5B). When both sides will be visible, there could be a bead on both surfaces.

Bed ends can be made with matched boards arranged horizontally or vertically (Fig. 10-5C). The general proportions can be the same as the last project.

For each end, cut grooves in the top and bottom rails (Fig. 10-5D) to make a reasonably tight fit on the boards. It is better to fit them dry than to glue them; this allows them to expand and contract.

Traditionally, the rails were tenoned into the legs (Fig. 10-5E). You can dowel them if you wish.

The legs could continue above the rails and be given conical ends, or turned finials might be ad-

ded. It is simpler to stop them level with the top rail and round the outer corners.

Make the lower foot end in a similar way. When you assemble, arrange the matched boards symmetrically and cut the outer ones squarely against the legs (Fig. 10-5F). There is no need to groove the legs, but the board edges could be glued to them.

Make the sides and other parts in the same way as in the last project. Casters could be fitted to the legs.

### Materials List for Matched-board Bed

| | |
|---|---|
| 2 legs | 2 1/2 × 2 1/2 × 34 |
| 2 legs | 2 1/2 × 2 1/2 × 24 |
| 4 rails | 1 1/2 × 2 1/2 × 48 |
| 2 rails | 1 × 3 × 48 |
| 16 matching boarding | 5/8 × 6 × 12 |
| 2 sides | 1 × 4 × 80 |
| 2 sides | 1 × 2 × 80 |
| 15 slats | 1 × 4 × 48 |

## VICTORIAN BED

Victorian furniture is characterized by curves, and this bed head (Fig. 10-6) is modified from a Victorian example. You might not favor very ornate work, but this design uses Victorian features without going to excess. The bed is shown without a visible foot, in the way preferred today, but you could make a lower version of the head, in the same way as the previous beds. They could be made with similar hidden foot ends to this one, if you wish.

Mark out the long legs with the positions of the rails (Fig. 10-7A) and the low rails with matching heights. Make rounded domed tops on the long legs. Moderately round the tops of the short legs.

Make all the crosswise rails with tenons or dowels into the legs. The ends of the top rail reduce to 2 1/2 inches for the tenon (Fig. 10-8A). Mark and cut its shape and the hole (Fig. 10-8B). Round all edges.

Make the central slat (Fig. 10-8C) and the three each side of it. They reduce in width and are shown 3 inches, 2 inches, and 1 inch, with 2-inch

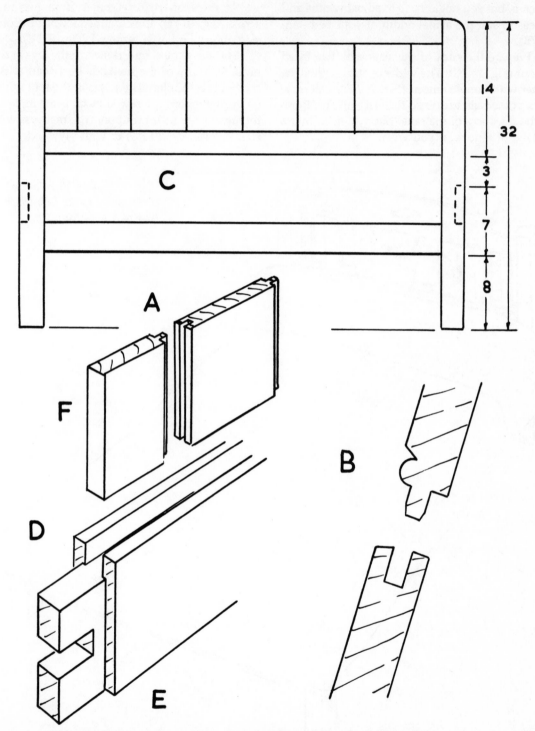

*Fig. 10-5. In a matched-board bed, the panels are formed with boards having tongue and groove joints, either plain or with a bead at each joint. The boards fit into grooved rails but have flat edges against the legs.*

spacing, but you might have to adjust widths and spaces to suit the actual width of your bed (Fig. 10-7B).

Prepare the ends of the slats with barefaced tenons (Fig. 10-7C). The wider central slat will be better with double tenons (Fig. 10-8D). Cut mortises in the rails to suit so the slats finish central in the thickness of the rails. Use 1/4-inch dowels instead of tenons, if you wish.

At the foot, rigidity comes from two rails across (Fig. 10-7D). One is at bed level at the outside and the other is centered (Fig. 10-7E).

The sides could be attached to the legs at the head with any of the methods described at the start of this chapter. The joints at the foot might be the same, but a screwed block is a simple alternative (Fig. 10-7F). Support the mattress with slats across (Fig. 10-7G) or with plywood.

*Fig. 10-6. This Victorian bed is without an exposed foot, which is generally preferred today.*

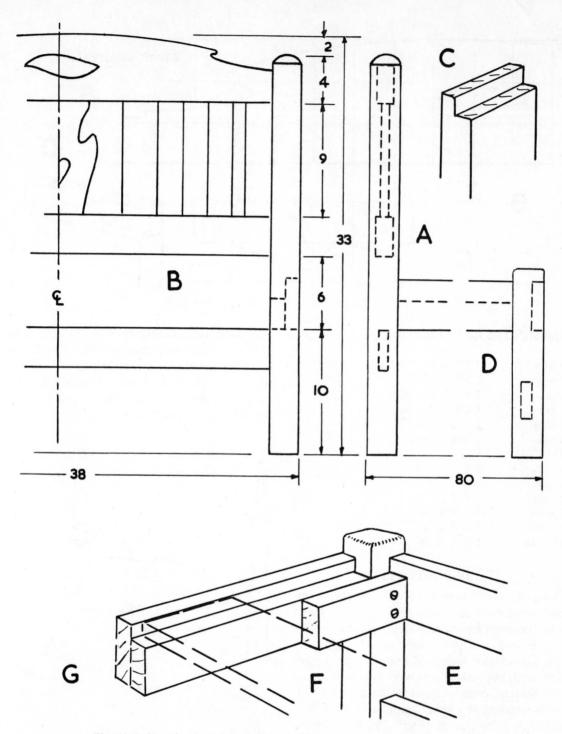

Fig. 10-7. Sizes for the bed parts and a method of joining the sides to the foot.

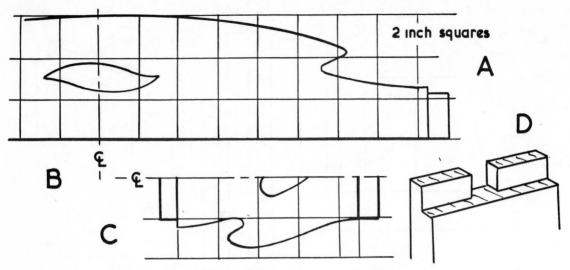

Fig. 10-8. The shapes and joints of bed head parts.

## Materials List for Victorian Bed

| | |
|---|---|
| 2 legs | 2 1/2 × 2 1/2 × 35 |
| 2 legs | 2 1/2 × 2 1/2 × 17 |
| 1 rail | 1 1/2 × 6 × 38 |
| 1 rail | 1 1/2 × 3 × 38 |
| 2 rails | 1 × 3 × 38 |
| 1 rail | 1 × 4 × 38 |
| 1 slat | 5/8 × 8 × 12 |
| 2 slats | 5/8 × 3 × 12 |
| 2 slats | 5/8 × 2 × 12 |
| 2 slats | 5/8 × 1 × 12 |
| 2 sides | 1 × 4 × 80 |
| 2 sides | 1 × 3 × 80 |
| 13 slats | 1 × 4 × 38 |

## FOUR-POSTER BED

Originally, posts at the corner of the bed were carried upwards to support a tester, or roof. These took hangings for curtains all around to provide privacy and as a protection from draughts. As home conditions improved there was no longer this need, but bed owners were reluctant to discard the posts completely, so beds were made with posts standing at a lesser height above the bed, although there was no practical need for them. They were often decorated by turning or carving or both. Decorated parts still provide charm and an air of quality. This bed is of the Jacobean period (Fig. 10-9) and is a fairly stout construction suitable for a queen-size mattress (Fig. 10-10). The headboard and footboard are divided to avoid very wide pieces of wood. The posts are divided where square changes to round, so the turned parts will be within the capacity of most lathes.

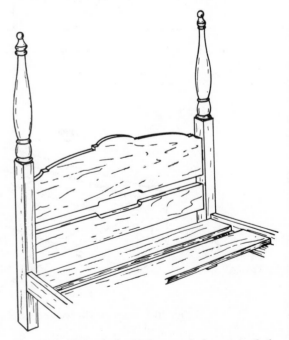

Fig. 10-9. The end of a Jacobean style four-poster bed.

A good quality hardwood is advised. An original bed would probably have been made of mahogany or walnut.

Start by making the square head posts (Fig. 10-10A) and foot posts (Fig. 10-10B) with the positions of the parts that will be attached to them. Carefully square and center the tops and drill 1-inch holes 1 1/2 inches deep for the dowels on the turned parts.

The shaped head and foot boards are the same

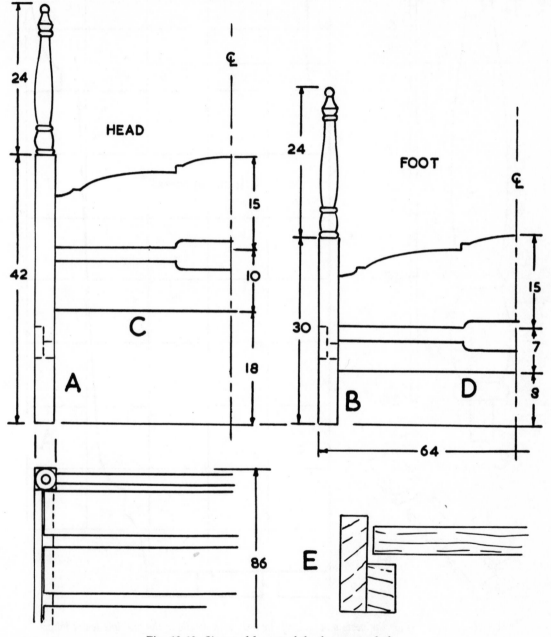

Fig. 10-10. Sizes and layout of the four-poster bed.

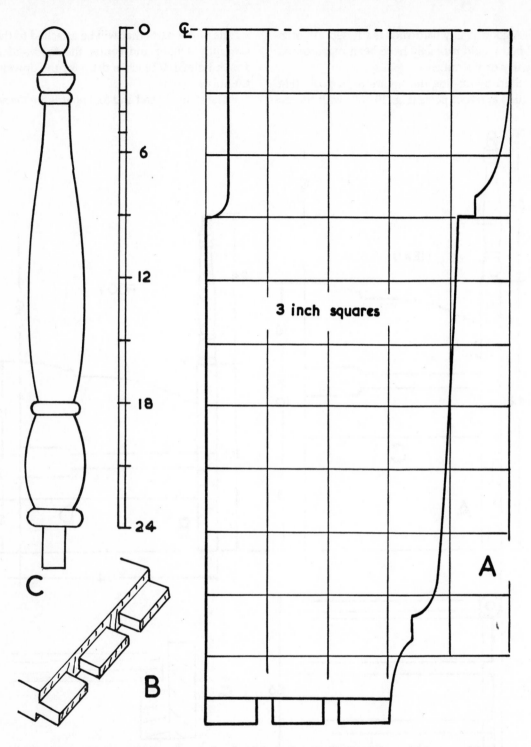

O

6

12

**3 inch squares**

18

24

C

B

A

*Fig. 10-11. Patterns for the posts and ends of the bed, with details of the multiple tenon joints.*

(Fig. 10-11A). Round the edges of the shaped parts. The ends could be joined to the legs with large dowels, but it is better to use tenons (Fig. 10-11B). Cut out the lower parts of the headboard and footboard so their edges match the upper parts, but remember that the head is 8 inches deep (Fig. 10-10C) and the foot is 5 inches deep (Fig. 10-10D). Cut divided tenons on the ends.

Use your own ideas for the turned parts of the posts, if you wish, but a suggested design is shown (Fig. 10-11C). All four should match.

If the bed is being built queen-size or larger, the sides should be stiff. They are shown made from 1 1/2-inch wood, 5 inches and 2 1/2 inches wide (Fig. 10-10E). Use a stiff wood for the slats across. In this larger and fairly heavy bed it will probably be best to use metal angle brackets to join the sides to the foot. Long bolts could be used at the head.

Glue in all the turned parts first and check straightness. Assemble the ends and see that they match. Check that diagonal measurements match when you join in the other parts.

## Materials List for Four-Poster Bed

| | |
|---|---|
| 2 legs | 3 × 3 × 42 |
| 2 legs | 3 × 3 × 32 |
| 4 legs | 3 × 3 × 28 |
| 2 end boards | 1 1/4 × 15 × 64 |
| 1 headboard | 1 1/4 × 8 × 64 |
| 1 footboard | 1 1/4 × 5 × 64 |
| 2 sides | 1 1/2 × 5 × 86 |
| 2 sides | 1 1/2 × 2 1/2 × 86 |
| 9 slats | 1 1/2 × 7 × 64 |

## TRUNDLE BED

A trundle or truckle bed is a low one that can be stored under a normal bed. It was originally used by a servant, who slept in the same room as her mistress. Today it might be regarded as a space saver, an extra guest bed, or a way of providing a child's bed that can be pushed out of the way during the day.

Size depends on available space. A narrow adult bed of sufficient length might be pushed in from the foot end of a large bed, but a trundle bed to go in from the side would have to be shorter,

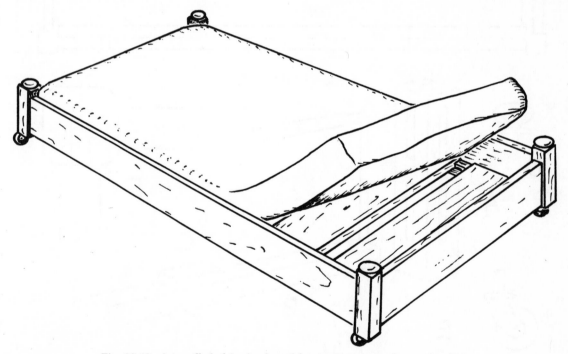

*Fig. 10-12. A trundle bed is simple and low so it stores under another bed.*

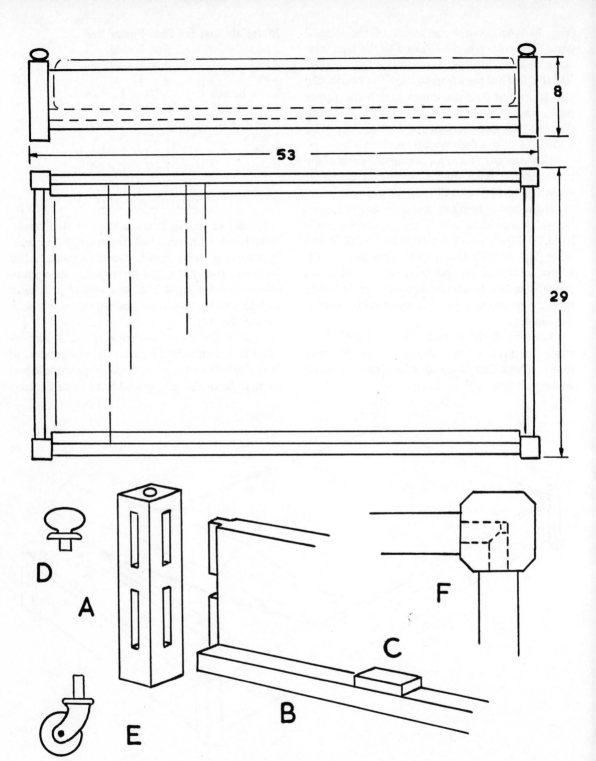

Fig. 10-13. Sizes and method of construction of the trundle bed.

although still ample for a child. Vertical clearance might be a deciding factor, as modern beds tend to be lower underneath.

The simplest trundle bed is little more than a box on wheels for a mattress. Many were made like that, but better beds had corner posts. This bed (Fig. 10-12) has posts and sizes to suit a child's mattress 24 inches by 48 inches, but any size could be made in the same way.

The sizes (Fig. 10-13) are for a mattress 5 inches thick, with casters 2 inches deep, and knobs projecting 2 inches; the total height is 12 inches. Depth could be reduced by omitting the knobs and using glides instead of casters.

Make the four posts (Fig. 10-13A) and mark on the positions of the rails. Traditionally the rails would have been tenoned, but you could use dowels. Fit square strips (Fig. 10-13B) to the insides of the side rails. Blocks can be added (Fig. 10-13C) to separate the slats.

You could turn knobs directly on the legs, but they are shown as drawer pulls (Fig. 10-13D) fitted into holes. If you use the type of caster with a peg (Fig. 10-13E), drill for that.

Take the sharpness off the inner corners of the legs (Fig. 10-13F). Do this all the way around if you wish. Miter the tenons to get maximum strength. Check squareness by measuring diagonals as you assemble. Make the slats to drop in loosely.

### Materials List for Trundle Bed

| | |
|---|---|
| 4 legs | 1 1/2 × 1 1/2 × 10 |
| 2 rails | 3/4 × 6 × 54 |
| 2 rails | 3/4 × 6 × 30 |
| 2 strips | 3/4 × 3/4 × 52 |
| 7 slats | 3/4 × 6 × 28 |

### ROCKING CRADLE

A young baby could be rocked by using a foot on a rocker below its cradle or by using a hand on a swinging cradle. Some rocking cradles were elaborately carved, particularly those with a German influence. Some were so enclosed that it seemed difficult to find the baby. Many had hoods or canopies. Today, the preference is for something more open, and this rocking cradle (Fig. 10-14) could be used for a baby or even as a means of displaying fabrics or flowers.

The sides and ends have a moderate flare. Corners could be nailed or screwed but would look best if dovetailed. A hardwood could be 1/2 inch thick, but softwood should be 5/8 inch. The rockers are better made of hardwood, in any case. The amount of flare both ways is shown as 100 degrees, but this is not crucial as long as you use the same angle throughout (Fig. 10-15A).

Mark out the two sides (Figs. 10-15B and 10-16A) but leave some extra wood at the ends until joint details have been arranged. Make the two end pieces with edge lengths to match the sides and curved top edges. Mark out the corner joints, either nailed or dovetailed, obtaining the angles for the edges by holding the four parts temporarily in position. Assemble these parts. Make the bottom to project enough all around for rounding or molding. Glue and nail or screw to the other assembly.

The two rockers (Figs. 10-15C and 10-16B) should have regular curves—a radius of 30 inches to 36 inches would be suitable. The projections on the ends prevent the cradle from being tilted too far. Round all exposed edges.

*Fig. 10-14. An open rocking cradle of simple construction.*

Fit a strip between the rockers (Fig. 10-15D) with tenons at the ends. Attach this assembly with screws through the cradle bottom.

## Materials List for Rocking Cradle

| | |
|---|---|
| 2 sides | 1/2 × 15 × 35 |
| 1 end | 1/2 × 13 × 18 |
| 1 end | 1/2 × 16 × 18 |
| 1 bottom | 1/2 × 15 × 32 |
| 2 rockers | 7/8 × 5 × 26 |
| 1 rocker strip | 7/8 × 2 × 26 |

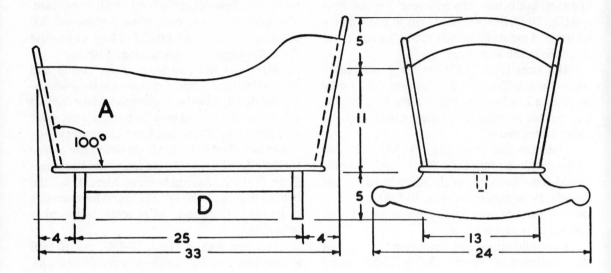

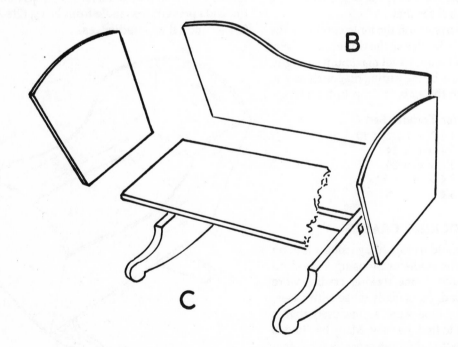

*Fig. 10-15. The cradle has a moderate flare and fits over a rocking base assembly.*

## SWINGING CRADLE

The alternative to rocking a cradle on the floor is to hang it so it can swing. This cradle (Fig. 10-17) hangs from supports that can be disassembled when not required or when it must be transported. Hardwood is advisable. The spindles are dowel rods. The sizes suggested (Fig. 10-18A) should suit most needs. If they are altered, make the feet broader than the cradle, which should hang low below its pivot but swing clear of the bar on the supports.

The cradle itself is made with two frames with the hanging uprights, as well as dowels, connecting them. Draw the main lines of an end view (Fig. 10-18B), with the top frame 20 inches and the bottom frame 16 inches across, to obtain the angles at the sides.

Shape the top ends (Fig. 10-19A) and make two sides (Fig. 10-19B). Cut open mortise and tenon, or bridle, joints at the corners but tilt the sides at the angle shown on your drawing. Cut the bottom parts (Fig. 10-19C) with similar corner

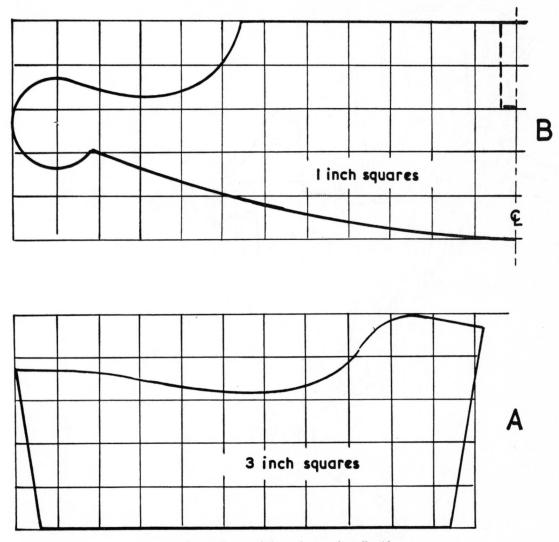

1 inch squares

B

3 inch squares

A

Fig. 10-16. Shapes of the rockers and cradle sides.

219

joints and the sides tilted. The cradle bottom could be plywood nailed underneath, but the sides might be grooved to take thin wood slats (Fig. 10-19D).

Mark top and bottom sides together for drilling to take 1/2-inch dowel rods at 2 1/2-inch intervals. At the ends, allow for the rods filling the space in a similar way (Fig. 10-18C).

Make the two hanging uprights (Fig. 10-18D and 10-19E). Notch them and the frame ends for accurate location. The notches need not be more than 1/8 inch deep.

Assemble the top and bottom frames including the bottom slats. Let the glue set, then level the joints and round edges.

Join the frames with the dowel rods and hanging uprights. Check that the assembly is square and symmetrical.

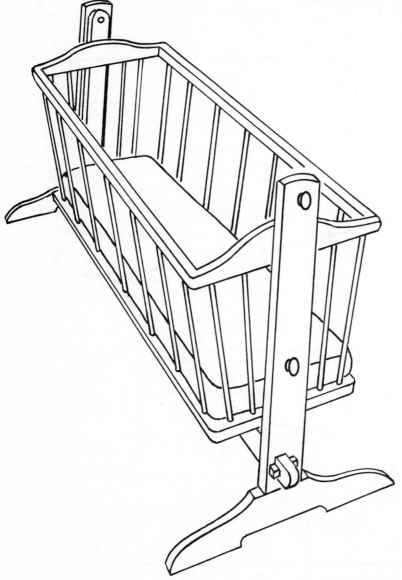

*Fig. 10-17. The cradle hangs from supports that can be taken apart when required.*

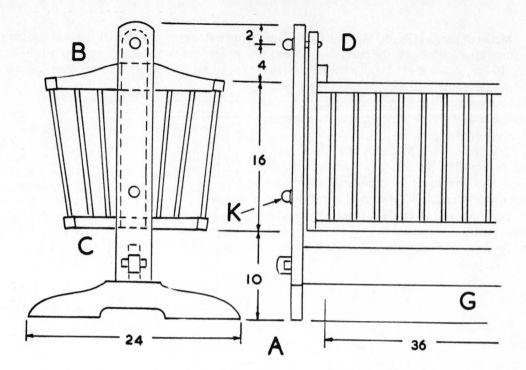

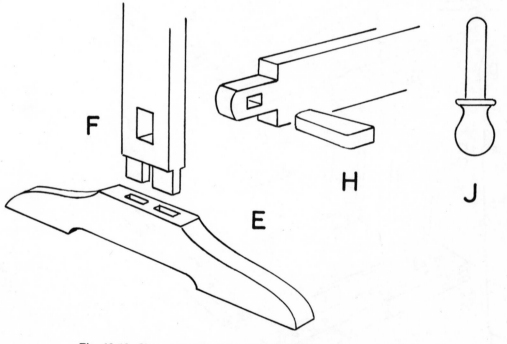

*Fig. 10-18. Sizes and support joint details for the swinging cradle.*

Mark out the feet (Fig. 10-18E), but leave shaping until after the joints to the posts have been cut (Fig. 10-18F). Make the bar with a length between the shoulders that will allow about 1/8-inch clearance between each post and hanging upright. Cut mortise and tenon joints to go through far enough to take a wedge (Fig. 10-18H).

The pivots could be pieces of 1/2-inch dowel rod, but it will be better to turn pivots with knobs (Fig. 10-18J) so they can be more easily withdrawn. When you assemble, it is worthwhile putting a fiber or fabric washer on each pivot between the wood parts.

So the cradle can be locked when it is not re-quired to swing, you can drill a hole into both parts at one end for another peg (Fig. 10-18K), which need go only partly into the inner piece.

## Materials List for Swinging Cradle

| | |
|---|---|
| 2 top ends | 1 1/4 × 3 × 22 |
| 2 lower ends | 1 1/4 × 1 1/4 × 18 |
| 4 sides | 1 1/4 × 1 1/4 × 40 |
| 38 spindles | 17 × 1/2 diameter |
| 9 bottom slats | 1/4 × 4 × 17 |
| 2 hanging uprights | 1 × 2 × 24 |
| 2 feet | 1 1/4 × 4 × 26 |
| 2 posts | 1 1/4 × 4 × 32 |
| 1 bar | 1 1/4 × 4 × 45 |
| 3 pegs | 1 × 1 × 6 |

Fig. 10-19. How the cradle parts are assembled.

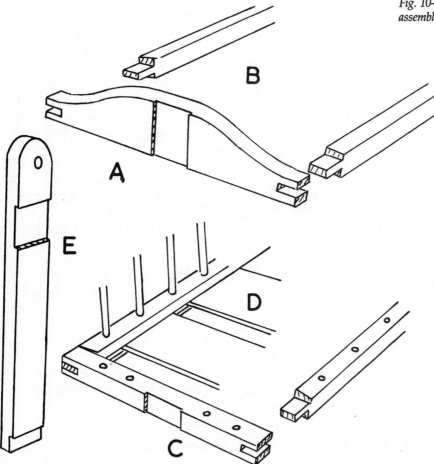

# Eleven

# Other Furniture

The basic range of furniture for any home, whether traditional or modern, has been covered in the preceding chapters. Besides eating, sitting, sleeping, and storing, anyone will find uses for other pieces of furniture not so easy to group with the main items. A few of these are described in Chapter 1 but more items, which are larger or require more skill, are described here.

All of the things described are based on designs used by our ancestors. Many have modern uses, while others, such as fire screens, have outlived their usefulness but are decorative or interesting enough to find a place in a room furnished in country style.

Many of these pieces will complement larger pieces of furniture. A room furnished only with tables and chairs, or other large essential items, will lack a lived-in look without things standing on the table or hanging on the walls. Some of these places will be taken by fabric or other materials, but there are several wooden items, such as picture frames and trays that are important accessories.

## BLOCK-CORNER PICTURE FRAME

Many early woodworkers did not have the means to cut the usual rabbet in picture frame molding, and they might not have trusted their ability to cut accurate miters. This frame (Fig. 11-1A) is built up to form rabbets, and the miters are hidden (Fig. 11-2). The result can look attractive and be made in any size.

To arrive at a size, add the widths of the back pieces to the picture size—for instance, 1-inch strips outside a picture 8 inches by 10 inches would give an overall size of 10 inches by 12 inches (Fig. 11-1B). Check the thickness of glass, picture, and backing, then allow a little more for the wood thickness.

Miter these strips and the corner pieces to overlap them about 1/4 inch (Fig. 11-1C). Glue the strips together, then glue the miters and cover them with thin squares (Fig. 11-1D). Extra strength can come from pins driven diagonally in the miters and from the back. If the grain is prominent, the corner squares look best with grain lines arranged diagonally.

**Materials List for Block-Corner Picture Frame**

| | |
|---|---|
| 2 strips | 1/2 × 1 × 11 |
| 2 strips | 1/2 × 1 × 13 |
| 2 strips | 1/4 × 1 1/4 × 11 |
| 2 strips | 1/4 × 1 1/4 × 13 |
| 4 corners | 1/8 × 1 1/4 × 1 1/2 |

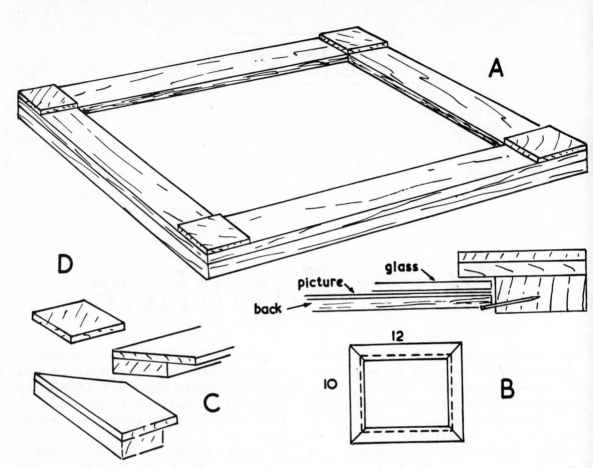

Fig. 11-1. In a block-corner picture frame, the narrow mitered pieces go under the wider ones and a square covers each corner.

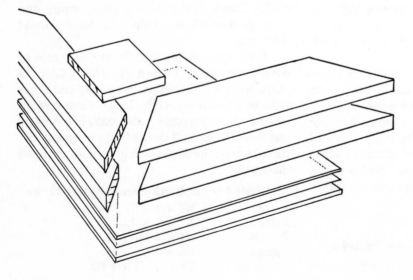

Fig. 11-2. The block-corner picture frame has squares over each corner. The picture and glass are held with pins into the frame.

## OXFORD PICTURE FRAME

A picture frame with the sides extending at each corner, known as an Oxford frame, was popular for framing religious texts, certificates, and samples of embroidery. The simplest frames had the paper tacked on the back of strips halved together. Another type had extra strips put around inside the crossed pieces to form rabbets, but the better made Oxford picture frames of Victorian and earlier days had the rabbets cut in the framed pieces (Fig. 11-3A). In such a frame the rabbets have to go into the half-lapped corner joints. This reduces the amount of wood left in one of the pieces, so it is very weak until the frame has been glued. With a modern router and a rabbeting bit, this problem is overcome by not cutting the rabbets until after the frame has been assembled.

For a picture 10 inches by 12 inches, wood 3/4

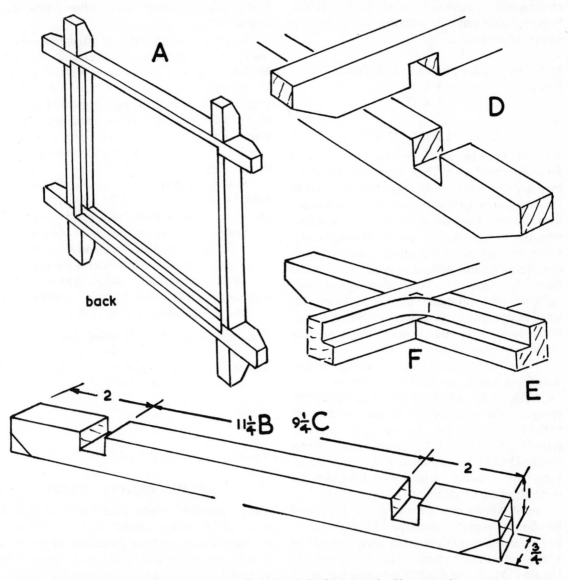

Fig. 11-3. An Oxford picture frame has halved joints and rabbets into them.

inch by 1 inch is suitable. Mark out two pairs of pieces (Fig. 11-3B and C) and cut halving joints (Fig. 11-3D). Slope the ends. Glue the joints and check squareness.

Make a rabbet with your router inside all round the back of the frame. It could be half the thickness of the wood and whatever depth is needed to take the picture, glass, and back—probably also half the thickness (Fig. 11-3E). At the corners, make a curve with a router bit (Fig. 11-3F). Square this by carefully working with a chisel to complete the frame.

### Materials List for Oxford Picture Frame

| | |
|---|---|
| 2 pieces | 3/4 × 1 × 15 |
| 2 pieces | 3/4 × 1 × 17 |

## LOOP-HANDLED BOX

A box that can be carried about is always useful for tools or gardening. There is an attraction about loop handles. Many early boxes had loops made from unseasoned ash or hickory, which bends easily. When dried out, the woods are much less flexible. You would not find "green" wood so easily today, unless you cut it yourself. There is a modern alternative that will get a similar result and is barely detectable. This takes advantage of modern glues that will make strong laminations. Instead of trying to bend a piece of 3/8-inch wood, probably unsuccessfully, you can bend and glue three, 1/8-inch thicknesses easily.

This box (Fig. 11-4A) may have a single lengthwise rigid handle, as shown, or two transverse loops (Fig. 11-4B and C) that pivot together for carrying or move apart when you want good access to the inside of the box. The box could be nailed together, have dovetails, or any other corner joints. The bottom is shown with pieces across with gaps between, which would let dirt fall through when gardening.

Most woods are suitable for the laminated handle but the pieces should be without flaws and have reasonably straight grain. Strips should be a little wider than the finished handle for smoothing after gluing. For this box use three pieces not more than 1/8 inch thick. The long handle has an

elliptical curve (Fig. 11-4D), but the other two may be semicircular. In both cases allow for straight ends and leave a little excess length to cut off after bending.

You need a former to bend the handles around. It could be one piece of wood (Fig. 11-5A) or several strips on a base. How it is made does not matter as long as the outside shape matches what the inside of the handle should be. Thickness should be about the same as the width of the strips.

Pull the glued strips (Fig. 11-5B) tight and hold them while the glue sets. Pad the clamps through the holes (Fig. 11-5C) with waste wood to spread the pressure. Tighten loops of rope with wedges (Fig. 11-5D). The parallel part might be held in a vise or with straight strips of wood under a bar clamp. Another good way of clamping all around is to let blocks pivot on screws so wedges can be driven (Fig. 11-5E).

Round the parts of the handle that will be held. For the swinging handles, the pivots could be nuts and bolts or roundhead wood screws, cut the best fastenings are copper rivets and washers taken through (Fig. 11-4E). Spread the rivet end on its washer inside the box. For the long handle, you can use wood screws and glue, although for a garden box there could be nails taken through and the points clenched (Fig. 11-4F).

### Materials List for Loop-Handled Box

| | |
|---|---|
| 2 sides | 1/2 × 4 × 16 |
| 2 ends | 1/2 × 4 × 11 |
| 3 bottoms | 3/8 × 4 1/2 × 11 |

*Handle*

| | |
|---|---|
| 3 pieces | 1/8 × 1 1/4 × 32 |
| or | |
| 6 pieces | 1/2 × 1 1/4 × 24 |

## RATCHET CANDLE STAND

The comparatively feeble light from a candle had to be used to the best advantage, and an adjustable stand allowed it to be positioned at the right height. Adjustable stands that used a ratchet adjustment were found in many early homes. The technique was very similar to that of one common

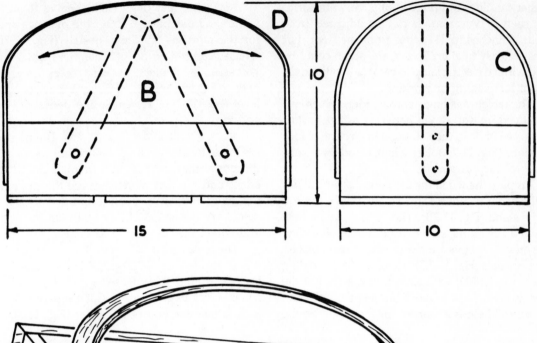

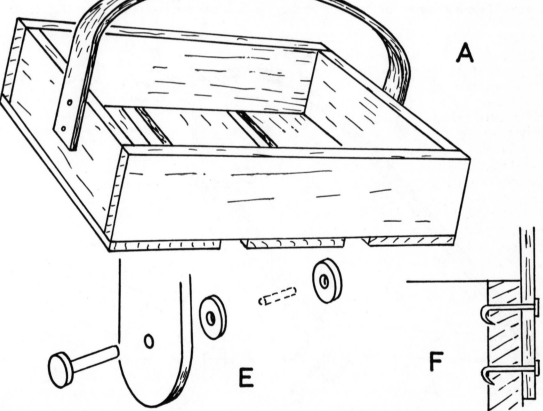

Fig. 11-4. *A loop handle on a box may be fixed lengthwise or a pair can pivot to be gripped together.*

wagon jack, so the idea was borrowed. This ratchet candle stand (Fig. 11-6) is very similar to one seen in Vermont. It can be adjusted from about 27 inches to 33 inches from the floor, but sizes are easy to alter. Today, the stand could be used with an electric lamp to get it to just the right height for reading or working.

The tabletop is on a central slider, which can be moved up and down between two pedestals supported on feet, then stopped in any one of four positions (Fig. 11-7A). Use a hardwood that is unlikely to warp or shrink.

Prepare the wood for the pedestals and slider to the same sections and straight. Make the top of the stand (Fig. 11-7B). The central square hole has to move on the slider without excessive play. The other two slots are mortises to take tenons on the pedestals (Fig. 11-7C). Make the lower sliding piece (Fig. 11-7D) with sizes that match, but the outer notches have to move on the pedestals, and the central hole is a mortise for the tenon on the slider.

Make the feet (Fig. 11-7E). Halve them together and use piece B to set the distance apart for the mortises for the pedestals (Fig. 11-7F), which need not go deeper than 3/4 inch. When you assemble the feet, put thin pieces under the ends to help the feet stand firmly if the floor is not level (Fig. 11-7G). Assemble the pedestals, feet and top.

Mark out the slider (Fig. 11-8A). The notches are made by first drilling 3/8-inch holes touching the edge, then cutting into them. Smooth the edges and see that all notches are the same. At the lower end, cut a tenon to fit into the sliding piece. Try the action of these parts in the stand and adjust the cutouts if necessary.

The tabletop could be round or octagonal, but it is suggested square (Fig. 11-7B) with a narrow lip put around the edges (Fig. 11-8C). Make a square block to go below it. Cut a square mortise in it to take the end of the slider (Fig. 11-8D).

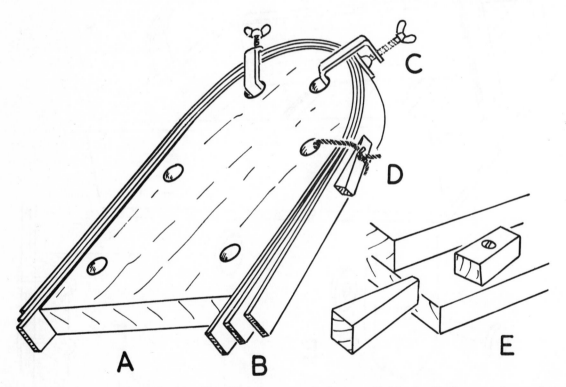

*Fig. 11-5. The strips to make the laminated handle are bent around a former and held to it with clamps, cord, or wedges.*

Make the ratchet with two pieces of 3/8-inch dowel rod (Fig. 11-8E). Drill for the ratchet in one pedestal (Fig. 11-7H) so the dowel through it will rotate freely.

Assemble the slider and its top and bottom parts in position in the stand. Wax may be used on the sliding parts to give a smooth action. Assemble the ratchet in position, with clearance each side of the parts it touches.

**Materials List for Ratchet Candle Stand**

| | |
|---|---|
| 2 pedestals | 1 1/4 × 1 1/4 × 25 |
| 1 slider | 1 1/4 × 1 1/4 × 21 |
| 1 stand top | 1 × 2 1/2 × 10 |
| 2 feet | 1 3/4 × 1 3/4 × 14 |
| 4 feet | 1/4 × 1 1/4 × 2 |
| 1 sliding piece | 1 × 2 1/2 × 8 |
| 1 table | 3/4 × 12 × 13 |
| 1 table block | 3/4 × 5 × 5 |
| 4 table lips | 1/4 × 1 1/8 × 14 |
| 2 ratchet sides | 3/8 × 1 × 5 |
| 2 ratchet rods | 4 × 3/8 round |

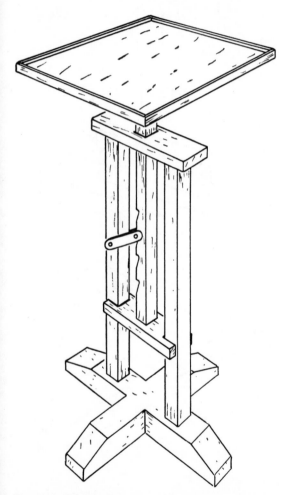

Fig. 11-6. To make the best use of the small amount of light from a candle, stands of adjustable height were made. One could be used today to place an electric lamp shining just as you want it.

## FIRE SCREEN CANDLE STAND

A screen to keep heat from the face while allowing heat from the fire to get to other parts of the body was considered essential, at least in the better class of homes. The actual screen could be moved up and down or rotated on a spindle. These screens were often decorated or used to display embroidery or other work. Some were quite elaborate.

You might not need a screen today for its original use, but it is decorative in a room of country furniture. The screen used in this project (Fig. 11-9) is based on one seen in Virginia. It has a shelf that was originally intended for a candle, but in a modern home, it could support a lamp or vase of flowers.

The screen itself is a comparatively wide, thin board. The shelf and the blocks at the back provide some stiffness, but the board should be a seasoned piece of hardwood so it will keep its shape. If you are not concerned about the screen being an authentic reproduction, you could use plywood, preferably with veneer on both sides. Other parts are solid wood. The spindle may be hardwood dowelling.

The sizes (fig. 11-10A) are as they would have been, but if you want the stand as a smaller display unit, parts can be reduced. Cut the board for the screen to shape (Fig. 11-10B). Make the shelf (Fig. 11-10C) and its bracket with the grain on the diagonal (Fig. 11-10D). These are the parts most visible, they should be well sanded and their edges rounded. Assemble with glue and screws through the back (Fig. 11-10E).

Make two rear blocks (Fig. 11-10F). They fit around the spindle and must slide in it. Provide

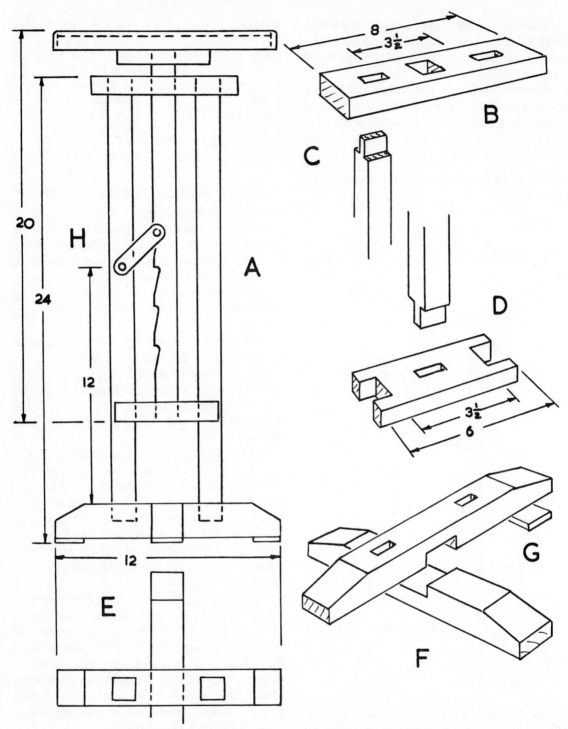

Fig. 11-7 Sizes and details of some parts of the ratchet candle stand.

friction to prevent slipping by gluing a strip of cloth to the board between the blocks. Allow for this when making the blocks. Glue and screw them to the screen.

The stand is turned and has three feet similar to the candle stand described in Chapter 4 (see Fig. 4-27). Turn the spindle with a maximum 3-inch diameter (Fig. 11-11A). At the top, drill to take the

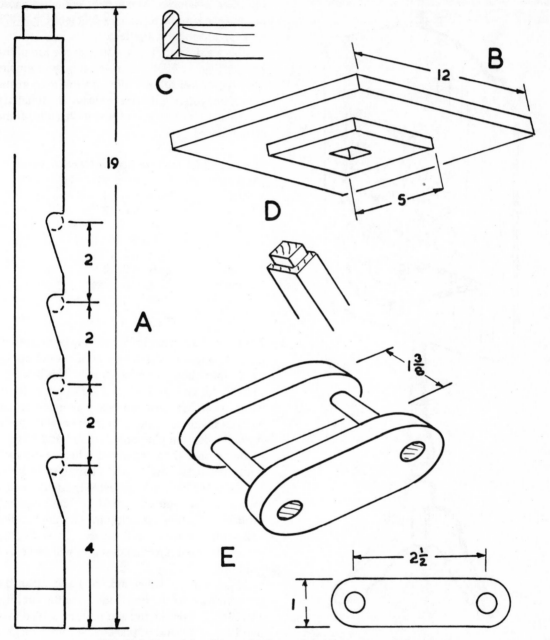

Fig. 11-8 Sizes of the slider and other parts of the ratchet candle stand.

Fig. 11-9. *An adjustable fire screen with a shelf makes a good display unit.*

1-inch spindle. At the bottom, turn down parallel to take the feet.

Cut the three feet (Fig. 11-11B). Leave on blocks for clamping (Fig. 11-11C), which you cut off after assembly. Make flats equally spaced around the spindle to take the feet (see Fig. 4-27F and G) and join on the feet.

Turn a finial to fit into a hole at the top of the spindle (Fig. 11-11D). When you finally assemble, glue the dowel rod spindle into the hole in the stand, but you might prefer to leave the finial dry as a push fit, in case you ever want to slide off the screen board.

## Materials List for Fire Screen Candle Stand

| | |
|---|---|
| 1 screen | 5/8 × 15 × 24 |
| 1 shelf | 5/8 × 5 × 14 |
| 1 bracket | 5/8 × 5 × 17 |
| 2 blocks | 1 × 2 × 10 |
| 1 stand | 3 × 3 × 19 |
| 3 feet | 1 1/8 × 5 × 14 |
| 1 finial | 2 1/2 × 2 1/2 × 6 |
| 1 spindle | 35 × 1 diameter |

## CARVER BOX

The edge of a carving knife needs to be protected, if it is to retain its sharpness, so it should not be tossed into a box with other cutlery. This box (Fig. 11-12) holds carving knife and fork with a sharpening steel. The original box was made of oak with an inside top and bottom lined with cloth. Assembly is with glue only. The lid and box are made as one, then separated where a 1/8-inch width is left for sawing and planing the edges.

Sizes will have to be adjusted to suit the knife, fork, and steel you wish to fit in. The knife will probably be longest, but clearance for the handles will settle the width and depth. The sizes suggested suit bent horn handles and will serve as a guide (Fig. 11-12A).

Mark out the sides and ends and make the dovetails clear of the lines indicating the cut (Fig. 11-12B). Glue on the top and bottom, which may overlap slightly and be planed level after the glue has set.

Saw the pieces apart and plane the edges. If

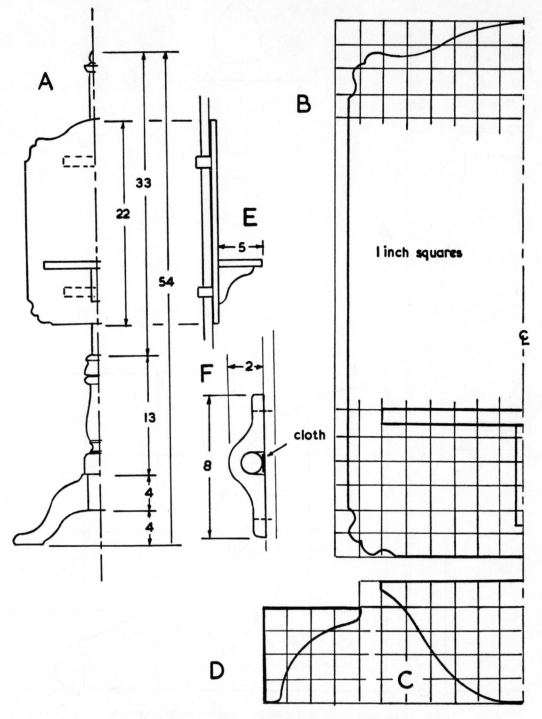

A

33

22

54

E

5

F

2

cloth

13

8

4

4

B

1 inch squares

3

D

C

Fig. 11-10. Sizes and shapes of parts of the fire screen with shelf.

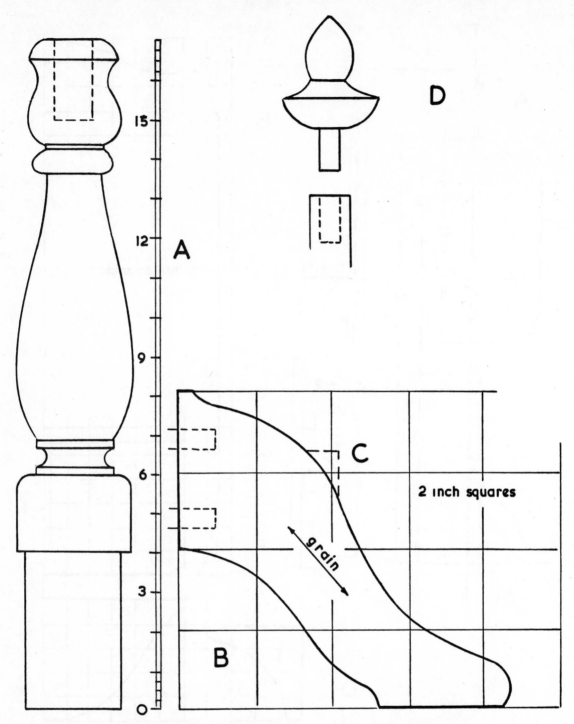

Fig. 11-11. Patterns for the turned parts and feet of the fire screen.

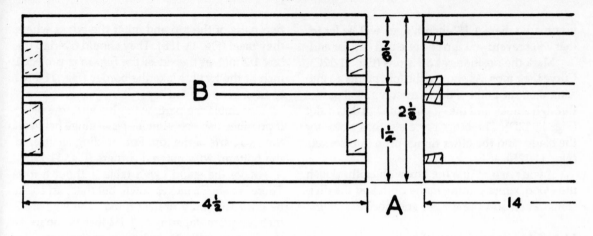

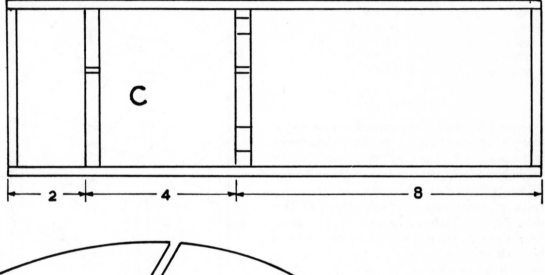

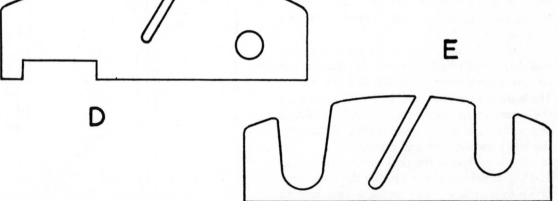

Fig. 11-12. Sizes of the carver box and shapes of the divisions to hold the knife, fork, and sharpening steel.

you mark where 1 1/2-inch hinges will be let in, that will prevent you turning one part end for end.

Mark the positions of divisions (Fig. 11-12C). Curve their tops. As shown, the fork points go into a low slot, the point of the sharpening steel passes through a hole, and the sloping knife tip has a slot (Fig. 11-12D). The other piece also has a slot for the blade, and the other things drop into sockets (Fig. 11-12E).

If you wish to line the box with cloth, polish the wood before putting in the cloth and the divisions. Then add the hinges and hook fasteners.

### Materials List for Carver Box

| 2 sides | 1/4 × 1 5/8 × 15 |
| 2 ends | 1/4 × 1 5/8 × 5 |
| 1 top | 1/4 × 4 1/2 × 15 |
| 1 bottom | 1/4 × 4 1/2 × 15 |
| 2 divisions | 3/8 × 1 1/2 × 5 |

### DESK

A sloping-top desk was regarded as essential in many early homes for the storage of documents and money as well as a writing surface. A desk might be portable and stand on a table or it could have legs. Some desks had surprisingly steep tops and papers must have frequently slipped off. This desk (Fig. 11-13) is based on a New England inn-keeper's desk, but it is arranged so the desk can be made without the legs, or if it is fitted with them, it can be lifted off. The sizes (Fig. 11-14A) are for a desk to be used while standing or sitting on a high stool.

Many early desks were nailed throughout, but this desk would be better with dovetails at the corners, even if other parts are nailed or screwed. The bottom is raised enough for locating pieces on the stand to fit inside (Fig. 11-14B). Molding around the outside covers nail heads and disguises the line between desk and stand.

The key parts of the desk are the ends (Fig. 11-15A), which are about 4 inches flat then slope down to 6 inches. Make the back and front to match the ends. Cut the corner joints, if you are using dovetails. Assemble the box with the bottom 5/8 inch up from the lower edge. Make the

two parts of the top and miter the edges where they meet (Fig. 11-15B). They should overlap the box 1/2 inch at the sides; the flap may project 1 inch at the front. Make the border (Fig. 11-15C) to fit around the flat top.

Assemble the parts with glue and fine nails. If possible, use a continuous *piano* hinge between the two parts of the top. Put molding all around the bottom, with mitered corners (Fig. 11-15D).

Make the stand like a table without a top. There is a shelf 6 inches down, but that part could be enclosed and a drawer fitted. The legs are 2 inches square, tapering to 1 1/2 inches square at the bottom from 11 inches from the top (Fig.

*Fig. 11-13. The top part of this desk will lift off its stand or could be made as a separate unit for use on a table.*

11-14C). The top rails are level with the outsides (Fig. 11-14D), but the shelf rails can be central. Cut the joints before tapering.

At the top use barefaced tenons on the rails (Fig. 11-16A). Cut back the front rail (Fig. 11-16B) for ease in reaching to the shelf. Under the shelf you can use ordinary tenons centered in the legs (Fig. 11-16C). Notch the shelf around the legs so it rests on its rails (Fig. 11-16D).

Compare sizes with the underside of the desk. Fit strips inside the rails (Fig. 11-16E), tapered slightly on the outsides for ease in positioning the

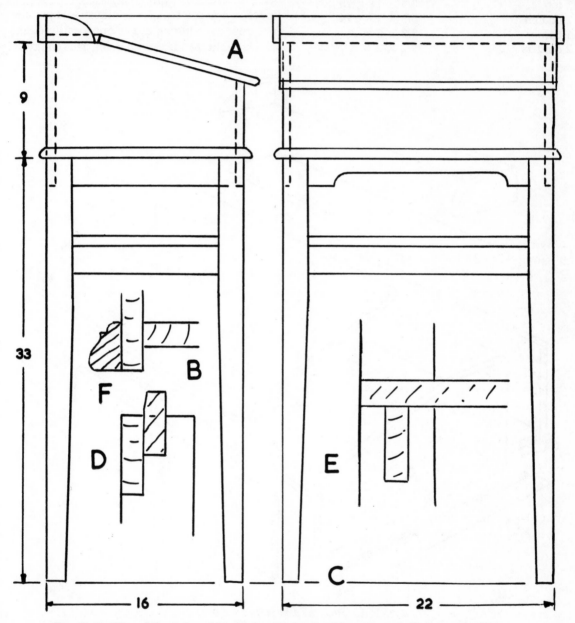

Fig. 11-14. Sizes of the desk and its stand, with details of how the parts fit into each other.

desk (Fig. 11-14F). Use the desk as a guide as you assemble the stand.

## Materials List for Desk

| 2 ends | 5/8 × 9 × 18 |
| 1 back | 5/8 × 9 × 24 |
| 1 front | 5/8 × 6 × 24 |
| 1 top | 5/8 × 4 × 25 |
| 1 top | 5/8 × 14 × 25 |
| 1 bottom | 5/8 × 15 × 24 |
| 1 border | 1/2 × 2 × 25 |
| 2 borders | 1/2 × 2 × 6 |

| 4 legs | 2 × 2 × 35 |
| 4 rails | 5/8 × 2 × 22 |
| 4 rails | 5/8 × 2 × 16 |
| 1 shelf | 5/8 × 16 × 24 |
| 2 locating pieces | 5/8 × 1 1/2 × 12 |
| 2 locating pieces | 5/8 × 12 × 18 |

## SETTLE/TABLE

Space-saving combination furniture was popular in European countries and amongst early settlers who brought the ideas with them. This combina-

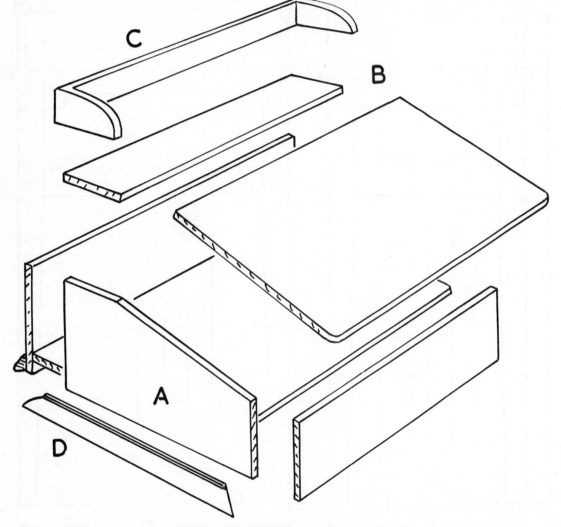

*Fig. 11-15. How the desk parts are assembled.*

tion of double seat, chest, and table has an English origin and was a type found in many early homes (Fig. 11-17).

Apart from its interesting historic appearance, it would be useful in a modern home; it could normally be kept against the wall as a seat and chest, then pulled out when you need a large table.

As drawn (Fig. 11-18), there is a double seat at normal height, storage below, and a table 33 inches by 54 inches and about 28 inches above the floor. Nearly all parts are made from 1-inch boards (finishing about 7/8 inch thick). They could be soft-

wood, but you will have a better piece of furniture if you use hardwood. Original tables were usually nailed, but you might prefer to use screws counterbored and covered with plugs.

Make the pair of ends first. The uprights (Fig. 11-19A) have semicircular tops with peg holes. They are notched for the back and front boards. For additional stability, glue on pieces at the bottoms of the uprights (Fig. 11-19B) and cut back the inner edges (Fig. 11-18A).

Groove strips to take panels (Fig. 11-19C) and cut tenons on the ends to fit into the uprights. As-

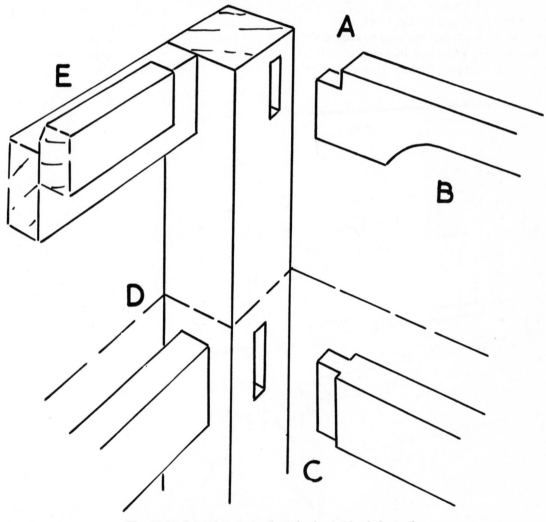

Fig. 11-16. Joints between rails and a leg in the desk stand.

semble the two ends and check that they match.

Make the back and front boards (Fig. 11-18B) to fit into their notches and a bottom to go between them. If you have to use two or more boards to make up the width of the bottom, put cleats across the ends inside. Assemble these parts to the ends.

The seat should project forward about 1 inch. At its ends, put strips across (Fig. 11-19D), shaped to match the seat, and a strip along the back (Fig. 11-19E). Its ends could be tenoned or dowelled. Make the seat (Fig. 11-19F) with a rounded edge. Cut recesses for two or three 4-inch hinges.

The two batten on the tabletop go outside the seat uprights (Fig. 11-18C). Allow about 1/4-inch clearance. Make them to within 2 inches of the width of the top (Fig. 11-19G). Mark the 3/4-inch pivot holes through the uprights so they match. See that the table will swing by pivoting each batten and watching that its edge clears the curve.

The top can be made up of any number of available boards, five are shown (Fig. 11-19H). They could depend only on the battens to hold them, their edges could be glued, or you could use tongued and grooved joints. Alternatively, dowels might be used between edges. Attach the battens securely with plugged screws.

The pivots could be plain pieces of dowel rod, but turned pieces with heads and rounded ends would be better (Fig. 11-19J).

**Materials List for Settle/Table**

| | |
|---|---|
| 4 uprights | 1 × 3 × 28 |
| 4 rails | 1 × 3 × 16 |
| 2 panels | 3/8 × 8 × 12 |
| 4 feet | 1 × 1 1/2 × 7 |
| 2 seat ends | 1 × 3 × 18 |
| 1 seat back | 1 × 3 × 38 |
| 1 front | 1 × 9 × 40 |

Fig. 11-17. A settle/table serves as a seat, chest, and table.

| 1 back | 1 × 9 × 40 |
| 1 bottom | 1 × 14 × 40 |
| 1 seat | 1 × 15 × 40 |
| 2 top battens | 1 × 3 × 31 |
| 5 top boards | 1 × 7 × 56 |
| 4 pivots | 1 1/2 × 1 1/2 × 5 |

## TAKE-DOWN BOOK RACK

Wedged tusk tenons were used for furniture that had to be disassembled for transporting. This book rack (Fig. 11-20) is typical of the method of construction. It is angular, but you could soften the outline of the ends with curves. The suggested length is 18 inches, and most usual book sizes can be accommodated (Fig. 11-21A). A compactly grained hardwood is advised.

The two lengthwise shelves are the same. Reduce the 4-inch width at the ends to 2 inches (Fig. 11-21B). The wedges go through holes about 1/2 inch square. Make the wedges 1/2 inch thick, tapering from 5/8 inch to 1/2 inch (Fig. 11-21C). Taper each hole to match its wedge and cut back the inner edge of the hole so it comes inside the thickness of the end and the wedge does not bear

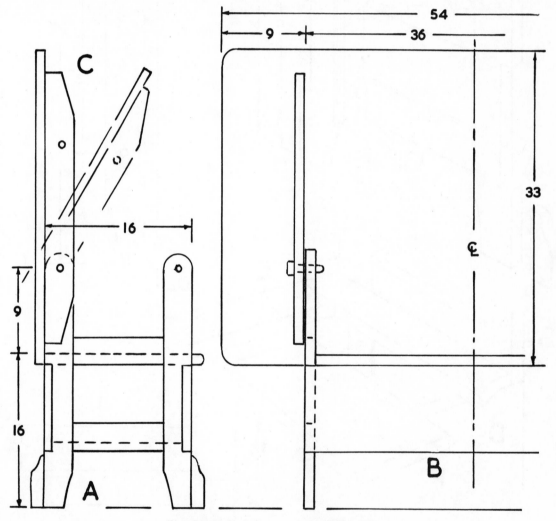

*Fig. 11-18. Overall sizes of the settle/table.*

241

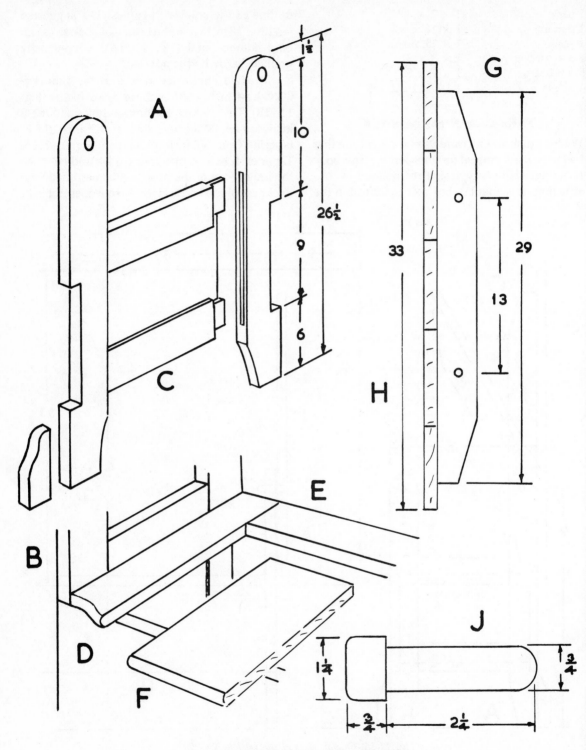

Fig. 11-19. *Details of parts of the settle/table.*

on it when it is pushed in. Trim the ends of the tenons leaving enough wood outside the wedge holes to take the thrust.

The drawing shows books tilted at 15 degrees, but that is not crucial. Use the grid as a guide to the end shape (Fig. 11-21D). Draw the book lines, then mark mortises to suit the tenons against them, followed by the outlines.

Round all expose edges of the ends and shelves. Make a trial assembly before polishing the wood.

**Materials List for Take-down Book Rack**

| | |
|---|---|
| 2 shelves | 5/8 × 4 × 22 |
| 2 ends | 5/8 × 11 × 12 |

## NESTING TRAYS

Trays have always been useful in the kitchen and dining room. A set of three that will fit into each other for storage or easy transport when empty are attractive. These three trays (Fig. 11-22) are the same, except that two of them nest into the large one. When they are in that position, the handle holes are in line to allow you to still push your fingers through and carry them.

The sizes suggested (Fig. 11-23A) for the large tray are 5 inches high, 14 inches wide, and 21 inches long. All parts are 1/2 inch thick. The frames should be a close-grained hardwood. The bases could be the same or you could use 1/2-inch plywood, as its edges will be hidden. It might be veneered, or you could cover it with cloth.

There are several, possibly more modern corner joints, but an early craftsman would have used dovetails. For the large tray, arrange three tails (Fig. 11-23B), but the other trays need only have two at each corner (Fig. 11-23C).

Draw at least half an end view of the large tray (Fig. 11-23D). From that make the two ends and use them as templates for marking the ends of the other trays. Allow 1/4-inch clearance at the sides and enough for the thickness of each bottom, so the hand holes will come level.

Make the sides and cut their corner joints. Round the top edges of all parts and the insides of the hand holes. Make the bottoms to fit inside. Be careful that all corners are square so the trays will fit neatly. Hold the bottoms in with glue and pins through the sides and ends.

Fig. 11-20. A tabletop book rack can be taken apart when the wedges are knocked out.

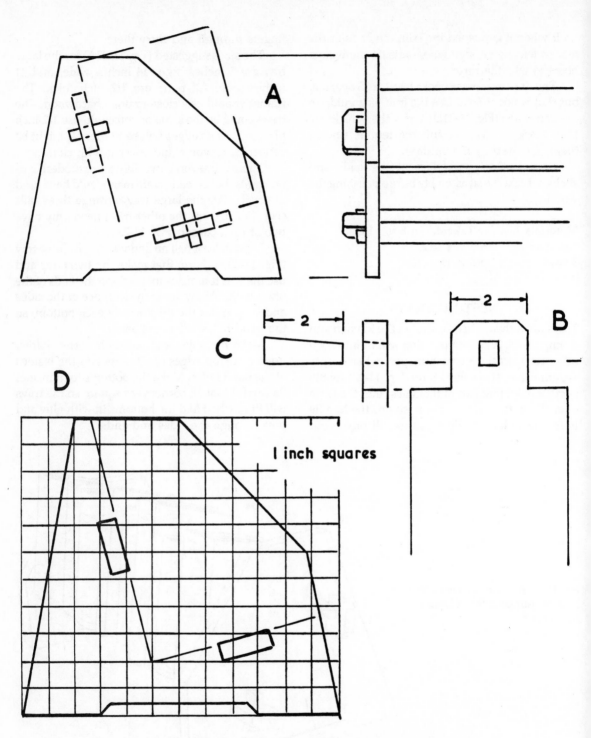

Fig. 11-21. Assembly details and end shape of the take-down book rack.

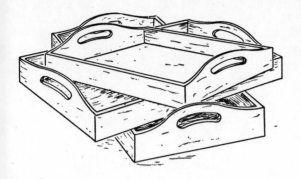

**Materials List for Nesting Trays**

| | |
|---|---|
| 2 ends | 1/2 × 5 × 15 |
| 2 ends | 1/2 × 4 1/2 × 14 |
| 2 ends | 1/2 × 4 × 13 |
| 2 sides | 1/2 × 3 1/2 × 22 |
| 2 sides | 1/2 × 3 × 21 |
| 2 sides | 1/2 × 2 1/2 × 20 |
| 1 bottom | 1/2 × 13 × 21 |
| 1 bottom | 1/2 × 11 1/2 × 20 |
| 1 bottom | 1/2 × 10 × 19 |

*Fig. 11-22. These three trays fit into each other and can be lifted together when not required for separate use.*

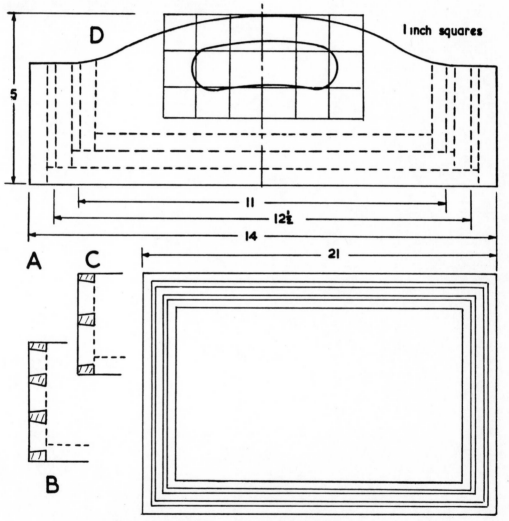

*Fig. 11-23. Details of the tray ends and joints.*

# Index

# *Index*

# Other Bestsellers From TAB

☐ **TROUBLESHOOTING AND REPAIRING SMALL HOME APPLIANCES—Bob Wood**

Author Bob Wood pairs step-by-step pictures with detailed instructions on how to fix 43 of the most common electric appliances found in the home. Following the illustrations and directions provided, you'll be able to quickly disassemble practically any electrical device to get to the trouble source. Among those included are: drill, garbage disposal, can opener, grass trimmer, vacuum cleaner, blender, and much more! This book supplies expert guidance for repairing popular household electronic entertainment items and appliances. 256 pp., 473 Illus.

**Paper $14.95**          **Hard $23.95**
**Book No. 2912**

☐ **THE ILLUSTRATED HOME ELECTRONICS FIX-IT BOOK—2nd Edition—Homer L. Davidson**

This revised edition of the bestselling home electronics fix-it handbook will save you time and aggravation AND money! It is the only repair manual you will ever need to fix most household electronic equipment. Packed with how-to illustrations that any novice can follow, you'll soon be able to fix that broken television and portable stereo/cassette player and "Boom Box" and intercom and . . . the list goes on! 480 pp., 377 illus.

**Paper $16.95**          **Hard $25.95**
**Book No. 2883**

☐ **BUILDING A LOG HOME FROM SCRATCH OR KIT—2nd Edition—Dan Ramsey**

This up-to-the-minute guide to log home building takes you from initial planning and design stages right through the final interior finishing of your new house. There's advice on selecting a construction site, choosing a home that's right for your needs and budget, estimating construction costs, obtaining financing, locating suppliers and contractors, and deciding whether to use a kit or build from scratch. 302 pp., 311 illus., Paperback.

**Paper $14.95**          **Book No. 2858**

☐ **SUNSPACES—HOME ADDITIONS FOR YEAR- ROUND NATURAL LIVING—John Mauldin, Photography by John H. Mauldin and Juan L. Espinosa**

Have you been thinking of enclosing your porch to increase your living space? Want to add a family room, but want the best use of the space for the money? Do you want information on solar energy and ideas on how you can make it work in your home? If "yes" is your answer to any of these questions, you'll want to own this fascinating guide! 256 pp., 179 illus.

**Paper $14.95**          **Hard $21.95**
**Book No. 2816**

☐ **101 KITCHEN PROJECTS FOR THE WOODWORKER—Percy W. Blandford**

These 101 practical as well as decorative projects for every level of woodworking ability are sure to provide pleasure and satisfaction for builder and cook alike! Included are bread and cheese boards, carving boards and butcher blocks, trays, cookbook stand and stacking vegetable bin, spatulas, forks, spring tongs, mug racks, pivoting and parallel towel rails, spice racks, tables, a hutch, and much, much more! 270 pp., 214 illus.

**Paper $14.95**          **Hard $23.95**
**Book No. 2884**

☐ **PROJECTS FROM PINE—33 Plans for the Beginning Woodworker—James A. Jacobson**

Easy-to-understand instructions and detailed drawings and photographs make this the perfect guide for beginning woodworkers! You'll find plans for cutting boards, a flower pot drop, a candle box, wood ornaments, a wine rack, shaker items, bookends, and shelves—all ideal gift ideas and many that you may want to produce in quantity and sell at craft shows. The author takes you from selecting suitable pine lumber for your project to a detailed discussion of the finishing process. 192 pp., 147 illus., 7″ × 10″.

**Paper $10.95**          **Hard $17.95**
**Book No. 2871**

☐ **DREAM HOMES: 66 PLANS TO MAKE YOUR DREAMS COME TRUE—Jerold L. Axelrod**

If you are planning on—or just dreaming of—building a new home, you will find this book completely fascinating. Compiled by a well-known architect whose home designs have been featured regularly in the syndicated "House of the Week" and *Home* magazine, this beautifully bound volume presents one of the finest collections of luxury home designs ever assembled in a single volume! 86 pp., 201 illus., 8 1/2″ × 11″, 20 pp. of full-color illus.

**Paper $16.95**          **Hard $29.95**
**Book No. 2829**

☐ **HOME PLUMBING MADE EASY: AN ILLUSTRATED MANUAL—James L. Kittle**

Here, in one heavily illustrated, easy-to-follow volume, is all the how-to-do-it information needed to perform almost any home plumbing job, including both water and waste disposal systems. And what makes this guide superior to so many other plumbing books is the fact that there's plenty of hands-on instruction, meaningful advice, practical safety tips, and emphasis on getting the job done as easily and professionally as possible! 272 pp., 250 illus.

**Paper $14.95**          **Book No. 2797**

# Other Bestsellers From TAB

☐ **40 EASY-TO-BUILD HOME FURNISHINGS—The Editors of School Shop** Magazine

A treasure of decorative, practical, and money-saving projects. Here's an intriguing collection of 40 easy-to-build, functional and decorative projects that you can make quickly and easily with a minimum supply of tools. From home furnishings and accessories, storage units, and office supplies to projects that will add to your indoor and outdoor hobby and sports fun, each project has been carefully selected for ease of construction and practicality. 144 pp., 67 illus.
**Paper  $9.95**                          **Book No. 2788**

☐ **HOW TO REPAIR HOME LAUNDRY APPLIANCES—2nd Edition—Ben Gaddis**

Covering both electric and gas versions of today's washers, dryers, and hot water heaters—as well as water softening and purifying units—Gaddis shows you, step-by-step, how the machines work and how to identify and repair problems as quickly and easily as possible. Covered are tools, professional troubleshooting tricks, and proper installation and repair procedures as well as specific repair procedures. 230 pp., 137 illus.
**Paper  $14.95**                         **Book No. 2662**

☐ **UPHOLSTERY TECHNIQUES ILLUSTRATED—Lloyd W. Gheen**

Here's an easy-to-follow, step-by-step guide to modern upholstery techniques that covers everything from stripping off old covers and padding to restoring and installing new foundations, stuffing, cushions, and covers. All the most up-to-date pro techniques are included along with lots of time- and money-saving "tricks-of-the-trade" not usually shared by professional upholsterers. 352 pp., 549 illus., Paperback.
**Paper  $17.95**                         **Book No. 2602**

☐ **MASTER HANDBOOK OF WOODWORKING TECHNIQUES AND PROJECTS—2nd Edition—Percy W. Blandford**

This classic guide to traditional furniture crafting is now completely updated to include the very latest methods, materials, tools, equipment, and techniques . . . while continuing to stress the importance of fine craftsmanship. Actual projects from simple bookcases, chests, and stools to advanced designs like a Queen Anne table and a glass-fronted cupboard are included so you can put the woodworking techniques you've learned to practical use. 368 pp., 349 illus.
**Paper  $15.95**                         **Book No. 2744**

☐ **ALL ABOUT LAMPS: Construction, Repair and Restoration—Frank W. Coggins**

You'll find step-by-step directions for making a wall lamp or a hanging lamp from wood, novelty lamps from PVC plumbing pipe, and designer lamps from acrylic or polyester resins. Shade projects range from needlepoint and fabric models to globes, balls, and tubular forms. There are suggestions for advanced projects, using salvaged and low-cost materials, and more! 192 pp., 267 illus.
**Paper  $16.95**                         **Hard  $24.95**
**Book No. 2658**

☐ **HOW TO TROUBLESHOOT AND REPAIR ANY SMALL GAS ENGINE—Paul Dempsey**

Here's a time-, money-, and aggravation-saving sourcebook that covers the full range of two- and four-cycle gas engines from just about every major American manufacturer—from Briggs & Stratton, Clinton Kohler, Onan, OMC, and Tecumseh to West Bend, and others! With this expert advice and step-by-step instructions you'll be amazed at how easily you can solve almost any engine problem. 272 pp., 228 illus.
**Paper  $10.95**                         **Hard  $21.95**
**Book No. 1967**

*Prices subject to change without notice.

**Look for these and other TAB books at your local bookstore.**

## TAB BOOKS Inc.
### Blue Ridge Summit, PA 17294-0850

**Send for FREE TAB Catalog describing over 1200 current titles in print.**
OR CALL TOLL-FREE TODAY:  **1-800-233-1128**
IN PENNSYLVANIA AND ALASKA, CALL:  **717-794-2191**